Fundamentals
of Planning
and Assessment
for Libraries

ALA FUNDAMENTALS SERIES

Fundamentals for the Academic Liaison
by Richard Moniz, Jo Henry, and Joe Eshleman

Fundamentals of Children's Services, 2nd ed.
by Michael Sullivan

Fundamentals of Electronic Resources Management
by Alana Verminski and Kelly Marie Blanchat

Fundamentals of Library Instruction
by Monty L. McAdoo

Fundamentals of Library Supervision, 3rd ed.
by Beth McNeil

Fundamentals of Managing Reference Collections
by Carol A. Singer

Fundamentals of Planning and Assessment for Libraries
by Rachel A. Fleming-May and Regina Mays

Fundamentals of Reference
by Carolyn M. Mulac

Fundamentals of Technical Services
by John Sandstrom and Liz Miller

Fundamentals of Technical Services Management
by Sheila S. Intner, with Peggy Johnson

Small Public Library Management
by Jane Pearlmutter and Paul Nelson

ALA FUNDAMENTALS SERIES

Fundamentals of Planning and Assessment for Libraries

Rachel A. Fleming-May
and Regina Mays

ALA
Neal-Schuman

Chicago   2021

RACHEL A. FLEMING-MAY is an associate professor in the School of Information Sciences at the University of Tennessee, Knoxville. Prior to earning her PhD from the University of Alabama in 2008. Fleming-May worked as a public and academic librarian for several years. Her teaching and research interests include academic libraries and librarianship, information sources and services, and library assessment. She has worked on two assessment-related Institute of Museum and Library Services funded grant programs: Experience Assessment: Building User Experience and Assessment Capabilities in Libraries and Information Centers (UX-A) (as co-principal investigator), and Value, Outcome, and Return on Investment of Academic Libraries (LibValue) (as a management team member).

REGINA MAYS is an associate professor and head of assessment programs and collection strategy at the University of Tennessee, Knoxville Libraries, where she has practiced, researched, and published on library assessment and planning for over a decade. She holds an MSIS from the University of Tennessee, Knoxville. Her research interests include library assessment and planning, with a particular focus on the organizational structure of assessment in academic libraries, assessment education for library professionals, strategic planning, and demonstrating library value.

Extensive effort has gone into ensuring the reliability of the information in this book; however, the publisher makes no warranty, express or implied, with respect to the material contained herein.

ISBNs
978-0-8389-4998-6 (paper)
978-0-8389-3781-5 (PDF)
978-0-8389-3779-2 (ePub)

Library of Congress Cataloging-in-Publication Data
Names: Fleming-May, Rachel Anne, author. | Mays, Regina, 1973- author.
Title: Fundamentals of planning and assessment for libraries / Rachel A. Fleming-May and Regina Mays.
Description: Chicago : ALA Neal-Schuman, 2021. | Series: ALA fundamentals series | Includes bibliographical references and index. | Summary: "This text provides a guide to responsive and responsible planning and assessment"—Provided by publisher.
Identifiers: LCCN 2020058614 (print) | LCCN 2020058615 (ebook) | ISBN 9780838949986 (paperback) | ISBN 9780838937815 (pdf) | ISBN 9780838937792 (epub)
Subjects: LCSH: Library planning—United States. | Libraries—United States—Evaluation.
Classification: LCC Z678 .F58 2021 (print) | LCC Z678 (ebook) | DDC 025.1—dc23
LC record available at https://lccn.loc.gov/2020058614
LC ebook record available at https://lccn.loc.gov/2020058615

Book design in the Melior and Din typefaces. Cover image © Adobe Stock, Inc.

♾ This paper meets the requirements of ANSI/NISO Z39.48-1992 (Permanence of Paper).

Printed in the United States of America
25 24 23 22 21   5 4 3 2 1

ALA Neal-Schuman purchases fund advocacy, awareness, and accreditation programs for library professionals worldwide.

Contents

Preface   vii

1   Introduction to Planning and Assessment   1

2   The History of Planning and Assessment in Libraries   19

3   Planning   41

4   Basic Principles of Assessment   63

5   Approaches to Assessment   81

6   Collecting Assessment Data   99

7   Collecting Direct Evidence   105

8   Collecting Indirect Evidence   123

9   Analyzing Data   157

10   Reporting and Presenting Data   173

11   Collaboration and Relationship Management   201

Appendixes

   A   *Sample Library Assessment Plan   221*

   B   *Sample Informed Consent Form   227*

   C   *Template for Recording Observation   231*

   D   *Suggested Journals and Conferences   233*

   E   *Sample Assessment Librarian Position Description   235*

Glossary   239

Index   247

Preface

G reetings! Welcome to *Fundamentals of Planning and Assessment for Libraries.* You've probably picked up this book for one (or more) of the following reasons:

- You are interested in planning and assessment and would like to learn the basics.
- You have been assigned work responsibilities related to planning and assessment, lack background, and need to learn the basics.
- You are a student in a library and information sciences program and would like a basic overview of the field.

You may have noticed that *basic* is the operative word here.

Indeed, as part of ALA's Fundamentals series, this text is aimed squarely at entry level. When we were asked if we'd be interested in writing about this topic for the Fundamentals series, the prospect held immense appeal for several reasons. First, it's fair to say that we both stumbled into the field of planning and assessment and could have used a text like this—Rachel became interested through her research and writing about the concept of "use," and Regina, through her work first as a graduate teaching assistant, then as a research associate working with Dr. Carol Tenopir. We both had the opportunity to think about planning and assessment more deeply through our involvement in the Value, Outcomes, and Return on Investment of Academic Libraries (LibValue) project, from which Regina segued into an assessment librarian position. Several years later, we revisited the subject to design and co-teach a planning and assessment course for the University of Tennessee's Master of Science in Information Sciences program.

We were also drawn to the Fundamentals approach because it mirrors Rachel's approach to teaching. Inclusivity is a principle that guides her pedagogy—she would rather provide students with content that is a little more basic than they need than to talk over their heads. She subscribes to a constructivist view of learning, meaning that knowledge is built (or "constructed") incrementally and in concert with each student's individual experiences and worldview. Constructivism also recognizes that developing more sophisticated skills and knowledge requires a foundation—it's simply not possible to build on empty air. Rachel will tell you what she tells students about this approach on the first day of class: please forgive us if we provide information that is a little too basic for you—we promise there is a reader for whom it is not. That being said, if you have previous experience with planning and assessment, you may find much of the content too rudimentary for you. You may wish to flip directly to the appendixes, which feature a collection of resources for further reading and professional development.

We also recognize that although we find planning and assessment topics endlessly interesting, they are not always popular concepts in the workplace, and libraries are no exception. For some, they carry an unpleasant whiff of corporate-speak. For others, they conjure images of additional workload being added to an already heavy burden. You may be embarking on this journey with some reluctance; if so, you wouldn't be alone! In fact, a recent article in *The Chronicle of Higher Education* described an incident in which a disgruntled professor sent an e-mail to "more than two dozen administrators and colleagues" with the subject line "A MANIFESTO FROM A PROFESSOR WHO IS BEYOND FURIOUS" (capitals theirs). Among other things, their tirade included a vow to (again, capitals theirs) "NEVER GO TO ANOTHER MEETING INVOLVING THE WORDS ASSESSMENT OR STRATEGIC PLAN."[1] While working on this manuscript, we've often wondered how many of our readers would feel the same. If you are nodding your head in agreement right now, please know we set out to make this text as practical and painless as possible.

In our view, planning and assessment can be tremendously valuable endeavors that enrich libraries' (and librarians') understanding of their own strengths, weaknesses, contributions, and areas that need improvement. When designed effectively, planning and assessment efforts can play an important role in building a library's profile with external stakeholders and, in turn, improving a library's position when it's time to allocate resources.

Most important, planning and assessment provide data that inform strategies for improving the services, resources, and facilities we offer our users.

Several years ago, we conducted a survey of librarians for whom assessment constituted a significant part of their jobs that asked them to identify the specific tasks they engaged in as part of their assessment work and how they learned to execute those tasks.[2] We learned that many of our respondents did not learn much about planning or assessment in their master's programs and some did not believe they had sufficient knowledge to plan effectively and assess performance with accuracy and precision. If this describes you, you've come to the right place. We designed our planning and assessment course to teach our students what we wish we'd known; in fact, Regina became the inaugural assessment librarian at her institution without having had formal instruction in the principles of planning and assessment and had to build her department from the ground up. It's also important to note that one does not need to have the title "planning and assessment librarian" to engage in these tasks. Everyone who works in libraries takes part in planning and assessment every day—the difference lies in the scale and formality of the endeavor. Our goal in writing this text is to provide practical, applicable information that is accessible to any librarian with limited knowledge of planning and assessment.

Specifically, this text will cover

- the history of planning and assessment initiatives in libraries
- the foundational concepts related to planning and assessment
- basic principles of planning, with an emphasis on strategic planning
- the basics of conceptualizing, designing, and executing assessment, including helpful research concepts
- important ethical considerations related to assessment
- a general overview of frameworks for library assessment
- a review of approaches to collecting data for library assessment and when each is appropriate
- the basics of data analysis and storage
- principles for organizing and presenting assessment findings
- approaches to effective management of planning and assessment programs, including placement within the organizational structure.

The text's appendixes include examples of tools and templates for planning and assessment, a glossary of terms, and resources for further study and professional development.

Throughout the text, we've tried to contextualize some pretty amorphous concepts with examples and case studies we've developed through considering our own experiences, conversations we've had with colleagues, and our immersion in the impressive professional and scholarly library planning and assessment scholarly communication ecosystem. In most cases, however, the examples we share are completely fabricated; regardless, any resemblance to actual people or situations is entirely unintentional. We should also note that although we are longtime collaborators, we have each had individual experiences that guided us in writing this book. In many cases throughout the text, the pronoun "we" actually refers to only one of us. We did this to avoid the ungainliness of having to specify whose point of view is being presented. In instances in which using the composite "we" would be more confusing than less, we've used the third person to identify which of us had the experience being described.

More important than these points of clarification, we hope this text conveys our excitement about and belief in planning and assessment for libraries. If **PROFESSOR BEYOND FURIOUS**'s manifesto resonates with you, well, we hope that reading this book will change your mind.

NOTES

1. Emma Pettit, "Her University Publicly Accused Her of Using Meth. Here's How It Came to That, and Here's What Happened Next," *The Chronicle of Higher Education*, September 3, 2019, https://www.chronicle.com/article/Her-University-Publicly/247062.
2. Rachel Fleming-May and Regina Mays, "Assessing Librarians' Preparation for Assessment: Development and Preliminary Findings from a Survey," in *11th Northumbria Conference*, Edinburgh, Scotland, 2015.

1

Introduction to Planning and Assessment

- The Concepts of Planning and Assessment
- Why Planning Matters
- Assessment That Matters
- Assessment in Context
- Rigorous Assessment
- Ethical and Just Assessment
- Assessment That Contributes to the Larger Conversation
- Don't Reinvent the Wheel
- Conclusion

In this chapter, we will define planning and assessment and describe their relationship to other concepts such as evaluation. We will explain why planning and assessment are connected concepts, and why these activities are important.

One idea we will return to again and again in this text is the importance of defining the phenomena, concepts, and entities you plan to measure. In the interest of setting a good example, it's important for us to explain what, exactly, we mean by the terms *planning* and *assessment*.

The Concepts of Planning and Assessment

Planning refers to the collection of processes, formal and informal, that an organization or department participates in to establish a baseline, record assets and deficits, and establish goals and strategies to achieve those goals. Planning also includes developing measures to assess your success in meeting those goals. In this way, assessment is closely related to planning.

Assessment versus Evaluation

Assessment refers to the systematic process by which an organization measures how well its resources and services are meeting the needs of its stakeholders. Assessment is sometimes referred to as *evaluation*, although to us that term carries a slightly different connotation of being reviewed by an entity outside one's organization (e.g., a programmatic accreditor). For example, Carol H. Weiss defines evaluation as "the systematic assessment of the operation and/or the outcomes of a program or policy, compared to a set of explicit or implicit standards, as a means of contributing to the improvement of the program or policy."[1]

Planning and assessment are, in our view, two sides of the same coin. Planning to implement a service or add a resource without prior assessment of needs, interest, and support increases the likelihood that stakeholders' needs will not be met. Similarly, launching an assessment of a resource or service without prior planning will generate a collection of meaningless data.

More accurately, planning and assessment are two phases in a process. There are many variations on the planning and assessment cycle depicted in figure 1.1, but this simplified version conveys its essence. *Plan* and *assess* are joined in the cycle by *implement* and *regroup* and *revise*. The latter two terms refer, respectively, to the actual placement of the service or resource being planned for and assessed, and the period of recalibration that (hopefully) comes after assessing preliminary results of the initiative in question.

In an ideal scenario, organizations embarking on a new initiative would follow some version of this process. First, the organization would gather data about constituents' needs and desires to inform project development and help establish goals for its execution. Throughout the new initiative, the organization would conduct formative assessment to gauge progress and incremental success in order to make adjustments. At a logical pause or the

FIGURE 1.1
The planning and assessment cycle

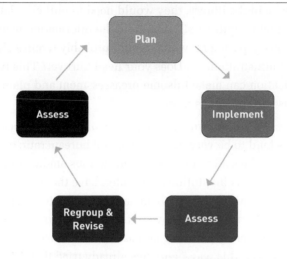

project's conclusion, a summative assessment measures the project's success in light of the goals set during its design and informs efforts at revising the next iteration of the project or new initiative.

Unfortunately, however, the process of designing and implementing a new service or resource more often resembles what is shown in figure 1.2. (The first and last steps are optional.)

Why do libraries so often forgo a robust planning process prior to new initiatives? There are a number of reasons.

1. *Libraries are complex organizations.* Effective assessment and planning can require input from employees in departments outside the area primarily responsible for the new initiative. For example, if a young adult services librarian wanted to plan

FIGURE 1.2
Typical implementation process

for a weekly program and needed to review circulation data to see which evenings large numbers of teenagers were most likely to already be in the library, they would need to pull circulation data, which might require assistance from the information technology or systems department, which would probably require clearance from administration. . . . Does your head hurt yet? This type of complication can make fulsome preassessment and planning onerous and time-consuming.

2. *Libraries are not known for being especially nimble.* Because libraries tend to be very hierarchical and bureaucratic organizations, it can be difficult to coordinate actions among multiple departments. As institutions they often have the momentum of several generations behind them, and reversing (or even shifting) course can be a challenge. Two of the biggest hurdles anyone involved in library planning and assessment must clear are "we've always done it this way," and "we already tried that." Those who utter those cursed phrases rarely include the unspoken coda: "even if it's not the best way," and "twenty-five years ago."

3. *Libraries operate within a number of constraints.* Libraries face near-constant scarcity of any number of essential resources—time, effort, money, and support from stakeholders are just a few examples. A library may be aware that it is a good idea to conduct a needs assessment prior to designing a new service, but staff may just not have the time or knowledge to conduct it effectively.

4. *"Need" is not always the motivating factor in developing new initiatives.* Sometimes, libraries create a new service or change an old one simply because it sounds like a good idea. Of course, this is often a function of our awareness of new and developing trends in library services, or of the availability of specific resources. It's part of a librarian's job to anticipate patrons' needs before they're even aware of them. This can work out well and result in popular and progressive services (e.g., an information commons or chat reference), but sometimes librarians misfire and end up investing a lot of resources in initiatives that are less fruitful (e.g., library presence in Second Life), which leads us to our next reason libraries might forgo planning and assessment:

5. *"Move fast and break things."* It can feel like some library administrators adopted Facebook's old motto as their guiding principle and have become obsessed with each new platform, app, or gadget that becomes available. Sometimes an organization's decision-makers just aren't interested in finding out that there really isn't a need for their pet project.

So, although it's understandable that one might want to avoid the planning and assessment process when developing and implementing a new resource or service, failing to do so creates complications down the road. For purposes of our discussion, the most significant of these is that without the information upon which the planning process is typically based, assessing the effectiveness of the service or resource in question post-implementation is far more difficult.

Why Planning Matters

Planning and assessment are responses to complexity. Ideally, they translate complexity into focused priorities and goals, outline effective and efficient action toward those goals, and clearly and simply measure progress and success.

Interest in the practice of planning has grown in tandem with the complexity of modern life. One of the earliest forms of formalized planning was urban planning. For those living in a nomadic band or a small village, not much planning is required. But the larger a city becomes, the more planning is required simply to keep it functioning, not to mention to avoid the looming potential disasters of communicable disease and infrastructure failure. Likewise, libraries were once much simpler organizations situated within a much simpler society. In that context, minimal planning was required. Planning is most important in an environment of high risk and high complexity, which is the situation in which most modern libraries and information centers find themselves.

Planning is a word that we all use a lot, in many different contexts. We have plans to go to dinner with friends, plans to go on a dream vacation next year, wedding plans, house plans, retirement plans. A lot of what we call plans are actually vague dreams or wishes. The ubiquity of the word is in some ways unfortunate because it obscures what we mean by planning and belies the incredible power that rests, waiting to be unleashed, in the formal practice of planning when it is well executed.

Effective planning, whether it is a plan for the perfect vacation or a plan for your organization, must always start with analysis. This analysis is often the most difficult part. Yet it is also potentially transformative, for it involves the powerful process of defining your purpose and priorities, as well as narrowing your focus. Narrowing focus is painful because it necessitates the exclusion of possible priorities and goals, and it requires giving up many worthwhile things you might wish to do to focus your energy and resources on a much narrower set of possibilities. This narrowed focus is the best and, some would argue, the only way to achieve great results. As the old saying goes, you can achieve anything you desire, but not everything you desire.

For libraries, narrow focus and clarity of direction have never been more important. Constant and accelerating change and advances in information technologies, competing priorities in civic and academic life, increasing social complexity, and the ever-present competition for funding all result in a maze of choices that organizations must make regularly, often with no real precedents and little or no hard data. Those choices can and have been made by sheer guesswork, which can and has gone terribly wrong. One major reason planning matters is it is the best way to minimize the risks of making the wrong choices, investing in the wrong technologies, implementing the wrong strategies, or not being able to quickly course correct in the face of unexpected challenges. This type of planning is not off the cuff, not the same as the whim to make "plans" to go to dinner next Saturday. It is a disciplined and powerful practice that can transform the course of an organization's future and can even change lives. That may sound like hyperbole, but it's this understanding of the power of planning and assessment, and our direct experience working with these practices over more than a decade, that informs our enthusiasm for the subject. Make no mistake, achieving transformative results can be challenging, but we aren't aware of any other way to achieve such results. The tools of planning and assessment provide a concrete path for achieving change and excellence within an organization. We'll go into more depth on the principles of planning in chapter 3.

Assessment That Matters

Like planning, assessment is a large and tremendously complex topic. Those with little formal experience with assessment can find the thought of developing a formal program of assessment, or even a smaller assessment project, quite daunting! We think considering some basic principles of assessment—why and when to do it, how to design it, and what to prioritize—can go a long way toward demystifying the process.

Two early guides to library assessment offer compelling answers to the questions of why and when libraries should engage in assessment (which is referred to as "evaluation" in both texts). In *Library Evaluation: A Casebook and Can-Do Guide*, Danny Wallace and Connie Van Fleet present a list of reasons libraries engage in assessment that we have referred back to many times.

According to Wallace and Van Fleet, libraries conduct assessment to:

1. Account for how they use their limited resources
2. Explain what they do
3. Enhance their visibility
4. Describe their impact
5. Increase efficiency
6. Avoid errors
7. Support planning activities
8. Express concern for their public
9. Support decision-making
10. Strengthen their political position[2]

"But," you might be thinking to yourself, "I thought the point of assessment was to, you know, *assess something*?" It is, at least nominally, but assessment can serve a number of additional purposes, and if you choose not to incorporate them into your planning, you have missed an opportunity. It's interesting to note that some of the reasons in Wallace and Van Fleet's list are internally focused, some are externally focused, and others are both (see figure 1.3). Effective assessment must involve stakeholders at some point(s) in the project's conceptualization, execution, or decision-making as a result of the project's findings. In our view, four of the nine reasons listed in figure 1.3 address external stakeholders, whereas an additional two are both internally and externally focused.

FIGURE 1.3

Internal and external purposes of assessment

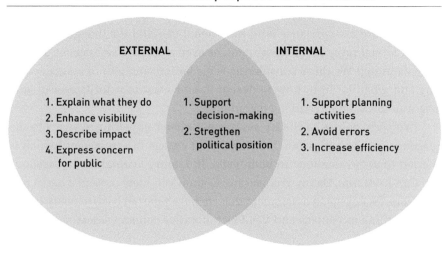

EXTERNAL   INTERNAL

1. Explain what they do   1. Support   1. Support planning
2. Enhance visibility   decision-making   activities
3. Describe impact   2. Stregthen   2. Avoid errors
4. Express concern   political position   3. Increase efficiency
   for public

In Wallace and Van Fleet's list, reason 10, which states that libraries conduct assessment to "strengthen their political position," explicitly acknowledges the fact that assessment is *always* political in that it requires commitment of valuable resources, especially in the form of time and person-power, two of a library's most valuable assets. It turns out that time actually *is* money in the sense that the time library employees spend on designing and executing an assessment project could be used in other ways and may create a deficit of effort elsewhere. Just as a library's annual budget is a statement of its priorities for that year, the focus of an assessment project indicates a library's most pressing concerns.

Because undertaking assessment is so labor-intensive and can have far-reaching consequences, a number of factors must be considered. José Marie Griffiths and Donald King's *Special Libraries: Increasing the Information Edge* provides a series of helpful guidelines for the important internal and external factors to consider in planning, including when a library should (and should not) undertake an assessment effort.

1. Evaluation must have a purpose; it must not be an end in itself.

2. Evaluation must be more than descriptive; it must take into account relationships among operational performance, users, and organizations.

3. Evaluation should be a communication tool involving staff
   and users.

4. Evaluation should not be sporadic but must be ongoing and
   provide a means for continual monitoring, diagnosis, and change.

5. Ongoing evaluation should be dynamic in nature, reflecting
   new knowledge and changes in the environment.[3]

All of these points offer helpful guidance, but items 1 and 2 resonate particularly strongly. As we've established, a meaningful assessment project is
resource-intensive. It is not possible to evaluate the utility and effectiveness
of every initiative and service, so some projects must be prioritized over others. Why would a library allocate a portion of its limited capacity to measure
something if it has no intention or ability to respond to what is discovered?
This applies to internal assessment, such as employee engagement or satisfaction surveys, as well. If a library distributes an employee survey to determine how the library could be improved as a workplace, then declines to
respond to any of their suggestions, there's a strong possibility that employees will be even less satisfied than they were before they were surveyed.

It's notable that several points in Griffiths and King's list seem to anticipate the *critical assessment* movement that has emerged over the past several
years. Grounded in the principles of cultural critical theoretical approaches
to research, critical assessment calls for its practitioners to engage in mindful-
ness and self-reflection in all stages of an assessment project. Critical assessment asks that we consider the cultural, social, and critical structures that
permeate tasks central to planning and assessment such as setting priorities,
values, and goals and allocating resources, while centering methods that rein-
force the precedence of quantitative data collection and analysis methods.

In addition to the idea that assessment must be actionable, Griffiths and
King's point that evaluation must consider relationships within the organization and with outside stakeholders is also central to critical assessment. We
agree that those engaged in library assessment must approach the decisions
they make in conceptualizing and executing assessment projects with keen
awareness of how the project might affect their colleagues, administrators,
and stakeholders.

Points 5 and 6 in Griffiths and King's list emphasize the need for assessment efforts to evolve and adapt, and preview the planning and assessment
cycle.

One assessment principle Griffiths and King do not list (explicitly, at least) is that assessment projects can provide an opportunity for positive public relations, a benefit we believe is often overlooked.

This can mean a couple of different things:

- First, an assessment project offers an opportunity to let patrons know that your library cares about their needs and wishes to explore how well the library is actually addressing those needs and wishes.
- Another unexpected benefit of assessment is that it can inform stakeholders about the service or resource being assessed.

If your library conducts a survey about patrons' satisfaction with your chat reference service, there's an excellent chance that some patrons will learn of its existence through the survey. For this reason, consider crafting your approach to assessing resources and services in a manner that also informs about the resource or service you're assessing. Of course, you shouldn't manipulate a survey instrument or other tool to such an extent that it no longer measures what it was initially intended to assess, but it can be helpful to include explanatory information about the service or resource being assessed for those who may not be familiar with it.

To these we would add a few guidelines of our own, which we'll cover in the rest of the chapter.

1. Assessment must be placed in context.
2. Assessment must be rigorous.
3. Assessment must be ethical and just.
4. Assessment must contribute to the larger conversation.
5. Assessment shouldn't reinvent the wheel.

Assessment in Context

Our use of the word *context* here is purposefully broad. In general, what we mean is that a library assessment project must reflect the needs and priorities of its community members.

Unsure how you might do that? The foundational documentation your library, university, municipality, or other organization has created is a great place to start. Mission, vision, and values statements can be frustratingly prosaic, but they should point to at least a few different institutional priorities.

Let's take, for example, the mission statement of our home institution, the University of Tennessee, Knoxville (UTK):

> The primary mission of the University of Tennessee is to move forward the frontiers of human knowledge and enrich and elevate the citizens of the state of Tennessee, the nation, and the world. As the preeminent research-based land-grant university in the state, UT embodies the spirit of excellence in teaching, research, scholarship, creative activity, outreach, and engagement attained by the nation's finest public research institutions.[4]

If you have been involved in writing one of these statements, you know that their authors (typically a committee) labor over them very closely and (usually) select each word with care. With that in mind, let's highlight what seems to be some of the statement's key words and phrases:

> The primary mission of the University of Tennessee is *to move forward the frontiers of human knowledge and enrich and elevate the citizens of the state of Tennessee,* the nation, and the world. As the preeminent *research-based land-grant university in the state,* UT embodies the spirit of excellence in *teaching, research, scholarship, creative activity, outreach, and engagement* attained by the nation's finest *public research institutions.*

From this, we can glean the following priorities:

- advancing knowledge
- enriching and elevating citizens of the state
- addressing the needs of a research-based public land-grant institution
- teaching, research/scholarship/creative activity, outreach, and engagement

And note that

> **Research is mentioned three times in the sixty-five word statement.** UTK is a Carnegie R1 institution (Doctoral University: Very High Research Activity), one of two in the state and Tennessee's only public institution with this designation (the private Vanderbilt University is the other). "Mov[ing] forward the frontiers of human knowledge" presumably also refers to research, as that is the primary method for a university's constituents to make such progress.

The statement refers specifically to *creative activity* alongside *research* and *scholarship*. This is fairly unusual among research institutions' mission statements and may reflect the fact that UTK has very strong academic programs in creative areas such as printmaking and theatre.

The statement does not mention *service*, which, along with research and teaching, forms the traditional "three-legged stool" of academic work. In its place, the statement addresses outreach and engagement—which are two types of service, to be sure, but exclude much of the more inwardly focused service work that universities (and particularly, their faculty) engage in, such as revising curricula, systematizing administrative processes, and reviewing colleagues' tenure and promotion materials.

The emphasis on outreach and engagement is in accord with the mission statement's emphasis on UTK's status as a public land-grant university (LGU). Established with the Morrill Acts of 1862 and 1890, LGUs were created to provide practical education in agriculture and the "mechanic arts," such as architecture, to a broader segment of American society than had previously enjoyed access to higher education. Part of that mission includes sharing the knowledge generated through research in areas such as agriculture to the practitioners who might benefit from it directly. Reference to UTK's LGU status, in combination with the specific reference to the state of Tennessee, make explicit the university's external focus on and commitment to the state's residents. The statement mentions enriching and elevating Tennesseans; while "elevating" is most likely a euphemism, "enriching" is situated in such a way that it's difficult to imagine that it is used metaphorically. We should consider that the university considers improving the financial prospects of the state's citizens to be a high priority.

How might we translate these priorities into assessment projects? Here are a few ideas:

Supporting Creativity: While demonstrating the library's support for research is already pretty well-trod ground, there has been less exploration of how academic library resources and services address the needs of faculty and students in the creative arts. Although we may not think of them as often, visual, literary, musical, and dramatic artists have information needs, too: they seek reference points and inspiration for new works, research the characteristics of different materials, seek exemplars for creating period-appropriate costumes, hair, and makeup, and so on. Many of these needs are likely addressed by library-provided resources and services, and there are many avenues for measuring the libraries' contributions to faculty's and students' creative output.

Enriching Tennesseans: This phrase seems to nod toward the university's status as a land-grant university that is tasked in part with transmitting faculty research findings to citizens who might use them to practical benefit. In some cases, this includes techniques for improving efficiency, some of which might be of financial benefit to, for example, farmers in the state. What library resources and services were employed in service to agricultural research?

Outreach and Engagement: If we assume that the mission statement uses these terms to refer to interactions outside the university's primary constituency, we might consider those library resources and services that are more outwardly facing, such as special collections. What impact do these, particularly those that are made accessible to the general public online, have on the attitudes about UTK held by those who are not among its immediate constituents?

Whose Context?

It is important to note that "community priorities" does not exclusively refer to those expressed by the leadership of your institution and its governing body. It's also vital to consider priorities expressed by constituents and those organizations representing constituents whose voices are not always heard. These should include groups representing members of traditionally marginalized groups such as

- Individuals and families experiencing homelessness
- Black, indigenous, and people of color (BIPOC)
- Members of the LGBTQIA+ community
- Community members with disabilities
- And so on, as appropriate to your community

With this in mind, and following our approach to the UTK mission statement, let's look at the mission statement for the university's office of Multicultural Student Life (MSL):

> Multicultural Student Life is dedicated to promoting a welcoming and inclusive campus environment while advocating for traditionally marginalized students by providing academic support, multicultural education, identity exploration, leadership development, and diverse and innovative programming through collaborative partnerships. We strive to assist in the retention and graduation of students who are empowered to positively impact a global society.[5]

This mission statement is packed! We've italicized some of the elements that might be actionable vis-à-vis planning and assessment; let's consider a few:

> *Promoting a welcoming and inclusive campus environment:* What programs and services does the library offer to support this goal? For example, does the library offer space that MSL might use for meetings or other activities?
>
> *Advocating for traditionally marginalized students:* How does the library support this goal locally? If the library has any sort of student advisory council, does administration ensure the students invited to participate are representative of the student body as a whole?
>
> *Multicultural education:* How does the library leverage its resources and programs to promote this goal? For example, does Special Collections curate exhibits and invite instructors of specific courses to bring their students for library instruction enriched by, say, materials related to social movements throughout the university's history?
>
> *Diverse and innovative programming through collaborative partnerships:* Does the library proactively pursue this type of relationship with organizations and units on campus that serve students, faculty, and staff from marginalized groups? What programs and events might the libraries co-sponsor or support by providing resources or space?

Because there is a significant danger that they may not be otherwise represented in the planning process in your organization, we want to emphasize the importance of consulting with stakeholders whose voices have traditionally been overlooked when considering how to plan for and assess the effectiveness of services and resources designed to support their needs. Consulting with users (and non-users) from marginalized groups should be an essential element of the planning and assessment process.

Rigorous Assessment

Rachel worked as an academic librarian prior to beginning her doctoral program and maintained close relationships with many of her former colleagues—her academic department was even located in the main library! She had not been working on her degree very long when she found herself in the library's elevator with one of its upper-level administrators. After exchanging small talk, the administrator leveled a penetrating look at Rachel and admonished her that no matter what she chose to focus her research on, she should make sure it was "rigorous—this field needs more rigor." Then the elevator doors opened, he nodded meaningfully and stepped out.

Rachel remembers feeling vaguely bemused and a little insulted: did he think she hadn't planned to be rigorous in her approach *before* his request? She suspected so; this particular administrator, who had earned his PhD in a field other than library and information science, had given the impression that he held LIS in somewhat low regard as a field of scholarship, one in which taking a rigorous approach to research was not, if you'll forgive the saying, *de rigueur.*

At this point, you might be confused—is *rigor* a good thing? Merriam-Webster defines rigor as "harsh inflexibility in opinion, temper, or judgment: severity (2): the quality of being unyielding or inflexible: strictness."[6] These are not positive qualities! In research, however, rigor is a quality to strive for. If a research project is described as having rigor, it was conceptualized well; data generation, collection, and analysis were executed carefully and precisely; and the findings were presented in an effective, honest, and ethical manner.

In the many years since Rachel's encounter with Administrator X, she has thought of his admonition often, especially when she's felt tempted toward expediency in an assessment project. Is she driven to prove him wrong? Perhaps in part, but regardless of motivation, both of us do try to design and execute our assessment projects as carefully and precisely as possible. When we have generated and analyzed our data, we are careful not to overstate our conclusions. Being able to come to small conclusions and support them with evidence is much more satisfying (and meaningful) than making a grand pronouncement that you can't back up. This idea ties into our next guideline.

Ethical and Just Assessment

Most of us can probably agree that misrepresenting the significance of evidence generated through an assessment project is unethical. There are many other places, however, when ethics in assessment can go off the rails. As many library-related assessment projects involve human beings who use library resources and services, ethical behavior is essential. First of all, approaching assessment from a critical perspective requires close consideration of the assumptions underlying the resources and services chosen for assessment and the approaches enlisted to conduct the assessment.

If you are affiliated with an academic institution, you may be familiar with its institutional review board (IRB). The purpose of IRBs is to protect the well-being of human subjects involved in research. First, the researcher submits a summary of the study and its potential dangers to human participants for review by the IRB. Some institutions' institutional review requests are processed by a faculty or staff representative in individual academic department before institution-level review; some ask that applications be submitted directly to the institution-level IRB. Although some institutions still rely on submission by e-mail attachment, most license access to one of the several different clients designed to facilitate the submission, review, and administration process.

If you are conducting an assessment project but don't intend to make your findings available outside your institution (e.g., in a publication or presentation), IRB approval is not strictly necessary. We would like to encourage you to go ahead and secure IRB approval for your project, though, for reasons we'll explain in the following section.

Assessment That Contributes to the Larger Conversation

This point may seem to contradict the earlier premise that assessment must be placed in context, but we believe it's possible for every assessment project to include connections to the benefits of library resources and services more generally. Your assessment project can provide useful information for librarians at institutions similar to yours in size and service community who are contemplating new or revised resources or services. Another librarian might choose to reproduce your assessment project or adapt your approach. They won't know how to do that unless you share your project outside your library.

Over the past several years, we've noticed a trend at conferences and, to a lesser extent, in publications, that we would like to encourage: sharing "failure stories." In the past, the convention for sharing the results of a research project has been to discard those results that don't support the original hypotheses. In other words, if the study doesn't "work," it should be scrapped. This might make sense for a biology research project (we honestly don't know if this is the case), but in an applied field like ours, sharing descriptions of failed initiatives can be as helpful as discussing those that were successful. If you hear from a colleague that the teen reading club they tried to launch to help decrease community members' experience of library anxiety had no effect, it might make you think twice about launching the same type of program at your library. This leads to our next point.

Don't Reinvent the Wheel

We assert that there is so much assessment work to be done that those embarking on a new assessment project should prioritize evaluating those services, resources, and user groups that have not been explored previously or have not been reviewed using a particular method or other significant change. If an assessment project is to be replicated, it should be tied explicitly to the project it's reproducing.

We have one more guiding principle, which we'll cover in chapter 4.

Conclusion

We hope that we've convinced you of the essential relationship between planning and assessment, or at least given you some food for thought. If you're still skeptical, read on to chapter 2, where we will discuss the history of the two enterprises and their development, which was largely in tandem.

NOTES

1. Carol H. Weiss, *Evaluation: Methods for Studying Programs and Policies* (Upper Saddle River, NJ: Prentice Hall, 1998), 4.
2. Danny P. Wallace and Connie Van Fleet, *Library Evaluation: A Casebook and Can-Do Guide* (Santa Barbara, CA: Libraries Unlimited, 2001), xx–xxi.
3. José Marie Griffiths and Donald W. King, *Special Libraries: Increasing the Information Edge* (Washington, DC: Special Libraries Association, 1993), 3.
4. The University of Tennessee, "Mission and Vision," Vol Vision Strategic Plan, https://volvision.utk.edu/mission-vision/.
5. Office of Multicultural Student Life at the University of Tennessee, Knoxville, "Mission of the Office of Multicultural Student Life," https://multicultural.utk.edu.
6. *Merriam-Webster*, s.v. "rigor (n)," https://www.merriam-webster.com/dictionary/rigor.

2

The History of Planning and Assessment in Libraries

- Planning
- Assessment
- Conclusion

We have a feeling that this chapter will be the favorite of some of our readers, whereas others will skip it entirely. We understand.

If you're a skipper, you might wonder why we're bothering to discuss the historical development of planning and assessment. Fair enough. Simply put, we believe the fundamentals of any topic include its origins, or at least some of them. The development of the profession is also important from the perspective of our organizations: both the ALA Core Competencies of Librarianship, drafted in 2009, and the ACRL Proficiencies for Assessment Librarians and Coordinators, drafted in 2017, established that a basic knowledge of the history of libraries and librarianship in general and a broad understanding of the literature, scope, growth, and role of assessment specifically were foundational to the profession.[1] Furthermore, 86.4 percent of our survey respondents indicated their job required "awareness of important library assessment initiatives, both current and past."

We both also believe it's important to know how and why a phenomenon developed in order to execute it successfully. Although an in-depth exploration of the history of planning and assessment in libraries is outside the scope of this text, we would like to discuss some of the more significant developments of the past 150 years or so.

This chapter provides a quick overview of the history of planning and assessment in libraries, including the development of planning and strategic planning; early efforts to standardize library data collection, such as the Gerould Statistics; the growth of surveys as the predominant approach to library assessment; and more recent efforts and approaches, such as ACRL's Value Report and the critical assessment movement.

Planning

The history of planning is inextricably linked with the evolution of assessment practices. As will become apparent throughout the whole of this book, the two are functionally inseparable. The history of planning in libraries and information centers is really the history of planning in modern western society. Both grew in parallel and developments in the library world tended to follow and adapt to what was happening in society as a whole. Although there are many different types of planning that happen in libraries, as we will explore further in chapter 3, in this history we will trace the evolution of planning in libraries in the broadest sense. The emergence of planning as a discipline arose in tandem with the emergence of managerial science in the latter part of the nineteenth and early part of the twentieth centuries. The need for managers, and therefore managerial science, essentially grew out of the Industrial Revolution and the rise of the factory system and the general increasing complexity of society. Prior to this, individuals tended to largely direct their own work or perhaps the work of a few apprentices or laborers, which is, of course, quite a different prospect than directing and managing large, complex organizations or communities. Likewise, a need for more complex and comprehensive planning also arose at this time. As Claude

S. George, Jr., wrote in *The History of Management Thought,* "Planning, of course, is not a separate recognizable act. . . . Every managerial act, mental or physical, is inexorably intertwined with planning. It is as much a part of every managerial act as breathing is to the living human."[2]

Management science and administrative science developed in tandem. Some terms may be used somewhat interchangeably in tracing their histories, but there are some important differences between the two that continue to reverberate to the present day. We will discuss these differences presently.

Management Science or Public Administration?

Increasing efficiency was the initial focus of administrative science, beginning with the Efficiency Movement of 1890 to 1932, also known as Taylorism, after its most enthusiastic adherent. Woodrow Wilson wrote "The Study of Administration" in 1887, which is widely considered the beginning of the discipline of public administration.[3] Increasing complexity in society, in government, and in business began at this time and was intensified by World Wars I and II. This was an explosive and hugely impactful movement at the time. As Charles Merriam said in 1912, "More attention has been given to the subject of efficient administration in our American cities during the last ten years than in any previous period of our history."[4] Textbooks for governmental administrators began appearing in the mid-1920s, and the American Management Association was founded in 1925. Both industrial and governmental administrators were "professionalized" around this time.

The formative tension between management science and public administration was also present in the library world. In 1887, Frederick M. Crunden, librarian of the St. Louis Public Library, gave a speech to ALA titled "Business Methods in Library Management"; in 1910, John Cotton Dana, founder of the Special Libraries Association and general library science pioneer, stated

> The librarian should have culture, scholarship, and executive ability . . .
> as a matter of fact the position of librarian is more of an executive business affair than a literary one . . . [S]uccess or failure of a library, as of a
> business, depends on the ability of the man or woman at its head, and
> only trained men and women should be in charge."[5]

Dana looked to the success of the (then) modern department store as a model for making libraries and museums more relevant to the lives of ordinary people, adding, "A great department store, easily reached, open at all hours, is more like a good museum of art than any of the museums we have yet established."[6]

Other prominent figures in the library world believed that public administration was the more appropriate model for library science. In 1938, the Library Institute at the Graduate Library School (GLS) of the University of Chicago devoted a third of its annual sessions to the topic of "current issues in administration," which drew more heavily from the field of public administration. GLS faculty member Carleton B. Joeckel wrote in 1938 that the topic of library administration

> is at once old and new. It is old in the sense that questions of organization and management have long been discussed by librarians. It is new in the sense that close and scientific study of library administration as a subject worthy of consideration in itself is only in its beginnings.[7]

Joeckel also believed that large libraries should, like government and industry, establish research departments or employ research assistants to aid in administrative decision-making, which may be one of the first explicit ties between administration, planning, and assessment in libraries.

Today, the question of whether management science or public administration provides the more appropriate model for running a library has largely been resolved in favor of management science. Guidance for applying business models to running a library abounds, whereas similar discussions of public administration's applicability in libraries are largely absent. Yet, as R. Kathleen Molz has said, "there may be a basic fallacy in assuming that the techniques for planning in a for-profit enterprise can be easily assimilated in a not-for-profit, or vice versa."[8] Although the idea of running a library like a business is currently very popular, the simple and obvious statement must be made that a library is not a business; even a special library, which may serve a business, is not in itself a business. The bottom-line goal of any business, by definition, is to generate profits, which are relatively straightforward to plan for and to assess. But a library, like any public sector organization, usually has multiple goals, some of which may conflict. A library's goals are also dynamic and may be obscure or poorly defined. It is important to keep in mind that planning concepts for the for-profit and not-for-profit sectors may overlap but are not always interchangeable in practice.

Standards and Goals for Libraries

In the late 1920s, Herbert Hoover commissioned the Research Committee on Social Trends, which eventually issued a massive two-volume report called *Recent Social Trends in the United States*. This report had far-reaching effects in all fields, and libraries were no exception. In response, Jesse Hauk Shera commented:

> What, then, taken by and large, has the librarian to learn from these two bulging volumes? . . . Obviously, it is the need for a basic, all-inclusive plan for future library development, co-ordinated with, and highly responsive to, the fluctuations, in our economic and social life.[9]

In the social and economic aftermath of the Depression and World Wars, the trend of planning swept the nation, and libraries were no exception. Throughout the 1930s and 1940s, national planning was ALA's top priority. ALA's Committee on Post-War Planning suggested developing standards and goals for all libraries, specific to their type: public, school, and academic libraries. These standards were first drafted and published in the mid-1940s. "A National Plan for Libraries" was published in the *ALA Bulletin* in 1935 and revised again in 1939.[10]

From Long-Range Planning . . .

The focus on programmatic and operational planning that developed in the early part of the twentieth century slowly shifted to a focus on long-range planning in the 1950s. Long-range planning was also sometimes known as corporate planning and was a precursor to strategic planning. It was from the practice of long-range planning that the concepts of goals, objectives, and performance measurement eventually came into use in libraries, which was fairly well established, particularly in public and academic libraries, by the 1970s. While the survey movement might be considered the earliest form of assessment in libraries, it was in the 1970s, with the growth of long-range and strategic planning, that library assessment as we know it today truly got its start.

One of the earliest works on strategic planning, Robert N. Anthony's *Planning and Control Systems: A Framework for Analysis*, was published in 1965.[11] Anthony's text proved highly influential, and the library world was not immune to its influence. Perhaps unsurprisingly, libraries' first push toward long-range planning was imposed from outside when, in 1970, an amendment to the Library Services and Construction Act of 1962 mandated long-range planning for state library agencies. It wasn't long before library-related organizations jumped on the long-range planning train: one of the first SPEC Kits ever published by the Association of Research Libraries (ARL) was titled *Goals and Objectives.*[12] Long-range planning became truly mainstream with the 1980 publication of Vernon E. Palmour's *A Planning Process for Public Libraries.*[13]

. . . To Strategic Planning

By the mid-1980s, many academic libraries had long-range plans that were beginning to include elements of strategic planning. In 1984 the first manual on strategic planning specifically for libraries was published, Donald E. Riggs's *Strategic Planning for Library Managers.*[14] *Strategic Planning Basics for Special Libraries* by Doris Asantewa followed in 1992.[15]

Public libraries followed suit. By the early 1990s, many library associations were publishing manuals or providing guidance for conducting formal planning, including the Public Library Association, a division of the ALA; the UK Library and Information Services Council Working Group on Public Library Objectives (1991); and the Association of Research Libraries.[16] Since the early 2000s, libraries have increasingly been required by parent institutions, legislators, and funders to perform regular strategic planning that aligns with the goals and strategic priorities of those stakeholders. These requirements go hand in hand with the calls for greater accountability that have made assessment and performance measurement even more crucial.

Assessment

If the professional literature of librarianship provides an accurate snapshot of the field, assessment is a term and concept that, although not new, has exploded in librarians' collective consciousness. Searching in Library and Information Science Source reveals that between 2011 and 2020, the database indexed 1,560 academic journal articles with "assessment" in the title. In the years between 1932 and 2010, "assessment" featured in the titles of 1,242 articles, the majority of which were published between 1990 and 2010.

Although we believe it is pointless to try and identify a single cause for this increased interest, it is worthwhile to consider a few of the circumstances that have likely contributed to it.

It also makes sense to distinguish those assessment efforts that are internally focused, including statistical reports and questionnaires completed by librarians, from those that consider the behavior, needs, and preferences of users.

James T. Gerould and the Association of Research Libraries Statistical Program

A significant example of the former is the initiative launched by James T. Gerould, librarian at the University of Minnesota and Princeton University. In a 1906 article published in the *Library Journal*, Gerould lamented that "year after year the American Library Association has discussed, at its meetings and in its committees, the question of library statistics, but no satisfactory plan has yet been evolved by which such figures can be made available."[17] Even if it were, Gerould said, the plan was designed to track statistics germane to public library services, not those provided by academic libraries. Then, as now, academic and public libraries differed in several significant ways; Gerould points out that circulation statistics were not an effective measure of academic library use as many libraries of the time severely limited user privileges.

Rather than continue to wait for ALA to finalize a plan that would be largely irrelevant to academic libraries, Gerould proposed his own approach. Although his *Library Journal* article provides a few reasons for his proposal, Gerould's primary interest seems to have been creating a regularly updated, comprehensive repository of the state-of-the-art of academic libraries. In Gerould's view, public libraries were responsible for a greater share of the progress in the field at that time; he believed academic librarians could mine their collections for data to strengthen their arguments for modernization.

These were the data points Gerould recommended collecting:

> *Building.* When was the building erected? What was its cost? What is its present and ultimate book capacity? How many seminar rooms? What system of stacks is used?
> *Books.* Total number? Additions during the year, by purchase, by gift? What special collections have you?

Finances. Income during the past year? Is the income the product of invested funds, legislative appropriations, or allotments from general university funds? How much has been spent for books, or periodicals, for building, for supplies and equipment? Are salaries chargeable against library funds or against the general funds for the institution? How are the funds allotted among the different departments of instruction? What classes of books does the librarian buy on his own motion? Do you charge a library fee?

Librarian. How elected? Does he have a seat in the faculty? Does he have the advantage of the sabbatical system? Does he give instruction in bibliography or library economy? Does he have the power of appointment and dismissal of subordinates?

Staff. Number of administrative and technical staff? How many doing order and accession work, reference work, cataloging, at loan desk, in other departments? Do you have a bindery? How many employees? Is promotion made by examination? Do you train your own assistants? Is the staff employed for the calendar or for the academic year? How much time allowed for vacations? Do you have a half holiday during the week?

Orders and accessions. What office records are kept? Do you have a regular agent for American books? Are your books ordered through a foreign or American agent? Number of periodicals received by purchase, by gift and exchange? Do you use an accession book? If not, what other scheme?

Catalog. In what form is your card catalog? Average cost of cataloging per title? Do you use Library of Congress cards? ALA cards? Have you duplicate departmental catalogs?

Loans. Do you loan books to all students? Is a deposit required? Is any restriction placed on faculty loans? What percent of your students use the library with any degree of regularity? What is your system of fines?

Reference. Have you a permanent reference library, and, if so, how large? Are the books largely duplicated in the main collection? Have you a separate room for serials? Have you the open shelf system for all students?

Departmental libraries. Do you have departmental or seminary
libraries, and do you distinguish between them? How are they
cared for? Have you any laboratory libraries not considered as
a part of the university library? Are the books in the seminary
library duplicated in the main collection? Are the seminary
libraries permanent or shifting collections?

Salaries. What is the payroll of the library?[18]

In response to Gerould's call, a group of prominent academic librarians
formed a committee to develop a plan for systematizing statistic collections.
It may surprise some readers to learn that the committee's work proceeded
with astonishing speed; Gerould began collecting statistics in the 1907/8 academic year and did so annually until he retired from Princeton University in
1938. The Princeton University Library continued the practice until the early
1960s, when the Association of Research Libraries took over the task.

Readers who are interested in learning more about the Gerould Statistics are
advised to read Robert E. Molyneux's *The Gerould Statistics, 1907/8-1961/2*, which
describes the history of the project and provides detailed analysis of the methodologies used over the years.[19]

The Gerould Statistics provided the seed from which the ARL statistics
program grew. In the years since 1962, the number and type of statistics collected by the ARL have expanded to encompass a vast assortment of metrics related to resources, expenditures, services, and staff. The model isn't
limited to the relatively small group of ARL-member libraries, either: ARL
has worked with other organizations, including the Association of College
and Research Libraries (ACRL), to shape their statistics programs, effectively
applying the ARL model to libraries associated with all types of academic
libraries.

Other Large-Scale Statistical Programs

In his 1991 review of efforts to build a national program for collecting library
statistics, Robert Williams asked "why does the library and information professional community still not have, after over 150 years of working on the
problem, a comprehensive and systematic national statistical data collection

system?"[20] That is not to say there hasn't been interest in developing such a program, however; as early as 1837, efforts were made to gather some measures of library resources and services on a large scale. The first significant effort was undertaken in 1849 by Smithsonian Institution librarian Charles Coffin Jewett, whom Williams refers to as "the true 'American father' of library statistics."[21] Jewett considered his effort to survey all public libraries as germane to the Smithsonian's mission. Williams considers Jewett's efforts impressive, though not enduring.

Although various agencies and organizations took a stab at developing and executing comprehensive statistical programs throughout the late nineteenth and early twentieth centuries, none were sustainable.

Passage of the Library Services Act in 1956 brought with it a renewed interest in a national statistical program. Perhaps believing that the US government was on the case, ALA and ACRL seem to have relaxed their statistics-collecting efforts in the early 1960s. Throughout that decade, the newly formed Library Services Branch of what was then named the Office of Education (now the US Department of Education) worked with ALA, state library agencies, and the National Council on Education Statistics (NCES) to develop plans for a national statistical program. The result was the Library General Information System (LIBGIS), under whose auspices school, public, and academic library surveys were conducted throughout the 1970s, until its efforts gradually collapsed. Its legacy lives on, however; the Department of Education has continued to collect and publish academic and public library statistics on an irregular basis first through NCES, and now through the Integrated Postsecondary Education Data System (IPEDS). The Special Libraries Association (SLA) and American Association of Law Libraries (AALL) have collected data from their members, but their data have not been aggregated with those of other types of institutions. Arguably, combining data from multiple types of libraries lacks a purpose beyond providing a single site for those interested in reviewing data from multiple types of libraries.

ACRL has collected statistics from academic libraries since 1998. Data is available by subscription through ACRLMetrics, an online platform.

The Survey Movement

Efforts at collecting standardized data were primarily accomplished by sending each library a form to complete. For this reason, the history of large-scale statistical programs relates directly to a phenomenon referred to as the survey movement, which emerged in the early twentieth century as a result of the recent push to gather empirical data to support planning and other efforts, particularly in Western Europe. Again, we can see an impetus in society's increasing complexity caused by industrialization and concomitant growth in population centers. These, in turn, led to the growth of charity organizations and massive social change.

During this time period, municipal surveys became extremely popular as a technique for managing change and gauging necessary social services. By the 1930s, survey research had begun to make its way into libraries, primarily as a tool for collecting data to support planning efforts (a trend, again, from management science). Endorsed by the American Library Association in 1936 as an effective tool for both public and academic libraries, the survey was the main instrument libraries used to plan organizational change from the mid-1930s through the 1940s. By 1940, one observer would note, "the library world appears to have broken out in a veritable rash of surveys."[22] Most of the library surveys conducted in the early decades of the twentieth century were not completed by community members, but rather librarians tasked with describing the facilities, resources, and services offered by their institution. Surveying stakeholders to ascertain their needs and how well libraries were meeting them was all but unheard of before the 1930s and 1940s—and was uncommon even then.

The Cognitive Turn

In fact, it wasn't until the 1970s that the library assessment world underwent a significant shift in thinking about why and how to evaluate library resources and services. Until that time, assessment was almost exclusively input- or output-based: how many books do you own, and how many times did they circulate last year? Enter the cognitive turn.

This phrase refers to a phenomenon much broader than the library world in which social scientists shifted (or "turned") their view of the role of human beings in social phenomena from one akin to cogs in a machine in favor of a model in which their subjects' thoughts, feelings, and experiences might be an important focus of their research. In library assessment, this manifested as a new interest in understanding patrons' wants, needs, and uses of the library and its resources.

ZWEIZIG AND DERVIN

Douglas Zweizig and Brenda Dervin were two of the most influential advo-
cates of this new approach. In a 1977 review of literature related to studying
public library users, they describe the current approaches as primarily falling
into two categories: "directive" approaches, which describe optimal services,
and approaches based on circulation statistics. Both of which, Zweizig and
Dervin argued, "tell us virtually nothing about who uses the library and how
much."[23] They point out that the statistical approach fails to provide any of
the essential information librarians need to plan programs or improve collections and services. Those studies that do delve more deeply into the characteristics of public library users tended to take what the authors call a "bullet"
approach, focusing on individual variables such as sex, age, race, educational
level, etc., as a basis for comparing levels of public library use, but essentially
providing little actionable data.[24]

Zweizig and Dervin call for a new approach to evaluating library effectiveness: one that moves beyond the premise that "the purpose of library use
is using the library" to exploring the underlying needs that prompted an individual to use the public library: "'Why did someone use the library? What
does the person find useful that the library might be able to provide?"[25] This
focus on the outcomes of public library use is reminiscent of the precepts
of the critical assessment movement, which began germinating in the early
2010s. In the meanwhile, though, the next major movement in library assessment developed: the focus on value, both financial and less concrete.

Return on Investment and Value

A number of factors have contributed to the increased interest in assessment over the past thirty years, but it's fair to say that an impulse toward
self-preservation has been chief among them. Although all types of libraries
have stakeholders for whom they must document their contributions, special
libraries feel this pressure especially acutely. Unsurprisingly, the movement
to strengthen library assessment began in special libraries. Special librarians,
whose facilities are often part of for-profit organizations, have long understood the need to demonstrate their contributions to the parent organizations
that fund them, but the push to establish the value special librarians add
to their organizations took off in earnest in the 1980s with a call to action
from Special Library Association (SLA) President-Elect Frank L. Spaulding.

At the 1985 SLA Annual Meeting, Spaulding established a presidential task force to explore the value of information and the work of the information professional. In his talk, Spaulding made the analogy that the information professional is to information what the spindle is to unprocessed material, like raw cotton, in that information professionals refine information to make it accessible and usable for their clients much in the same way that yarn is wound on a spindle to make it easier to work with. Spaulding asked: "What is the spindle—the information professional—worth, what is the *difference* in value between the information in a jumble on the floor, and the information in usable form—wound on a spindle?"[26]

Because special librarians often work in the for-profit sector, much of the task force's focus had to do with demonstrating how information professionals increase efficiency, support time savings, or directly improve the organization's profit margin by increasing income or decreasing expenditures. The task force's report includes suggestions that were undoubtedly helpful to other less profit-oriented libraries.

Arriving just a few years later, José-Marie Griffiths and Donald W. King's *Special Libraries: Increasing the Information Edge* presents findings from value-related studies conducted in twenty-three companies and federal agencies over the course of a dozen years.[27] Although much of Griffiths and King's text focuses on monetary calculations of value, as in the case of the SLA Task Force, many of the studies the authors share are based on conceptual models that could easily be adapted to other types of organizations. For example, the text includes methods for calculating the actual cost of acquiring specific information if it's not owned by the organization and methods for connecting library resource and service use with desirable qualities, such as individual productivity; provides an overview of the basics of assessment for special librarians; and presents a course of action for librarians in public and academic settings to adapt. While much of Griffiths and King's modeling focuses on economic aspects of information and information services' value, many of the approaches Griffiths and King describe are adaptable to other types of settings.

At the time, focusing on the financial benefits of working with an information professional may have seemed foreign to public and academic librarians. Just a few years later, however, the large-scale shift in how information is published, presented, and accessed would make focusing on materials expenditures and the potential income generated as a result of library resources more practical and logical even for organizations that didn't previously consider such issues.

Electronic Resources Assessment

Throughout the 1980s and 1990s, public, academic, and special libraries shifted information resources and services online at a steady, but measured clip. Right around the beginning of the twentieth century, however, the pace that had been akin to a brisk walk accelerated into a sprint. In very short order, much of libraries' materials budgets were reallocated to electronic resources subscriptions. Why? With the introduction of high-speed internet home connectivity, information seekers could suddenly conduct sophisticated searches of scholarly material relatively quickly—at home. In-house reference statistics dropped precipitously as formerly active library patrons discovered the World Wide Web. Publishers stepped in to meet consumers on the web; librarians, formerly tasked with connecting information seekers with information sources, found they were somewhat extraneous in this new world; or, at least, that information seekers could find a sufficient amount of "good enough" information on their own.

In short order, academic libraries in particular shifted all kinds of resources to make high-quality electronic resources available to their patrons. They moved all kinds of services—interlibrary loan, reference, instruction—online. People continued to visit the physical space of the library, but often for different reasons.

PROJECT COUNTER

A major consequence of this change is that much of patrons' information behavior concerning the most high-cost materials (i.e., the materials that libraries and their stakeholders most wanted to confirm were being used) moved outside library walls and outside librarians' observation. Although vendors of electronic information products provided information about how frequently their products were accessed, the data was messy and inconsistent. It was impossible to compare usage of two similar databases because each might track usage in a different way.

Enter Project COUNTER (Counting Online Usage of NeTworked Electronic Resources) and SUSHI (Standardized Usage Statistics Harvesting

Initiative). Introduced in 2002, COUNTER's Code of Practice provided a standardized collection of statistical measures of electronic resource usage, whereas SUSHI provided the mechanism to automatically harvest the data.[28] Vendors were encouraged to become COUNTER-compliant, and most did. Today, COUNTER's Code of Practice is in its sixth iteration (Release 5).[29]

Dr. Carol Tenopir

Any discussion of the development of library assessment would be incomplete without mentioning Dr. Carol Tenopir. Tenopir was one of the first in the field to really focus on the large-scale shift of scholarly communication—both in terms of content and as a means of access—into the online space. In 2000, she and Donald W. King published *Towards Electronic Journals: Realities for Scientists, Librarians, and Publishers*, a synthesis of decades of research into scientists' scholarly reading and sharing habits.[30] Among their conclusions: the idea that electronic journals make editors, publishers, and librarians obsolete is a myth. Tenopir has continued to have tremendous impact in library assessment; we will revisit her work throughout this text.

Academic Library Assessment Movement

The early 2000s saw something of a watershed in the realm of academic library assessment. Throughout the first decade of the twenty-first century, some of the most influential figures and organizations in librarianship, including ARL, ACRL, and the Institute of Museum and Library Services (IMLS), all sparked initiatives that pushed the field forward by leaps and bounds.

ASSOCIATION OF RESEARCH LIBRARIES

As we've already discussed, ARL inherited the benchmarking model that would set the standard for academic library statistical measures. Nearly ninety years after James Gerould published his call to begin a program to collect comparable statistics, the ARL resolved to develop new approaches to research library assessment that would stretch beyond the input measures they'd relied upon to incorporate approaches that focused on outcomes (i.e., the impacts) of library facility, service, and resource use.

The ARL New Measures Initiative (NMI) was a multi-pronged effort to explore the value of new library resources and services as well as to look at traditional resources and services through a new lens. NMI was composed of several separate tools and frameworks, but the three with the most significant impact and longevity are arguably LibQUAL+, a survey designed to collect library users' impressions of a standardized list of services and resources; MINES for Libraries, a brief automated point-of-use survey for patrons accessing electronic resources; and the E-Metrics Project, a collaborative effort to identify a common collection of statistical usage measures related to electronic resources—not unlike an e-version of J. T. Gerould's call for a group of peer institutions to collect and share data of a different sort nearly 100 years earlier. Each of these will be discussed in greater detail in subsequent chapters.

ARL also launched the Library Assessment Conference in 2002. In the years since, the biennial event has grown in size and notoriety, affording attendees and presenters opportunities to network, learn, and share their own research.

THE INSTITUTE OF MUSEUM AND LIBRARY SERVICES

In addition to their own projects, ARL has also collaborated with other organizations and institutions to promote the importance of library assessment; in 2009, IMLS partnered with researchers from the University of Tennessee, the University of Illinois, Syracuse University, and Bryant University on an IMLS-funded grant project entitled Value, Outcomes, and Return on Investment of Academic Libraries (LibValue).[31] The goal of LibValue was to develop a suite of tools academic libraries could use to demonstrate their contributions to the mission of the larger institution. These included models for assessing impacts related to research, prestige, teaching, learning, and student success.

IMLS has funded a number of other assessment-related projects designed for academic and public libraries, as well as programs supporting professional development and master's-level education.

THE ASSOCIATION OF COLLEGE AND RESEARCH LIBRARIES

ACRL's Value of Academic Libraries Initiative was launched in 2009 and almost immediately set in motion what was to be a tremendously significant development in the library assessment. In 2010, Megan Oakleaf published the ACRL-commissioned *The Value of Academic Libraries: A Comprehensive Research Review and Report* (known as the "Value Report").[32] Oakleaf's report stands out as a singular achievement, as well as an overview of the significant concerns, approaches, and tools for assessment from special, academic, public, and school libraries, Oakleaf outlined an agenda for future work to demonstrate academic library value. The Value Report left an impression that can be seen in much of the academic library assessment research conducted in the ten years since the Value Report was published. The Value of Academic Libraries Initiative has since sponsored research, continuing education opportunities, and practical tool development—a variety of helpful resources for academic librarians to develop their assessment-related knowledge and skill.

The Critical Assessment Movement

In the years following publication of the Value Report, academic library assessment in particular seemed to develop a laser focus on demonstrating value—often in a monetary sense. Unsurprisingly, some practitioners and authors began raising concerns about the pervasiveness of this framework. Three years after publication of the Value Report, Meredith Farkas issued a gentle rejoinder against what she observed to be a growing tendency to "conflat[e] library assessment and library value research as if they [are] the same thing"[33] and an emphasis not on assessment to inform developing services to support student success, but on "showing a relationship between the library and indicators that are meaningful to campus administrators."[34]

As described by authors such as Veronica Arellano Douglas and Ebony Magnus, Jackie Belanger, and Maggie Faber, the critical assessment movement combines concerns like Farkas's with a call to reflect upon the larger cultural, social, historical, and justice-related context for and implications of library assessment efforts.[35]

Because critical assessment is situated primarily (at this point) in academic librarianship, it's natural that much of the discussion of its origins focuses on what many consider the "neoliberal" priorities dominant in today's higher education practice in the United States. Jeff Lilburn describes neoliberalism in higher education as a movement away from the idea of the "university as a public good devoted to critical social analysis, civic education, and meaningful scholarship" and toward "a utilitarian and market-driven approach to higher education characterized by flexible and efficient program delivery designed to produce an employable workforce and commercially relevant research."[36] Indeed, today's institutions of higher education, particularly high-profile public universities, operate in an environment of reduced financial support (outside of tuition) and greater scrutiny from stakeholders, many of whom are wary of higher education both as an institution and as a collection of individual employees. As the *Chronicle of Higher Education* documented in a recent series of articles, state higher education governing boards are often politicized through the nomination and appointment process, which is frequently dominated by one political party.[37] In many cases, governing board members come from the business world; their qualifications seem to stem primarily from success in that milieu rather than from special knowledge of higher education systems.[38] As a result, practices and values from the corporate world (increasing efficiency, cost savings, profit maximization) have influenced higher education institutions' practices and values, including those related to assessment.

Among other things, the critical assessment (CA) framework calls for shifting assessment efforts from efforts that focus on demonstrating how the library provides value to stakeholders. Rather, a critical approach to assessment emphasizes efforts to understand how users' needs and how library resources and services meet them, reminding us of Douglas Zweizig and Brenda Dervin's efforts in the 1970s. (See "Further Reading" at the end of this chapter for a selection of CA-related works.)

Other Important Initiatives

Of course, this review is not meant to be comprehensive, and we have neglected to discuss important library assessment developments such as the Ithaka S+R Surveys of faculty research, teaching, and publishing practices that have taught librarians so much about how faculty view the library, its resources, and services; and professional development opportunities like the biennial International Conference on Performance Measurement in Libraries (LibPMC—formerly known as "The Northumbria Conference"). The truth is, assessment (and its close companion, planning) occupies a central position in the view of almost all types of twenty-first century libraries. Gerould would be so proud!

Conclusion

Taking a few minutes to consider the long view of libraries' efforts in planning and assessment is diverting (to us, anyway), but is it instructive? We think so, and can see several lessons in the events of the past 175 or so years, such as:

> *The principles and practices of the business world influence planning and assessment efforts, even for not-for-profit institutions.* "We should run [universities/public libraries/the government/ etc.] like a business!" Although it feels like the pervasiveness of this attitude is a relatively new development, evidence shows us that this kind of thinking was common in the early days of management science. The private sector can certainly offer some useful models and efficiencies, but it's important to maintain perspective and resist attempts to assess libraries exclusively using models designed for understanding for-profit entities.

> *Don't reinvent the wheel.* Find a model that kind of works and modify it. Throughout this discussion, we've highlighted several instances in which people working on library planning and assessment have "borrowed" models and approaches from other fields or made use of data collected for a different purpose. There's no shame in that! Save time and other resources by adopting and adapting existing, vetted approaches for your own needs.

> *If an existing model isn't available, don't be afraid to team up.* Find partners. Pool your resources. Identify others—libraries, researchers, organizations—that share your interests and compliment your skill set. Work together!

> *Don't forget to seek institutional support.* Many of the advances outlined here happened only with the support of a large organization. Seek out sources of funding for equipment, travel, stipends, expertise, labor. These will come in handy.

> *Agility is key.* Many of these developments were predicated on an organization's willingness and ability to shift gears and devote resources to something different. Think about ARL anticipating the coming sea change resulting from a large-scale shift to electronic resources—back in the mid-1990s! One could argue that

the writing was already on the wall, but we only remember it being written in chalk at that point. Permanent marker came later.

That being said, *don't be afraid to take a minute to step back and look at the bigger picture.* Planning and assessment consume a significant amount of resources—time, money, staff hours—if done well. That kind of investment is a statement of priorities—where your organization allocates its limited resources says something. Have a larger plan and check in with it often.

NOTES

1. "ALA's Core Competencies of Librarianship" (Chicago: American Library Association, 2009; 2017); "ACRL Proficiencies for Assessment Librarians and Coordinators" (Chicago: Association of College and Research Libraries, January 23, 2017).
2. Claude S. George, Jr., *The History of Management Thought*, 2nd ed. (New Delhi: Prentice Hall of India Private Limited, 1974), 164–65.
3. Woodrow Wilson, "The Study of Administration," *Political Science Quarterly* 2, no. 2 (1887): 197–222.
4. Charles E. Merriam, "Investigations as a Means of Securing Administrative Efficiency," in *Efficiency in City Government*, Emory R. Johnson, ed. (Philadelphia: American Academy of Political and Social Science, 1912), 281.
5. John Cotton Dana, *A Library Primer*, 5th ed. (Chicago: Library Bureau, 1910), 21, 134.
6. Dana, *Library Primer*, 21, 134.
7. Carlton B. Joeckel, "Current Issues in Library Administration," in *Papers Presented before the Library Institute at the University of Chicago* (Chicago: The University of Chicago Press, 1938).
8. Redmond Kathleen Molz, *Library Planning and Policy Making: The Legacy of the Public and Private Sectors* (Metuchen, NJ: Scarecrow Press, 1990), ix.
9. Jesse Hauk Shera, "Recent Social Trends and Future Library Policy," *The Library Quarterly: Information, Community, Policy* 3, no. 4 (1933): 349.
10. "A National Plan for Libraries," *Bulletin of the American Library Association* 29, no. 2 (1935.): 91–98; "A National Plan for Libraries"; *Bulletin of the American Library Association* 33, no. 2 (1939): 136–50.
11. Robert N. Anthony, *Planning and Control Systems: A Framework for Analysis* (Cambridge, MA: Harvard University Press, 1965).
12. *ARL SPEC Kit: Goals and Objectives* (Washington, DC: Association of Research Libraries, Systems and Procedures Exchange Center, 1973), 2.
13. Vernon E. Palmour, *A Planning Process for Public Libraries* (Chicago: American Library Association, 1980).

14. Donald E. Riggs, *Strategic Planning for Library Managers* (Phoenix, AZ: Oryx Press, 1984).
15. Doris Asantewa, *Strategic Planning Basics for Special Libraries* (Alexandria, VA: Special Libraries Association, 1992).
16. Charles R. McClure, Public Library Association New Standards Task Force, Amy Owen, Mary Jo Lynch, Douglas L. Zweizig, and Nancy A. Van House, *Planning and Role Setting for Public Libraries: A Manual of Options and Procedures* (Chicago: American Library Association, 1987); Setting Objectives for Public Library Services, Library and Information Services Council Working Group on Public Library Objectives (London: HMSO, 1991); Susan Jurow and Duane E. Webster, "Building New Futures for Research Libraries." *Journal of Library Administration* 14, no. 2 (1991): 5–19, https://doi.org/10.1300/J111v14n02_02.
17. James T. Gerould, "A Plan for the Compilation of Comparative University and College Library Statistics," *Library Journal* 31 (1906): 761.
18. Gerould, "Plan for the Compilation of Library Statistics," 762–63.
19. Robert E. Molyneux, "The Gerould Statistics 1907/08-1961/62," Association of Research Libraries, 1986; 2nd ed., 2010.
20. Robert V. Williams, "The Making of Statistics of National Scope on American Libraries, 1836-1986: Purposes, Problems, and Issues," *Libraries and Culture* 26, no. 2 (1991): 464.
21. Willliams, "Making of Statistics," 465.
22. L. P. Latimer, "Surveyitis," *Library Journal* (October 1940): 787.
23. Douglas L. Zweizig and Brenda Dervin, "Public Library Use, Users, Uses," *Advances in Librarianship* 7 (January 1977): 233.
24. Zweizig and Dervin, "Public Library Use," 234.
25. Zweizig and Dervin, "Public Library Use," 247; 251.
26. James M. Matarazzo, *President's Task Force on the Value of the Information Professional*, Preliminary Study: Final Report, 1987, 5.
27. José Marie Griffiths and Donald W. King, *Special Libraries: Increasing the Information Edge* (Washington, DC: Special Libraries Association, 1993).
28. Oliver Pesch, "Usage Statistics: About COUNTER and SUSHI," *Information Services and Use* 27, no. 4 (2007): 207–13.
29. "Project COUNTER—Consistent, Credible, Comparable," Project Counter, https://www.projectcounter.org/.
30. Carol Tenopir and Donald W. King, *Towards Electronic Journals: Realities for Scientists, Librarians, and Publishers* (Washington, DC: Special Libraries Association, 2000).
31. *Value, Outcomes, and Return on Investment of Academic Libraries*, www.libvalue.org.
32. Megan J. Oakleaf, *The Value of Academic Libraries: A Comprehensive Research Review and Report* (Chicago: Association of College and Research Libraries, 2010).

33. Meredith Farkas, "Accountability vs. Improvement: Seeking Balance in the Value of Academic Libraries Initiative," *OLA Quarterly* (January 5, 2013).

34. Farkas, "Accountability vs. Improvement," 4.

35. Veronica Arellano Douglas, "Moving from Critical Assessment to Assessment as Care," *Communications in Information Literacy* 14, no. 1 (2020); Ebony Magnus, Jackie Belanger, and Maggie Faber, "Towards a Critical Assessment Practice," *In the Library with the Lead Pipe* (October 31, 2018), www.inthe librarywiththeleadpipe.org/2018/towards-critical-assessment-practice/.

36. Jeff Lilburn, "Ideology and Audit Culture: Standardized Service Quality Surveys in Academic Libraries." *portal: Libraries and the Academy* 17, no. 1 (2017): 93.

37. Lindsay Ellis, Jack Stripling, and Dan Bauman, "The New Order," *The Chronicle of Higher Education*, October 2, 2020.

38. Sondra N. Barringer and Sheila Slaughter, "University Trustees and the Entrepreneurial University: Inner Circles, Interlocks, and Exchanges," in *Higher Education, Stratification, and Workforce Development*, Sheila Slaughter and Barrett Jay Taylor, ed. (Springer International Publishing, 2016), 151–71; Arthur Taylor, "Perspectives on the University as a Business: The Corporate Management Structure, Neoliberalism and Higher Education," *Journal for Critical Education Policy Studies* 15, no. 1 (2017): 108–35.

FURTHER READINGS

General

Fleming-May, Rachel A., and Jill E. Grogg. "The Concept of Electronic Resource Usage and Libraries." *Library Technology Reports* 46 (6): 1–35, 2010.

Critical Assessment

Folk, Amanda L. "Reframing Information Literacy as Academic Cultural Capital: A Critical and Equity-Based Foundation for Practice, Assessment, and Scholarship." *College and Research Libraries* 80, no. 5 (2019): 658–73.

"Keeping Up with . . . Critical Assessment." Association of College and Research Libraries, June 11, 2019.

Planning

- Types of Planning
- What Is Strategy?
- Understanding Strategic Planning
- Strategic Analysis (SWOT Analysis)
- Goals
- Creating Your Assessment Plan
- Conclusion

This chapter focuses on the fundamentals of planning, with an emphasis on strategic planning, and includes a discussion of the importance of strategic assessment. First, we'll define different types of planning. Next, we'll provide an explanation of what strategy is, its importance in assessment, the elements of good strategy, and how to recognize bad strategy. A general overview of strategic planning will be presented, including the elements of a strategic plan and the process of planning, as well as an explanation of how strategic planning differs from tactical and operational planning. We'll end this chapter with a discussion of the elements of an assessment plan, with an emphasis on how organizational-level planning is the foundation for developing your assessment goals.

Types of Planning

Planning is crucial to an effective assessment program. There are an endless number of things one could assess in the average library, and most libraries generate an astronomical amount of data each year without even trying. If you do not approach assessment strategically, you will likely be wasting your time and efforts for little or no payoff.

To approach assessment strategically means tying your efforts to your community's and organization's plans and goals as well as being able to think and plan strategically for your own assessment activities. If you are not proficient at planning, your assessment efforts will be a headache at best, a disaster at worst. While it's not uncommon for someone charged with a general or specific assessment assignment to feel pressured to jump into the actual practice of assessment or into a big project, laying the groundwork with sound planning first will exponentially increase your odds of success.

One big obstacle to effective planning comes from a confusion about different types of planning and when to use each. In the library environment, many types of planning are sometimes mentioned: budget planning, space planning, succession planning, program planning, and more. Although each of these have their own particular concerns, to a large extent, the processes necessary for each can all more or less fit into one of three categories. Thus, for our purposes, we will divide planning into three main categories: operational, tactical, and strategic.

Operational Planning

In an ideal world, all plans would start with strategic planning and progress from tactical to operational planning. But in reality, planning often begins with the operational. Operational planning is best understood as planning that keeps business as usual happening efficiently. It is quite literally planning for the operation of the organization or department on a daily basis. In the library context, operational planning keeps many supervisors busy, and indeed, although strategic planning tends to happen at a higher level, operational planning is generally done by middle managers. It includes things like work and operating schedules, staffing needs, ordering supplies, and basic communications processes. Without operational planning, most organizations of any complexity simply cannot function, so it tends to go on pretty consistently, and most people have a basic understanding of how it works.

Tactical Planning

Operational planning is about what happens day to day; tactical planning is used for more complex, multi-step projects to be accomplished over a longer time period. Project management includes more than just planning, but it may be helpful to think of tactical planning as the type of planning you would use in project management. It includes coordinating a team, defining the objectives and scope of a project, estimating costs, and tracking progress and project milestones. Tactical planning also requires the ability to adjust in real time to the unexpected.

Strategic Planning

Strategic planning is perhaps the most misunderstood of all types of planning. In a nutshell, strategic planning is a process used to envision a new and different future and then to identify the key strategies you will follow to make your vision a reality. Where operational planning is daily in nature and tactical planning is short or mid-term, usually a year or less, strategic planning takes the long view and looks into a future sufficiently far away to manifest the strategic vision. Strategic planning does not focus on small details or lay out the daily steps required, but rather sees the big picture and focuses on broad goals and objectives.

The Mix in Practice

An example may help further differentiate the types of planning. Imagine you work at a mid-sized academic library that is concerned with staying relevant and valuable in a time when budgets are shrinking and some stakeholders question the value of a library in the age of the internet. Your organization starts to address this situation through strategic planning. As part of that process, the organization first does an analysis of the external environment that includes a careful consideration of the priorities and goals of the library's parent institution; the needs and preferences of your users, both faculty and students; and the values and agendas of any other external stakeholders, such as alumni, donors, parents, state and federal legislators, and accrediting bodies. The library also performs an analysis of your organization's internal strengths and weaknesses, including elements such as staff, spaces, and budget. After undertaking this process, the library identifies the most pressing opportunities and challenges facing the organization, both now and projecting into the future three to five years, and begins to construct possible strategies to meet the challenges and take advantage of the opportunities. One area of focus that emerges is the importance of assessing and meeting user needs in order to stay current with how users work now. The organization decides to explore offering new services, based on a concrete assessment of user needs, as well as an understanding of what needs the library is uniquely situated to address with its particular combination of spaces, reputation, and staff skill sets. After performing this analysis, your organization concludes that one action you will take in employing this strategy is to create a makerspace in the library.

Once the strategy and specific goal have been decided, it's time for tactical planning. This might be the task of a new group or a continuation of work by those who laid the strategic foundation. They will begin constructing a plan to bring the goal of a new makerspace in the library to realization. This will include the need to evaluate library spaces and decide where the makerspace should go. They will need to resolve questions such as

- What equipment, hardware, software, furnishings, etc., will be offered in the space?
- Who will staff the space and will they need to hire new staff?
- Are there special skills the staff working there will need?

Next, the team formulates a plan to transform the chosen space, which may include hiring architects, designers, and construction companies. All of those things may, in turn, require putting projects out to bid.

Another aspect of planning will include implementation of the new space. After determining staffing needs for the new service, both in terms of number, skills, schedules, and responsibilities, there must also be a plan for new procedures and workflows for the new service.

Other planning needs may include coordinating advertising and communication about the new service, as well as assessing the service. In addition,
the planning team must also respond to any issues that arise during implementation in real time, adjusting on the fly.

The work of bringing all of these smaller steps to completion to finish
the larger project—creating the makerspace—is the work of tactical planning.
All of this planning for and the rollout of the new service would happen
over weeks or months and would require coordinating the work of multiple
people, on multiple aspects of the project. If key decisions arise during this
process, the team may refer back to the strategic plan to help make those
decisions, but other decisions may be purely tactical, or even operational, in
nature.

Once the space is completed and the grand opening ceremony has
occurred, running the space on a day-to-day basis will require operational
planning. This type of planning includes things like deciding the hours the
space will be open, the kind of staffing needed during hours open to users,
and even a daily schedule for staffing. In this case, operational planning could
also include procedures for updating the software and hardware in the space,
and for making decisions about repairing and replacing the equipment. If the
library will offer instruction related to the makerspace, there must be plans
for an instruction schedule as well as a procedure for scheduling instruction.
Operational plans could also include procedures for communicating to internal staff about the space, as well as communicating basic or daily information about the space to users (such as unexpected closings, etc.). All of these
things fall into the realm of operational planning. If you want to plan special
programs for the space, you may need to dip back into the world of tactical
planning. If you want to decide whether or not to expand the space, you may
need to do some more strategic planning. And if you want to know if the
space is successful and is accomplishing the goals you set for it, you would,
of course, do some assessment.

What Is Strategy?

Most libraries find they must do some sort of strategic planning these days.
The results, however, are often less than satisfactory. Many in the field can
relate to the experience of spending a lot of time and effort to go through an

often long and laborious strategic planning process that results in a sometimes dense and overly specific plan or in other cases a vague and airy plan,
either of which tend to go into a drawer for three to five years, after which
time the organization dusts it off and enjoys the surprise of seeing how many
of its strategic goals were accomplished.

The point of our discussion of strategic planning is not to provide a guide
for "doing" strategic planning as an organization; many of these already exist.
Rather, our goal is helping the assessment practitioner understand the common elements of a strategic plan, to know when and how to use these elements in creating your own assessment plan, and most importantly, to be
able to recognize the difference between good strategy and bad strategy and
to begin to develop the crucial skill of strategic thinking.

Strategy Defined

Before we dive into the details of strategic planning, let's begin with a basic
question: what is strategy? The word originates from the Greek *strategos*,
which refers to both an army and its commander; that it has a solidly military
origin is instructive. Although we frequently use the term *strategy* in every-
day conversation, it has a specific significance in planning-related literature.
Joseph Matthews defines strategy as "a plan of action with a shared understanding designed to accomplish a specific goal that focuses on how a given
objective will be achieved."[1] To understand strategy, the first step is to understand when a strategy is necessary. Strategy is only necessary in the face of a
problem or challenge, or when you want to manifest something new. In the
absence of a problem, your best course of action is to simply maintain the
status quo until one arises. Similarly, for a very long time, libraries did not
really need strategies. They had no real competitors and fulfilled an essential
function for the communities they served. The information world did not
materially change for centuries, so there was no real need to develop new
processes or procedures. Basically, libraries did what they did very well and
had no competitors or other threats, apart from perhaps fires or natural disasters, or the occasional funding crisis. In this atmosphere, the smartest course
of action was simply to maintain business as usual.

So, what are the characteristics of good strategy? And how do you recognize bad strategy so that even if you aren't in a position to change it, you
don't waste your time on it? Richard Rumelt, in his excellent book *Good*

According to Matthews, libraries employ strategy to "move the library toward the vision of the library and to eliminate the gap that exists between where the library is today and where it wants to be tomorrow." Matthews points out and clarifies a common misapplication of the term: "Strategies are *not* the programmatic goals and objectives that most libraries have historically developed."[2]

Taking a more metaphorical approach, Gordon R. Sullivan asks readers to imagine strategy as "a bridge; values are the bedrock on which the piers of the bridge are planted, the near bank is today's reality, the far bank is the vision."[3]

Richard Rumelt takes a more practical approach, describing strategy as "a way through a difficulty, an approach to overcoming an obstacle, a response to a challenge." He makes the important point that developing strategy requires making tough decisions, as it is "about deciding what is truly important and focusing resources and action on that objective. It is a hard discipline because focusing on one thing slights another."[4]

Strategy, Bad Strategy: The Difference and Why It Matters, defines four major hallmarks of bad strategy. When any one of these is present, you know you have more work to do (or, if it's out of your control, you'll at least be able to predict that this particular strategy is likely to fail and judge how much of your energy to invest in it).

Four Characteristics of Bad Strategy

The first characteristic of bad strategy is *fluff*. This is essentially a lot of purple prose, current buzzwords, or other jargon that sound good, but upon further inspection have no real content. A completely made-up example of fluff might be a library vision statement that says something like: "XYZ Library will create a synergistic experience of information excellence that energizes interdisciplinary evolution, leveraging actionable analytics and personalization of the library-centric environment." What does it mean? No one knows, but it includes many buzzwords, so it must be good, right? Unfortunately, no.

The second characteristic of bad strategy is *failure to face the challenge*. This one can be a common pitfall for new assessment professionals. Often, you may be asked to assess something only to discover that everyone involved knows what the problem is and they also know what needs to be done to fix it, but they don't have the will to do it. They are hoping that you will come in, perform an assessment, and somehow magically change the fact that they don't have enough staff to do everything they are doing; or that their manager is incompetent and mean; or that Joe just won't come in on time. These are challenges that people may hope you will somehow fix by doing a survey or other assessment, but in reality, they simply need to face the problem, have a difficult conversation, or do tough things like impose consequences and enforce them, or accept that they can't do everything with current staffing levels and let go of the legacy services someone is sentimental about, but no one is still using, etc.

The third hallmark of bad strategy is *mistaking goals for strategy*—this one can be harder to spot. After all, we are frequently reminded of the importance of goals and goal-setting, admonished to create SMART (specific, measurable, achievable, relevant, and time-bound) goals, and very often our goals and whether we met them are tracked from year to year. With this sort of focus on goals, it can be easy to confuse them with strategy, and it's not uncommon for an organization's strategic plan to really be nothing more than a list of goals, in effect more of a checklist than anything approaching strategy.

The fourth characteristic of bad strategy is *bad strategic objectives*. A classic example of this is when Kodak invented the digital camera but chose not to release it for over fifteen years so as not to hurt its film sales. They focused on the short-term objective of meeting sales goals, completely missing an incredible strategic opportunity to lead a technological revolution that was going to take place with or without them.

Elements of Good Strategy

Good strategy, on the other hand, can be recognized by "at a minimum, three essential components: a diagnosis of the situation, the choice of an overall guiding policy, and the design of coherent action."[5] If your strategy doesn't include a careful definition of the problem or challenge you are trying to address, it's not a good strategy. This is, in our experience, the element of good strategy that is most often overlooked in libraries. We tend to assume that we know what users want and how they think, and perhaps most damningly, what is best for them (even if they disagree). We can also be quite reactionary—for instance, waiting until our budget is slashed to decide, in the heat of the moment, what to do about the problem. If your library administrators are doing their due diligence in strategic analysis and planning on a regular basis, they should be able to see that a budget cut is a looming possibility before it happens, and if they are true strategic thinkers, they will have contingency plans even if there is no apparent danger. The times when it is most important to be strategic are often the times when it is hardest to be so. But these are the moments when it is most important to keep a clear head and take the time to truly understand the challenge that you face.

The second element of a good strategy, the choice of an overall guiding policy, is also crucial. The first word to pay attention to in that sentence is *choice*. Strategy does require choice, which means there are several possibilities of how to manage a challenge that you will leave on the table in order to try the one that you do choose, that you deem most likely to be effective given your careful analysis of the situation. Choice does involve risk, but the great thing about strategy is that although you do need to commit wholeheartedly to your chosen guiding policy as you attempt to enact it, you are also free to abandon it completely once you see that it isn't working and go with plan B (or C or D). So, your guiding policy will be your chosen approach to the challenge, given what you know about it in the present moment. If the situation changes or you learn new facts, you can and should adjust or even change your approach. Going back to the bridge analogy, if your challenge is to cross a river and you decide that building a bridge is your best strategy, you put your all into building that bridge. If situations change and you need to get across faster than you thought, you might decide to take a boat instead. But then the boat springs a leak midway, so then your best strategy may be to swim the rest of the way.

The final element of good strategy is the design of coherent action. This is where your goal-setting skills can come back into use, but you must also never lose sight of the big picture. Perhaps the most important word in that sentence is *coherent*, although *action* is a close second. Good strategy requires that all parts of an organization are working in tandem and no one is working at cross purposes.

Thinking and acting strategically are crucial skills for assessment professionals. Being able to cut through the noise of competing agendas and demands will help you maintain your sanity, even if you can't always affect the outcome. But we encourage you to see your position in assessment, whatever it may be, as an opportunity to be an influencer in your organization and help guide your colleagues toward good strategic objectives and evidence-based decision-making. Assessment can be a powerful tool by which to steer an organization, particularly when it is used strategically.

Understanding Strategic Planning

> "Strategic planning isn't strategic thinking. One is analysis, and
> the other is synthesis."
>
> —Henry Mintzberg[6]

In an ideal world, strategic planning is a process that allows an organization
to implement the insights gleaned from careful strategic thinking and analysis. In the real world, it often falls short of this. One reason for this is that
those leading the strategic planning process often don't understand its true
purpose, its elements, or how to effectively communicate these things to key
stakeholders. After reading this section, it's likely that you will understand
more about strategic planning than at least 90 percent of the people in your
organization. Although often misused and misunderstood, strategic planning
can be a powerful tool when used correctly.

Strategic Planning Defined

In the words of John Bryson, strategic planning is "a deliberative, disciplined
approach to producing decisions and actions that shape and guide what an organization (or other entity) is, what it does, and why." Or, in other words, "what to do,
how, and why."[7]

There are several common elements of strategic planning, and these, too,
are often misunderstood or confused with each other. For instance, people
often confuse a mission statement with a vision statement. But these are two
distinctly different things with different purposes. The mission statement,
vision, and values are commonly considered the core of a strategic plan. One
way to understand these three elements is as a way to model visionary and
transformative leadership styles.

Mission Statement

People often confuse the vision and mission statements, but they are very
different. A mission statement defines the core purpose of your organization
or program. What is the fundamental reason it exists? What is its purpose?
Although a vision statement will change over time (as one vision is achieved,
a new one will emerge), a mission statement should stay fairly consistent
over time.

For libraries, their mission may seem obvious. But, as David Osborne and Ted Gaebler point out, there are benefits to organizations coming together and hammering out a shared understanding:

> The experience of hashing out the fundamental purpose of an organiza-
> tion—debating all the different assumptions and views held by its mem-
> bers and agreeing on one basic mission—can be a powerful one. When it
> is done right, a mission statement can drive an entire organization from
> top to bottom.[8]

Especially in this time of fast-paced change, it could be a very powerful and potentially transformative exercise to genuinely ask the question: what is our core purpose? A good mission statement not only defines what you do, but it also, by default, defines what you don't do. This can be a vital thing to define.

An example of a mission statement for a library assessment program would be: "The mission of the assessment program is to facilitate continual improvement in library services and resources by empowering all staff to make evidence-based decisions; and to illustrate the value of the library to our funders and to the community we serve." Many different activities are encompassed by these two core purposes, but many other possible activities are excluded by them.

Vision Statement

Although the elements of a strategic plan each depend on the other, one place to start a plan is with a vision statement. A vision isn't just a goal. The true point of a vision is to transform an organization. A goal might be looked at as a stepping-stone from where you are now to the next logical place you want to be. A vision is a giant leap to a place or way of being that is so far or different from where you are now that most people can't see it from where you are. Visionary leaders hold this vision of a reality that does not yet exist for a whole organization and guide others toward it. Because not every organization is blessed with an effective visionary leader, the vision statement might be seen as a way to make this mysterious charismatic form of leadership into a standardized process that anyone can follow. The reality is, however, that at some point, someone needs to think outside the box in order to create a compelling vision.

Imagine that you wanted to create a strategic plan for a new assessment program at your library. Your vision for your library would be to bring into existence something that does not yet exist: an assessment program. Great, you have a vision, you're done. Just kidding! What does that program look like? What does it accomplish? How does it transform your organization? This is a place to let your imagination run wild. In a perfect world, where all the stars aligned just right, what would your assessment program look like a year from now? Three years from now? Five years from now? How will you know when you've achieved your vision? A good vision statement will answer all of these questions.

Guiding Principles (Values)

Knowing your mission and having a vision are key to strategic action, but it's also important to define guidelines for how the organization fulfills its mission and works toward the vision. That's where guiding principles come in. Although the word *values* is more commonly used in strategic planning and can hold the commonly understood meaning of the word—a deeply held belief about what is right or wrong or good or bad—generally it may be more useful to think of them as guiding principles. Some of your guiding principles may actually be ethical guidelines for behavior, but they may also be more practical or process oriented.

Consider the following guiding principles for a library assessment program.

The library assessment program is guided by the following guiding principles:

> *Meaningful*—Assessment activities should look at issues that matter, in ways that will yield meaningful evidence.
>
> *Necessary*—Assessment activities should be necessary, focusing on areas where improvement or information is needed and will make a difference.
>
> *Actionable*—Assessment should focus on areas where action can actually be taken based on the results.
>
> *Simple*—Although research and solutions should be as complex as necessary to adequately address issues, the simplest approaches and solutions that meet all needs are best.
>
> *Evidence-based*—Assessment activities should begin and end with well-conducted research. Our activities should be guided at all times by evidence.

Inclusive—Assessment activities rely on participation by all members of the library staff and should include and value the input of departments and staff throughout the library, as well as the input of our users.

User-centered—Our ultimate goal is to improve the user experience and help the library to constantly improve at meeting user needs.

Integrity—Assessment activities should be guided by ethical behavior, accountability, and honesty. At all times, the program will be faithful to methods and evidence considered scientifically rigorous and accurate.

For instance, if you need to choose between doing a website usability study in the next six months or focusing on a wayfinding study, you can use these values to help you make a decision.

There may be pressure from different stakeholders to do every one of these. How do you decide and how do you defend and explain your decision? Apply the values to each possibility.

Are they both *meaningful*? Yes, potentially. Both issues are currently very important to your organization and could be studied in a way that would yield meaningful evidence.

Are they *necessary*? The wayfinding study is very necessary. Your organization has tried lots of different signage over the years, but user surveys and focus groups still show that users have a hard time finding resources and even service desks. Is the usability study necessary? Perhaps a heuristic evaluation would be a better place to start. Have you applied the fundamental principles of good web design? Will you learn anything through a usability study that you couldn't discern with a fair degree of certainty through a heuristic evaluation? Probably not.

Are both studies *actionable*? You are planning a remodel next year and there is a budget for new signage. A wayfinding study would be very actionable. Your website, on the other hand, is centrally administered, was just redesigned a few months ago, and it's unlikely your web team would be willing to make significant changes any time soon.

These guiding principles are a powerful tool for decision-making as you build your program and your plan. Applying guiding principles can help make tough decisions and provide concrete reasons to explain and defend that decision. This is the true purpose of values in strategic planning.

Strategic Analysis (SWOT Analysis)

A strategic analysis, also known as a SWOT analysis (SWOT stands for strengths, weaknesses, opportunities, and threats) is the single most important part of any strategic plan. Without a thorough and competent strategic analysis, it is not possible to formulate an effective strategy or to think strategically about a challenge. Yet, the strategic analysis is often skimmed over in strategic planning. Perhaps that's because the analysis is generally not included in forward-facing strategic plan documents. Perhaps it's because carrying out a competent strategic analysis is just plain hard work. It requires in-depth research, analytical thinking, and synthesis. It also requires being able to explain the results of the analysis in a compelling and engaging way. And there is no real way to know if the analysis is correct until long after it's done. A strategic analysis is an attempt to predict the future, based on the best evidence available in the present. If this were easy to do, the world might be a very different place!

A strategic analysis is the point in strategic planning where strategy can begin, by carefully defining the problem or challenge.

Remember, if there is no problem or challenge, you don't need a strategy and you don't need a strategic plan. The purpose of a strategic plan is to respond proactively and effectively to anticipated opportunities and threats, and to leverage any advantages you have, while minimizing the impact of any weaknesses.

It's common to see a grid like the one below when doing a SWOT analysis:

FIGURE 3.1
SWOT analysis grid

Internal	Strengths	Weaknesses
External	Opportunities	Threats

Let's discuss each element in turn. The *opportunities* and *threats* refer to the external environment of an organization. (The word *challenges* is sometimes used in place of threats.) But the essential point is the same. In this part of the analysis, you look carefully at all the opportunities and challenges in your external environment, understand them as deeply as you can, and speculate about how they may affect your organization or program.

If you were doing an analysis in preparation for planning your assessment strategy, for instance, you'd want to look at some essential elements in your external environment. The first thing to ask yourself is, who are the external stakeholders of your library and what is important to them? For an academic library, this could include your institution's administrators, perhaps your state legislators, alumni and donors, any accrediting bodies, your faculty, the students, their parents, and the surrounding community.

Being thoroughly familiar with your institution's strategic priorities is crucial, but you also need to keep an eye on accreditation requirements, not just for your main body, but also for all the individual programs that are accredited through different organizations. If you are a state institution, knowing what your state legislators are up to in regard to higher education may be important. If you are at a private institution, understanding your major donors' priorities will also be crucial. And, of course, understanding the needs of your users will always be key.

So, as an example, imagine that you work in an academic library that serves a state institution facing budget crunches brought on by reduced state funding, increased competition for students from more online colleges and options, as well as reduced enrollment brought on by a shrinking middle class. Your institution's response is to try to grow enrollment (as a strategy for dealing with reduced state funding) by focusing on undergraduate student success, as well as increasing student retention. The external challenges have been defined above, but they also provide you with some opportunities because previous assessments have shown that undergraduate students prefer to study in the library, and your gate counts have consistently gone up for the last several years. So, a possible strategy for your library and your assessment program could be to focus on better understanding undergraduate students' needs, as well as attempting to measure the library's contribution to undergraduate student success. This could provide your library with important data to guide decision-making, with a focus on increasing the library's value to students, as well as preparing you to demonstrate your contribution in the event that you need to make a case for more resources in the form of increased budget (or even just to avoid budget cuts).

The *strengths* and *weaknesses* refer to your internal environment. This is also crucial to analyze before you decide on any strategies. The first thing to consider is your library's strategic plan and priorities. Next, consider any unspoken priorities that your administrators may have. How will you find out about those? Good question. This is one compelling argument for assessment programs to be housed within administration or report to the library director or another senior administrator. In order to do your job well, you need to be having regular discussions with your leadership. Even if you are working on a one-off assessment project and it's not your full-time position, for the duration of the project having face time with your leadership will be invaluable. Your director will know things that you can't find out any other way, for instance, that your library board chairperson hates qualitative data but is a big fan of pie charts. Never underestimate the importance of individual personalities in the functioning of large, complex systems!

So, in your work to create an assessment plan and strategy, perhaps a strength is having the full support and cooperation of your library administrators. If you don't have that, you need to be realistic about it and not choose a strategy that requires a lot of top-down support. Perhaps a weakness is that you are the only person working in assessment, your organization does not have a culture of assessment, your assessment committee hasn't met in three years, you are currently understaffed, and everyone is overworked. Be realistic about that too. Don't choose a strategy that will require thirty people to work ten hours a week on your assessment goals. If, on the other hand, you are magically blessed with a large staff dedicated solely to assessment work, then don't think small. Use your resources effectively and strategically, whatever they may be. Especially when trying to start an assessment program and create a culture of assessment, small wins are powerful. But at any point, people like to bet on winners and will be more likely to get on board with a project or plan if you can demonstrate proof of concept from the beginning. In assessment, it is almost always more effective to show rather than tell, whether that's showing how a plan can be effective or how the data might be used, or whether it's literally illustrating your assessment results through effective data visualizations or even video or transcriptions of actual assessment studies.

Goals

Goals are another important aspect of a strategic plan. Yes, now we finally get to actual goals. These should ideally go from broad to more narrow: strategic priorities > long-term goals > shorter-term action items. In your assessment plan, one strategic priority might be focusing on undergraduate student needs and success. One long-term goal for this strategy could be to conduct a survey in the following year to better understand undergraduates' use of the library and their information needs. The shorter-term action items could include forming a team to plan and conduct the survey, doing a literature review on library user surveys or the library's contributions to student success, or investigating existing survey services that would allow you to pay a third party to conduct a survey. Your strategic priorities will likely remain the same for a while, particularly if you have done your strategic analysis well. Your long-term goals may be somewhat general and broad but should still have a timeline and be fairly well-defined. Your shorter-term action items will be very specific and may change fairly often. That's okay. This is the place to be flexible and adjust on the fly in order to be as strategic and effective as possible. But if your internal or external landscape changes drastically, you may also need to change your big-picture strategies. Never forget that your strategies and goals are about an effective response to a challenge. The famous saying "no battle plan survives first contact with the enemy" should never be forgotten. To be truly strategic, you have to adapt in real time to what is actually happening.

Creating Your Assessment Plan

Now that you understand the different types of planning, as well as strategic thinking and planning, you can create your own assessment plan. Although there is still no standard model for an assessment plan and plans will vary based on institution type, size, configuration, and needs, the "typical" assessment plan may contain any or all of the three types of planning previously discussed: operational, tactical, and strategic. If you have a large organization with a dedicated assessment department, it may not be necessary for you to define the operational aspects of planning, such as who is responsible for doing assessment, whom they report to, or how assessment results are communicated; however, it can be useful to define this, especially in organizations where it may not be obvious.

Much like a strategic plan, an assessment plan will typically cover a defined period of time, generally anywhere from one to three years. Because assessment priorities can change quickly, we've found a two-year plan, updated annually, to be the sweet spot. This aspect of the plan may contain details of tactical planning such as what projects you plan to undertake and when, who will perform them, and what resources you need to complete them. It's highly recommended that you include some aspects of strategic planning in your assessment plan and that your starting point for creating an assessment plan should be performing your own strategic analysis of your organization's assessment needs.

It's important to remember that assessment is a collaborative process. Just as an organization needs buy-in to accomplish its strategic goals, you will need buy-in and support to accomplish your assessment goals. As you develop your goals and timeline, we recommend you engage in a scaled-down version of strategic assessment planning, engaging your entire organization for feedback and input in developing your plan. At the very least, you should seek input from your library administrators and from all those you will need to work with to accomplish your stated goals.

Elements of an Assessment Plan

The following are possible elements of an assessment plan. It may not be necessary for you to include all of these elements in your plan. Every library is different, so there may also be elements not mentioned here that you find helpful or necessary to include in your plan. Ideally, your plan will be a dynamic and living document that actually functions to guide and promote your assessment activities, so design it to work for you and reserve the right to adjust it as you progress and learn.

MISSION AND GUIDING PRINCIPLES

This section will include an explanation of the purpose and aims of assessment in your organization, as well as any principles or values you have developed to guide your assessment program. (See our earlier discussion of strategic planning for more on these elements.)

RESPONSIBILITY AND STRUCTURE FOR ASSESSMENT

This section would include an explanation of the structure of assessment in your organization. This would include identifying who is responsible for assessment, the reporting lines for assessment, and any groups or committees involved in assessment, including the text of or links to the charges of any assessment groups. It can also include information about how assessment results are communicated, etc.

LINKS TO LIBRARY AND PARENT INSTITUTION STRATEGIC PRIORITIES

Because your assessment plan should be explicitly tied to and guided by the strategic priorities of your organization (which, in turn, should be based on the strategic priorities of any parent institution or funding body), it may be helpful to outline how your assessment plan reflects those other strategic elements.

ASSESSMENT STRATEGIC PRIORITIES, GOALS, AND OBJECTIVES

In this section, you will define your strategic priorities for assessment and briefly explain your assessment strategy if you have not already done so in the previous section. You will also define your specific goals and objectives for assessment for the period of time covered by the plan. Goals and objectives may also include information about who will be responsible for the goals, the timeline, and the expected outcomes.

ASSESSMENT TIMELINE

It can be helpful to visualize the timeline for specific assessment projects and activities. This may include both recurring assessment activities, such as statistical reporting, as well as one-time or semi-regular assessment activities and projects, for instance, a user survey or data inventory. Because one-off projects are subject to timeline changes, however, it may be best to reserve the timeline for annually recurring activities as a way to include these in your plan but also distinguish them from specially planned projects.

FIGURE 3.2
Sample assessment timeline*

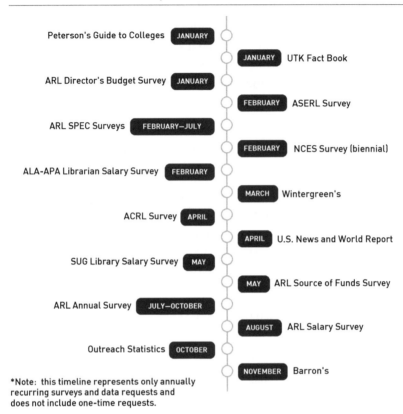

Peterson's Guide to Colleges [JANUARY]

[JANUARY] UTK Fact Book

ARL Director's Budget Survey [JANUARY]

[FEBRUARY] ASERL Survey

ARL SPEC Surveys [FEBRUARY–JULY]

[FEBRUARY] NCES Survey (biennial)

ALA-APA Librarian Salary Survey [FEBRUARY]

[MARCH] Wintergreen's

ACRL Survey [APRIL]

[APRIL] U.S. News and World Report

SUG Library Salary Survey [MAY]

[MAY] ARL Source of Funds Survey

ARL Annual Survey [JULY–OCTOBER]

[AUGUST] ARL Salary Survey

Outreach Statistics [OCTOBER]

[NOVEMBER] Barron's

*Note: this timeline represents only annually
recurring surveys and data requests and
does not include one-time requests.

RESOURCES

Assessment takes resources, which can include staff time, training, equipment, and funding. In this section, you can define the resources required for your planned assessment activities. One benefit of doing so is to make the need for such resources explicit early in the planning process and help ensure they will be available when needed.

DATA POLICIES

In this section, you can define any policies and procedures for collecting, storing, managing, reporting, and sharing assessment data. Developing and sharing data policies for assessment data is a good way to encourage transparency, which, in turn, increases both confidence and buy-in in assessment, as well as encouraging the effective use of assessment data.

ASSESSMENTS AND OUTCOMES

As time goes on, you may find it helpful to include a section in subsequent assessment plans that documents the previous assessments you performed and how your library responded to those findings (see figure 3.3). This will close the loop on your assessment efforts and emphasize the benefits that assessment has to your organization. Over time, this can be a powerful factor in fostering a culture of assessment. (For more on developing a culture of assessment, see chapter 11.)

FIGURE 3.3

Assessment effort and subsequent outcomes

Assessments and Outcomes—FY2017–2019

Date	Assessment Effort	Outcomes
2017	Hours Study	Extended library hours; opened entire building 24 hours, as opposed to just the Commons, to avoid overcrowding.
2018	User Survey	Increased customer service training; expanded Scan on Demand services; increased equipment checkout.
2019	Website Usability Tests	Redesigned interlibrary loan website interface; featured library hours more prominently on website.

For an example of a library assessment plan, see appendix A.

Conclusion

As we've discussed, planning and assessment are inextricably linked. In chapter 4, we will begin discussing what to do when you've moved on from planning to assessment.

NOTES

1. Joseph R. Matthews, *Strategic Planning and Management for Library Managers* (Santa Barbara, CA: Libraries Unlimited, 2005), 25.

2. Matthews, *Strategic Planning and Management*, 25–26.

3. Quoted in Matthews, *Strategic Planning and Management*, 3.

4. Richard Rumelt, *Good Strategy, Bad Strategy: The Difference and Why It Matters*, 1st ed. (New York: Currency, 2011), 310, 40.

5. Rumelt, *Good Strategy, Bad Strategy*, 268.

6. Henry Mintzberg, "The Fall and Rise of Strategic Planning," *Harvard Business Review* (January 1, 1994): 107.

7. John M. Bryson, *Strategic Planning for Public and Nonprofit Organizations: A Guide to Strengthening and Sustaining Organizational Achievement*, 4th ed. (San Francisco: Jossey-Bass, 2011), 19.

8. David Osborne and Ted Gaebler, *Reinventing Government: How the Entrepreneurial Spirit Is Transforming the Public Sector* (Reading, MA: Addison-Wesley, 1992). Quoted in Matthews, *Strategic Planning and Management*, 14.

Basic Principles of Assessment

- Assessment or Research?
- The Scientific Method
- Concepts Related to Data Analysis
- Grounded Theory
- Working with People
- Critical Perspectives in Assessment
- Data Integrity
- Conclusion

In this chapter, we will discuss the basic principles of assessment and its relationship to research. Although not an in-depth treatise on research methods, this chapter will explain important terminology such as dependent and independent variable, operationalization, validity, and reliability.

You may recall that in chapter 1 we outlined our guiding principles for assessment:

1. Assessment must be placed in context.

2. Assessment must be rigorous.

3. Assessment must be ethical and just.

4. Assessment must contribute to the larger conversation.

5. Assessment shouldn't "reinvent the wheel."

We have one more to add. At the risk of sounding unambitious:

6. Assessment shouldn't oversell.

How many times have you read an abstract from an article about an assessment project and thought, "This is it! The assessment project that will finally show that A (some use of the library) causes B (some positive outcome)!" then read the article itself and discovered the assessment project did not prove that A caused B at all? As we discuss the relationship between the principles of assessment and research, we will discuss the danger of confusing a correlative relationship with a causative one. Let's say you uncover the fact that small business loan applicants who attended your library's small business loan application workshop are more likely to have had success securing a loan. Did attending the workshop provide the small business owners with the skills and knowledge they need to create a successful application (causative)? Or are the characteristics of small business owners who take the time and effort to learn all they can about creating successful business loan applications (including by attending a library workshop) more likely to create a successful application (correlative)? In other words, did A cause B, or do A and B just appear together?

Demonstrating that A caused B is often the goal of assessment, particularly assessment that is focused on demonstrating the value and impact of the library and its services. Unfortunately, it's rarely possible to definitively prove causation in research involving human behavior—and almost never possible to do so with a single assessment project. On the other hand, if you would like to demonstrate that your workshop provided (some) small business owners with (some of) the knowledge necessary to create a successful loan application, why not give it a shot?

In our opinion, the best way to develop an assessment project that demonstrates a significant impact is by applying some of the principles of research design. Now, assessment needn't always follow a strict research protocol, but a general awareness of the basic characteristics of carefully constructed research can provide a helpful guide.

Assessment or Research?

At conferences, in professional journals, and online, it's not uncommon to hear discussions about the distinction between assessment and research. Most of these arguments center on the localized nature of a typical assessment project and differences in intent between the two approaches: whereas assessment is conducted to guide policy and practice, the purpose of research is developing theory and testing hypotheses. Those distinguishing between assessment and research also point to the role of the investigator as a major difference—while a researcher should be as objective as possible, an individual conducting an assessment project has a more active role and has often been involved in the program under consideration. Once the assessment project is complete, they may also have an obligation to make judgments and present recommendations based on their analysis.

Nevertheless, some of the concepts related to research design are very instructive in discussions of assessment and can provide helpful guidance in thinking about assessment and designing an assessment project. Understanding and following these general principles can also help ensure that assessment will be rigorous. Remember, a project is considered rigorous if the project design and execution are of high quality. A rigorous research project's findings are considered more likely to be trustworthy, and future researchers will feel more confident replicating a research protocol, or design, that adheres to accepted standards. From a strictly pragmatic point of view, time spent on the assessment design front-end typically reduces time spent in data gathering and analysis. Meticulous research design also makes it more difficult for those who would dismiss your findings to do so.

Careful research design is especially important for projects that deal with human subjects, or research participants. A note about research with human subjects: typically, if findings from research involving human participants are to be shared outside the organization (i.e., in a professional or scholarly publication, or presented at a conference), researchers are required to submit the research design to an institutional review board to ensure the project will not be harmful to the people who participate. The policies and procedures for institutional review will differ depending on the organization.

If you are designing an assessment project, we encourage you to take the extra time and effort to complete the institution's approval process so that researchers can share findings from their study widely. There are so many excellent assessment projects that generate findings which would be extremely helpful to librarians in similar organizations or others with similar assessment needs. By securing institutional approval for these projects and then sharing the results through publication or conference presentations, librarians make a significant and meaningful contribution to the larger professional community.

The Scientific Method

A typical research project has several phases that, in aggregate, comprise the scientific method. In this section, we will discuss the scientific method, as well as several key terms and their significance to assessment.

The core structure of the scientific method is now part of the standard K–12 curriculum in many US states. No later than middle school, children learn about theories, research questions, and hypotheses. The scientific method as a concept, however, is a little harder to pin down. One of the best descriptions we have found comes from SAGE's Encyclopedia of Case Study Research, which asserts that the scientific method stresses three elements: (1) assumptions, or the theoretical and epistemological structures that shape research questions and hypotheses; (2) procedures, or the concrete steps researchers follow in conducting research; and (3) consistency, or the importance of testing research findings to determine their applicability outside the original setting.[1]

The basic steps of the scientific method are as follows:

1. The researcher develops one or more questions they wish to explore (research questions).

2. They create hypothetical answers (hypotheses) to those questions, usually on the basis of a larger theory of the nature of knowledge within their field (theoretical framework).

3. The researcher tests their hypotheses for accuracy.

If the hypotheses are determined to be accurate, the procedure is duplicated by the same or other researchers to establish the hypotheses' applicability (generalizability) in other settings, with other subjects.

Assessment Projects, the Scientific Method, and Terminology

The scientific method model can help us think about structuring assessment. For example, let's say we work in a library that is considering deaccessioning a collection of print atlases that are, according to table studies, rarely removed from their shelves. A group of our colleagues object to this action. They believe the atlases are rarely used because they are shelved in a remote area of the library where they are unlikely to be noticed by patrons. Their theory, or educated guess, is that moving the books would increase patron awareness of them, and a subsequent change in the amount of use the atlases enjoy would be a natural consequence of such an action. Because our colleagues believe the atlases to be useful, they might further hypothesize the change in frequency of access will be an increase rather than a decrease.

VARIABLES

Our research questions are informed by these hypotheses and the variables we want to measure. An assessment project is concerned with two main types of variables: dependent and independent. The dependent variable is the thing you are interested in measuring, in this case, patrons' accessing the books that have been moved. The independent variable is the thing that's been changed. In this example, moving the books' location is the independent variable.

RESEARCH QUESTIONS

Respondents to our survey of librarians with assessment responsibilities indicated that 79.8 percent held positions that required they know how to analyze an assessment need and use it to develop a research question. This section of the text will provide some guidance in that regard.

Returning to the use of our atlases: we might formulate a research question like, "will more patrons access the atlases if they are moved?" Let's say that we work in the library of a university with a small number of geography graduate students but a large number of undergraduate students who are required to complete an introductory geography course as part of their general distribution requirements. In this case, we might also hypothesize that graduate students would be more likely to know about the atlases and more motivated to make the trek to the far corner of the basement to use them, whereas undergraduate students might be less likely to go out of their way. Therefore, we might further speculate that the increase in atlas use by undergraduates will be disproportionately higher than the increase of use by geography graduate students. Our second research question might be "will any one group's use of the atlases increase more than others' after they're moved?"

OPERATIONALIZATION

Another important but often overlooked aspect of a research or assessment project is operationalization. Operationalizing your dependent variable refers to determining how, exactly, you are going to measure a change, which is necessary to avoid presenting your variables as primitive concepts.

> A primitive concept in research is an idea that is so fundamental as to be indefinable. Commonly provided examples include time and specific colors (e.g., blue). Some disciplines treat certain concepts as primitive almost by default because they lack a consensus definition. Examples of this include information for information scientists or culture for anthropologists.

So far, we've discussed changes to patrons' accessing or using the atlases that will be moved. Now, we need to operationalize "access," or determine what it means to us for the purpose of this assessment project: how will it be measured? What is the action that will serve as a proxy for the concept of "access"?

Gathering Evidence

Because the atlases are reference materials and can't be checked out, we can't use circulation to operationalize use. This complicates things! If we decide that "removal from the shelf" can be our proxy for "use" or "access," that is how we've chosen to operationalize those concepts, and a table study is the method we've chosen to address our research questions.

Measuring in-house use of the materials gathers the type of data we refer to as direct evidence—it is tied directly to the phenomenon in question.

Let's say we lack the human resources to pull off a meaningful table study. We can still collect indirect evidence, or secondhand documentation of the phenomenon we're studying. For example, we could ask patrons leaving the building to tell us if they used the atlases. Surveys, interviews, and focus groups are well-known examples of methods for gathering indirect evidence.

All three of these methods also use what's called an instrument. A survey's questions and structure constitute the instrument, as does the protocol, the list of questions (and their order) a focus group moderator or interviewer use to collect responses.

Types of Data

Whether we decide to count the number of atlases left on nearby tables before and after the move, ask people to self-report having used them, or check students' papers for citations to the atlases, we are gathering data. Speaking very broadly, numeric data, such as that generated by a table study, is quantitative, and data presented in the form of words or other, non-numeric forms, is qualitative. Different questions call for different types of data; often, the best research or assessment projects collect data in more than one way to strengthen the ultimate argument. For example, as illustrated in figure 4.1, we might choose to conduct both a table study to measure the number of times our atlases are removed from the shelf and also review works cited lists from papers written by high school geography students to see if they cited a larger number of atlases after the move.

This principle—approaching one question from multiple perspectives or data points—is called triangulation. Triangulation is especially important for answering questions that might be a little more slippery, such as anything involving human behavior.

FIGURE 4.1
Research question approached from single data point versus triangulated data point

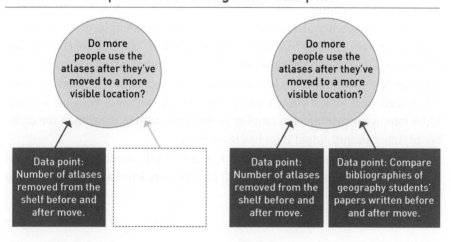

Concepts Related to Data Analysis

Depending on the type of data being analyzed, the tactics for doing so will differ. In subsequent chapters, we will discuss data analysis for surveys, interviews, focus groups, observation, and other approaches to assessment, but for the moment, we will focus on introducing some terminology related to specific goals for meaningful data analysis.

Validity

Validity, very simply, is the extent to which findings from your project support the hypotheses you developed prior to conducting the project. More broadly, validity describes the overall quality of a research project. There are two important types of validity, internal and external.

Internal validity is the extent to which a researcher can be certain the independent variable has had a causal effect on the dependent variable; in other words, the extent to which the original hypotheses can be judged correct.

External validity is the extent to which findings from a research project can be said to extend to settings and situations outside the specific setting and situation in which the original project was conducted. It is synonymous with generalizability. Returning to our atlas assessment project, if colleagues at a different institution moved a collection from an isolated area of the library to a more visible location and observed the same change in usage as we did in our library, we could say that our findings were generalizable.

Reliability

Reliability is the degree to which the tool or instrument chosen actually measures the phenomenon it's intended to measure. For example, circulation statistics are a very reliable—indeed, the most reliable—measure of the number of times an item has been checked out. On the other hand, the number of times an item has circulated is a less reliable measure of the number of times it has been read, as we know patrons often check out items they never read. Therefore, we would need to employ another measure to determine the number of times an individual item has been read.

Inter- and intra-coder reliability are important considerations for analyzing qualitative, or textual, data. Typically, text from survey comments, interview and focus group transcripts, and other written material should be coded by more than one individual. If multiple individuals analyze a collection of texts and agree on their findings, a project can be said to have a high degree of inter-rater reliability. On the other hand, intra-rater reliability refers to a single researcher's consistency of analysis throughout a project.

Grounded Theory

Grounded theory is generated through the process of data analysis. This approach stands in direct contrast to the traditional research question, theory, hypothesis, data generation, and analysis model of research design. An excellent example of grounded theory in LIS research is Constance Mellon's theory of library anxiety.[2] Mellon developed her theory after reviewing a collection of research journals kept by undergraduate students with whom she was working. Mellon expected that the students would record their research processes and progress in a technical sense, for example, listing the indexes and search terms they'd used. Instead, she found that many of the students used their journals to express their stress and fear about conducting research in the library. Through analyzing the journal contents, Mellon developed her grounded theory of library anxiety, which hypothesizes that students experience library anxiety due to a number of factors related to the size, staff, and process of locating information and resources in the library. Grounded theory can be thought of as a bottom-up approach; Mellon's theory is grounded in the data rather than a theory structuring the research project, as it would in a more traditionally designed study.

Working with People

As is the case with more formal research, there are important ethical considerations inherent in assessment. Many of these have to do with the people who are often the focus of assessment. Elsewhere in the chapter, we've touched on the role of the institutional review board (IRB) for guiding ethical treatment of assessment participants, but we'd like to go into a little more depth here. This is a topic 73 percent of our survey respondents indicated was important.

Protection of Human Subjects

The twentieth century saw significant growth in the social sciences and inquiry into human behavior. Much of this new knowledge was generated through experimentation and other types of research that involved human beings—and not all of it was in the best interest of the people involved. In fact, some research projects inflicted lifelong suffering on their participants. The National Research Act, which was passed in 1974 to address some of these abuses, allowed for creation of the National Commission for the Protection of Human Subjects of Biomedical and Behavioral Research to develop basic principles for conducting research with humans in an ethical and non-harmful fashion. After research and deliberation, the commission published the *Belmont Report* in 1976, which codified expectations and guidelines for researchers.

The report is worth reading and goes into much more detail than we will share here, but we do want to call attention to the three overarching principles for ethical research established by the commission and detailed in the report:

> Respect for Persons: Individuals should be treated as autonomous agents, and second, that persons with diminished autonomy are entitled to protection. The principle of respect for persons thus divides into two separate moral requirements: the requirement to acknowledge autonomy and the requirement to protect those with diminished autonomy.
>
> Beneficence: Persons are treated in an ethical manner not only by respecting their decisions and protecting them from harm, but also by making efforts to secure their well-being . . . beneficence is understood . . . as an obligation. Two general rules have been formulated as complementary expressions of beneficent actions in this sense: (1) do not harm and (2) maximize possible benefits and minimize possible harms.
>
> Justice: The selection of research subjects needs to be scrutinized in order to determine whether some classes (e.g., welfare patients, particular racial and ethnic minorities, or persons confined to institutions) are being systematically selected simply because of their easy availability, their compromised position, or their manipulability, rather than for reasons directly related to the problem being studied.[3]

These three principles have significant and direct impact on the design and execution of research involving human subjects. For example, "respect for persons" includes the principle of informed consent, or the idea that prior to joining a study, research participants should understand the risks and benefits as well as the fact that they can leave the study at any time. "Beneficence" refers to the idea that research should not be harmful to participants, and ideally should present them some benefit. "Justice" addresses previous unethical approaches to identifying research participants from vulnerable populations. The principle of justice requires researchers to explain strategies for recruiting participants, including why specific members of specific groups are being sought, if that is the case.

The *Belmont Report* outlines principles, whereas the Common Rule, established in 1991, also outlines the policies and procedures necessary to ensure research projects meet ethical standards prior to execution. The *Belmont Report* focuses on principles, whereas the Common Rule describes procedures, including the composition and role of the institutional review board, additional protections for specific groups (including children and the incarcerated), and the nature and content of mechanisms for securing informed consent from participants. (See appendix B for a sample informed consent form.)

If you intend to publish or formally present the results of your assessment project involving human subjects, you must secure IRB approval from your home institution. Specific requirements and processes vary significantly, and it's worth looking into the particulars well in advance.

Most library assessment projects are eligible for what's called expedited review, meaning they have limited potential for harm or significant benefit to participants. As the name implies, expedited review typically results in more timely approval.

Critical Perspectives in Assessment

The past fifteen or so years have seen an interest in critical approaches to librarianship, particularly in the area of instruction. Critical librarianship is often referred to as critlib, especially on social media, where robust discussions of this important perspective take place regularly. Critical librarianship calls for approaching the practice of librarianship with an awareness of the power structures inherent in the library as institution, in librarianship as a profession, and in the larger information ecosystem. As stated on the critlib website, critical librarianship recognizes "that we all work under regimes of white supremacy, capitalism, and a range of structural inequalities" and asks, "how can our work as librarians intervene in and disrupt those systems?"[4]

An interest in critical assessment as a concept, and in critical approaches to library assessment, seems to be ascendant. Critical assessment "pushes us to consider the roles of power and privilege in the design of our learning measurement methods, and to give voice to the people involved with the assessment."[5] Critical assessment reminds us of the importance of centering the needs, preferences, and satisfaction of those stakeholders who may typically be overlooked. To do so, we must consider the structural, political, social, and economic contexts in which everyone involved in an assessment process operates. One drawback to considering the traditional elements of research when designing assessment is the illusion of neutrality. Critical assessment asks us to pause and remember that humans insert bias into any effort they undertake.

> There is some very insightful, meaningful work being done in the area of critical assessment. Please see some of our recommendations at the end of chapter 2.

Data Integrity

We will go into more detail on this topic in chapter 10, but it's worth touching on here, too. One important component of an IRB application involves storage and preservation of data. Even if you won't be seeking IRB approval for your project, if you are collecting data on human subjects, it's essential that you consider how and where your data will be stored. If there is identifying information attached to, say, survey responses, you should either figure out how to remove identifiers from those responses or develop a system for storing them securely.

Honesty in Data Presentation

You may find this heading confusing (and a little insulting). You might be thinking to yourself, "Of course, I would never falsify data!" We know! We are discussing the type of dishonesty involved in over-reporting the number of reference questions patrons asked on a Friday morning—which you would never do! Rather, it is possible to present data that is factually accurate in a manner that is dishonest. An illustration of this point may be helpful; please indulge us.

Let's pretend that we own a theme park that has a problematic safety record. The local authorities informed us last fall that our permit will not be renewed in the upcoming spring because five of the park's most popular rides, the Crown Coaster, Peach Pit, Quartz Mine, Buzzin' Bee, and Bulldog Blaster, have had too many accidents to be considered safe. We have the winter to make repairs for inspection in mid-May.

We delay making the repairs, changing plans several times, and failing to provide the supplies that maintenance teams require. Before we know it, it's almost time for inspection. We spend the last week of April and beginning of May running tests on the five rides. As figure 4.2 shows, our results are not great:

FIGURE 4.2

Top five rides with the greatest number of accidents between April 26 and May 9

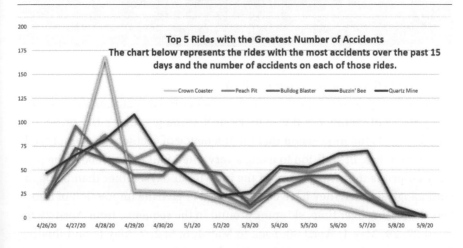

Although we appear to have made some progress in reducing the number of accidents on the rides, there is not a clear and consistent downward trajectory for all five rides. The Quartz Mine in particular had a significant number of incidents just two days prior to the end of the testing period; it's also unlikely that our accidents declined so precipitously on the last two trial days, so there may have been a problem with data collection. Regardless, the data as presented in this chart is unlikely to encourage the Office of Permits to allow us to open the park by Memorial Day weekend. So, we have a moment of inspiration: what if we just present the data differently?

FIGURE 4.3

Top five rides with the greatest number of accidents between April 26 and May 9: alternative presentation 1

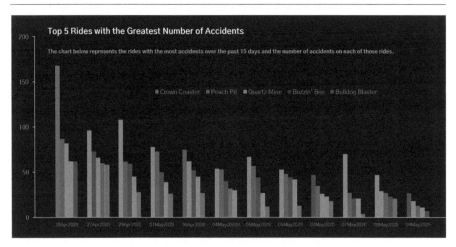

Looks better in figure 4.3, doesn't it?

The data presented in this chart is factually correct. Each day's and ride's accident counts are the same as in the line graph; it's the presentation that lends the impression that the frequency of accidents has improved more than it has. In addition to using a very small font for the labels, the primary culprit is the arrangement of the individual days: rather than being in chronological order, they have been arranged to give the impression of numbers decreasing over time, skipping around in the sequence from April 28 to April 27, 29, May 1, April 30, back to May 4, 6, 5, 2, 7, May 8, and finally, May 9. If the codes inspector skims this chart without paying close attention to the labels, that's not our fault, is it?

Before you say, "That's outlandish! No one would ever do such a thing!" allow us to tell you about the state of Georgia. In early May 2020, some individual US states began to ease restrictions put in place in prior months to slow the spread of COVID-19. Georgia was one of the first states to allow some of these non-essential businesses to reopen, a move that concerned many outside observers and Georgians alike. In mid-May, the state of Georgia released a chart illustrating the "Top Five Counties with the Greatest Number of Confirmed COVID-19 Cases: Cobb, DeKalb, Fulton, Gwinnett, and Hall." The chart label describes it as representing the number of cases in these counties "over the past 15 days and the number of cases over time," implying that the data is represented chronologically. If you just scan the chart quickly, things look to have improved in Georgia between April 26 and May 9.[6]

(A note: we'd initially planned to use Georgia's charts, but you may not be surprised to learn that the state was rather embarrassed by the public outcry over the charts that were initially released and we thought the prospect of securing permission seemed unlikely. Instead, we decided to create our own versions, using different data, to illustrate Georgia's approach. However, the data and presentation are nearly identical to our rearranged ride accident chart in figure 4.3. We did not anticipate how difficult it would be to arrange the data and dates to create a chart that gave the impression accidents were decreasing over time. For example, we had to make deliberate alterations to the date format to prevent the program from automatically ordering the days chronologically. We are not sure how Georgia's first chart was created "by mistake.")

Unfortunately for the individual who created this chart, more than a few eagle-eyed Georgians went beyond giving it a cursory glance and realized the dates are not arranged in chronological order. Rather, the days are arranged in descending order by numbers of cases, and the counties' arrangement for each day are in descending order. Remember our assertion that assessment is always political and it's conducted and shared in at least one context? The chart's release coincided with activation of Governor Brian Kemp's policy to expand reopening even further. It's easy to imagine the chart was designed to give the impression that cases had declined over time, making it seem less dangerous to reopen public spaces than it had fifteen days prior. The data is factually correct but is presented in a manner meant to direct the viewer to an incorrect conclusion that more closely supports the creator's objective.

It's difficult to imagine a scenario in which such an arrangement would be helpful to those trying to grasp the disease's spread "over the past 15 days," especially when one also inspects the x-axis labels, which are printed in a font that is both very small and in a difficult-to-read color. Unsurprisingly, the public assumed nefarious intent on the part of Georgia officials, who insisted there had just been a mistake. After public outcry, the state reissued the chart.[7]

Here is our ride data presented in a manner that mimics Georgia's rerelease. It makes more sense, although we'd argue that the line graph in figure 4.2 is much easier to read than figure 4.4's clustered column chart.

FIGURE 4.4
Top five rides with the greatest number of accidents between April 26 and May 9; alternative presentation 2

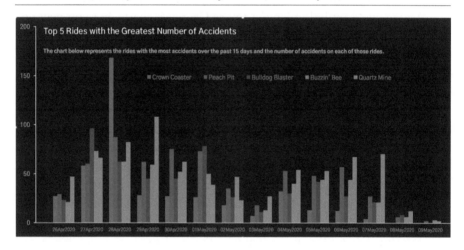

Both charts present data that is factually correct, but only one represents the data honestly by arranging it in a manner that makes sense.

The x-axis label font is still difficult to read, however.

Conclusion

Assessment is hard work! It consumes significant resources of many types—financial, labor, political, and social capital—therefore, it is essential that an assessment project be well-planned and executed. Assessment and planning do not have a linear relationship; rather, they are points on an iterative cycle.

It's also important to remember that assessment does not occur in a vacuum; all assessment is political and occurs in a context. Sometimes, there's really no point to conducting an assessment project if there's no possibility of acting on what you discover to improve the library's resources, services, or environment for your constituents. Remember, assessment can be a powerful vehicle for both positive and negative public relations.

Although some would argue "assessment is not research," we're of the opinion that the principles of research design can provide helpful guidance for assessment projects. Making sure you know what you are measuring and why you are measuring it is essential. It's also important to keep the user in mind while planning and conducting an assessment project. This may mean submitting your plan to an institutional review board for review and approval.

NOTES

1. Ricardo Alexandre Morais, "Scientific Method," in *Encyclopedia of Case Study Research*, ed. Albert J. Mills, Gabrielle Durepos, and Elden Wiebe (Thousand Oaks, CA: SAGE Publications, Inc., 2010), 841–42.
2. Constance A. Mellon, "Library Anxiety: A Grounded Theory and Its Development," *College and Research Libraries* 76, no. 3 (2015): 276–82.
3. *The Belmont Report* (National Commission for the Protection of Human Subjects of Biomedical and Behavioral Research, 1979).
4. "About/Join the Discussion," Critlib, http://critlib.org/about/.
5. Candice Benjes-Small, Maura Seale, Alex R. Hodges, and Meg Meiman, "Keeping Up with . . . Critical Assessment," Association of College and Research Libraries, June 11, 2019.
6. Stephen Fowler, "I've deleted this tweet...," Twitter, May 17, 2020, https://twitter.com/stphnfwlr/status/1262171592932589569.
7. Willoughby Mariano and J. Scott Trubey, "'It's Just Cuckoo': State's Latest Data Mishap Causes Critics to Cry Foul," *The Atlanta Journal-Constitution*, May 19, 2020.

Approaches to Assessment

- Metrics-Based Approaches
- Economic Models
- Standards-Based Assessment
- Outcomes-Based Models
- Conclusion

Chapter 4 focused on the foundational principles of conceptualizing, designing, and implementing an assessment project, but we haven't yet discussed the specific approaches or frameworks one might use to design assessment and the specific areas of library quality each might assess most effectively. Over 82 percent of respondents to our survey of librarians with assessment responsibilities indicated their position required them to determine the best research model for a particular question; in this chapter, we will discuss specific frameworks for assessment, including metrics such as inputs, outputs, and outcomes; and models such as standards-based assessment and benchmarking. We will also make an overview of economic models, including return on investment (ROI) and their applicability in not-for-profit institutions such as libraries.

Although there is an abundance of approaches to assessing the effectiveness and value of library resources and services, let's focus on the most common: metrics-based assessment, standards-based assessment, outcomes-based assessment, and economic approaches.

Metrics-Based Approaches

Metrics-based approaches constitute the most longstanding approach to library assessment. Metrics-based assessment focuses on quantitative measurements of inputs and outputs. Inputs are the things that go into a system to make it function, while outputs come out of a system as a result of combining inputs with the work done by library staff.

Examples of inputs include:

- hours of operation
- budgets
- number of programs
- number of instruction sessions offered
- number of items added to the collection

Examples of outputs include:

- door counts
- reference queries
- item circulation
- e-resource usage statistics

Specific inputs and outputs are closely associated, but it's often possible to mix and match, that is, to measure an output resulting from more than one specific input, and vice versa.

Figure 5.1 provides an illustration of inputs and outputs associated with the traditional approach to assessing reference and information services. In this case, the inputs are the financial expenditures on the reference materials required to provide information sought by patrons, the hours that reference services are available (e.g., the number of hours that the library is open or reference chat is running), and staff availability to provide reference services. The primary output measured to assess quality is the number of reference queries asked (and sometimes, the number of answers provided) within a specific time frame. Each of these inputs and outputs can be associated with other metrics if we cared to do so.

FIGURE 5.1

Example of input and output measures associated with a specific library service

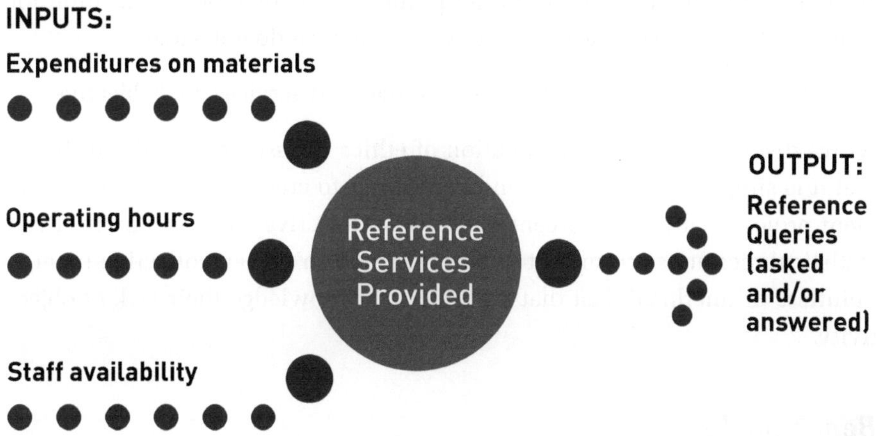

INPUTS:

Expenditures on materials

Operating hours

Reference Services Provided

OUTPUT:

Reference Queries (asked and/or answered)

Staff availability

Libraries rely heavily on input- and output-based assessment for a number of reasons:

- It's straightforward and easy. Metrics like circulation and e-resource log-ons and downloads are often recorded automatically in integrated library systems and COUNTER reports. When automatic recording is not available and metrics must be recorded by hand (e.g., the number of reference queries fielded in a given day), it is fairly simple to train staff to record statistics accurately.
- Inputs and outputs are also easily understood by stakeholders inside and outside the library. Reporting to your library board president or your city's mayor that 150,000 children participate in summer reading programs each year is impressive, and the number can be compared to participation in other programs offered through the school system

or park district, as well as participation in programs offered by peer
library systems.

- Inputs and outputs are also requested or required by governmental
  and professional organizations such as the Association of College and
  Research Libraries and the US Department of Education.
- Because input- and output-based assessment is so common, most
  libraries will already have prior records of specific measures, which
  facilitates tracking and comparison of circulation, expenditures,
  program attendance, and other metrics over the years.

We would like to add another bullet point with a common justification for
input- and output-based assessment with which we do not agree:

- Statistical measures of library resources and services are "objective."

As we discussed in our consideration of ethics in assessment, it's our belief
that it is simply not possible for human beings to create a research or assessment project that is 100 percent objective. "Objective data" is a myth. Even
statistical measures are subject to bias. That doesn't mean collecting them is
pointless or unethical, just that we need to acknowledge their lack of objectivity.

Benchmarks

This is perhaps most evident in a subtype of metrics-based assessment, the
comparison-based approach known as benchmark-based assessment, or
benchmarking. Benchmarking compares metrics between institutions or organizations of similar size or with a similar mission, such as public university
libraries in a specific geographic region. One of the most well-known examples of benchmarking is the Association of Research Libraries (ARL) Library
Investment Index (LII), a formula that considers the following metrics, all of
which are inputs:

1. Total expenditures

2. Salary expenditures

3. Materials expenditures

4. Number of professional + support staff

Each year, ARL uses the LII formula to develop a numbered list of its member libraries. Although ARL is hesitant to call this list a ranking, its order is calculated annually based on the statistical information gathered from member libraries. The LII was adapted from the previously used metric, the Membership Criteria Index (MCI), which used the following metrics:

1. Volumes held
2. Volumes added (gross)
3. Current serials (number of subscriptions)
4. Total expenditures
5. Professional + support staff (number)

It's interesting to note that although the LII is strictly an input-based approach, the MCI incorporated volumes held and current serials—both outputs—and volumes added, which can be considered an input or an output, depending on the focus of assessment.

Economic Models

Libraries, special libraries in particular, have employed economic approaches to measuring the value of library resources and services for decades (see Griffiths and King). It is unsurprising that this approach originated in libraries of businesses and other for-profit enterprises; their librarians have long been expected to demonstrate their contributions to the organization's bottom line. In recent years, however, libraries—public, then academic—have adopted this framework for demonstrating value.

Revisiting our discussion of critical assessment, it's important to note the significant and legitimate objections to focusing on the "value"—especially in a monetary sense—a library brings to its parent organization. Primary among these is that grafting private sector priorities onto a public good distorts our understanding of libraries' fundamental mission. We find this argument resonant but would be doing the reader a disservice if we were to ignore these approaches to assessment.

Cost-Benefit Analysis and Return on Investment

Cost-benefit analysis (C/BA) employs both inputs and outputs to create a measure of value. The principle of C/BA is fairly straightforward: if an institution makes an investment in a specific resource or service, what kind of financial benefit might it expect? Return on investment (ROI) is perhaps the best-known approach to C/BA; ROI is the specific rate of return on a financial investment. This approach is best illustrated by a project conducted by Carol Tenopir, Paula Kaufman, and Judy Luther. The team gathered information about faculty who had successfully applied for grant funding within a specific time period and contacted them directly to ask if they had utilized library resources to prepare their grant application. The researchers calculated the total grant funds awarded to faculty who indicated having used library resources and divided that figure by the library's budget during the time period during which the grant application was being prepared. They found that for every dollar spent by the library, faculty were awarded $4.38 in grant funds.[1]

ROI is also a popular approach for public libraries and a bit easier to conceptualize than in academic library settings. Most typically, public libraries have calculated ROI by dividing the number of dollars a patron might have spent on the books they checked out during a year by the number of dollars allocated to the library from the patron's property taxes, for example. More recent models have incorporated services like internet and wireless access, programming, and research databases.

What about those benefits that don't have a financial value attached to them directly? It might still be possible to calculate a financial return by considering things like time savings. For example, Prestigious University's Professor Jones is a very heavy user of the library's electronic resource subscriptions, which they typically access from their campus office or home, located about one-half and ten miles from the library, respectively. If, when they needed a journal article, they were required to visit the library, locate a bound volume, find a photocopier, and copy the article, that would constitute a significant time expenditure. This would consume a significant amount of their work time that could be spent on other tasks.

Because they typically read academic journal articles for research and teaching and not for pleasure and their university pays them to complete this work, it would be possible to approximate the financial benefit to Prestigious University of providing faculty electronic access to academic journals. First, Professor Jones would record the number of hours required to physically acquire a copy of a print article (x), and perhaps multiply that number by the number of library-subscribed resources they accessed during their last research project (y). They would then use their annual salary to calculate a rough approximation of their wage if they were paid hourly (z)·(xy)z = the total cost to Prestigious University of Professor Jones finding and duplicating print journal articles. By making a similar calculation of the time required to gather the same number of items in electronic format (w), it's possible to estimate the total salary savings to Prestigious University facilitated by providing access to electronic resources: (xy)z − (wy)z = savings.

This model makes a number of assumptions. First, that the time Professor Jones saved by accessing articles online would be spent on another work-related task, which may not be the case. Instead, they may spend that time reading for pleasure or taking a walk. Second, calculating the value of time on the basis of salary creates the assumption that the time of individuals with higher salaries is more valuable. As such, this approach could backfire; in academic institutions, salaries are not uniform across campus. For example, the salaries for tenure-line faculty at the University of Tennessee range from just over $50,000 to nearly $370,000. Would that mean that the e-resources typically used by the faculty member whose salary is at the higher end are more valuable than those used by those at the lower end of the scale?

Contingent Valuation

Contingent valuation (willingness to pay) is a bit trickier as an approach for measuring the value of library resources and services. The basic premise of the methodological framework is asking users to assign a monetary value to the resources and services they use ("what would you be willing to pay to access chat reference services?"), or asking them to estimate their monetary savings by virtue of using a resource or service ("if you were unable to access the library's cookbook collection, what might that cost you?"). Of course, many patrons will be unable to estimate the value of a resource or service that has always been provided to them at no cost, or they might believe they only use the resource or service in question because it's provided at no cost, and they would decline to pay anything if required to do so and could forgo the service or resource with little or no discomfort or inconvenience.

In addition, some library resources and services have simple analogs among for-profit resources and services. For example, you can check out a novel from your local library, or you can pay Amazon $9.00 to purchase the

Kindle format version of the book. You can send your teenager to watch a movie that your local library has licensed for teen night, or you can rent the same movie from Redbox for $2.99. Other resources and services are less easy to pin down. Most people have no idea what it might cost to hire an assistant to locate genealogical information or gather data related to the business climate in a specific community. How then might they estimate the value of such a service with any kind of accuracy? Estimating the cost to access the information resources necessary to answer such questions would also be impossible for most laypeople.

THE MATTHEW EFFECT

Sociologists Robert K. Merton and Harriet Zuckerman named the phenomenon behind the aphorism "the rich get richer, while the poor get poorer" the "Matthew Effect," referring to the parable of the talents from the New Testament of the Bible.[2] In the parable, Matthew is one of three servants given a sum of money by his employer prior to the employer's leaving for a trip. Matthew and one of the other two servants chose to invest the money they were given to potentially increase the sum, while the third servant buried his money for safekeeping. Upon the employer's return, the two servants who invested the original sum are rewarded, but the third servant is ridiculed for laziness and punished. The crux of the parable is as follows: "For to all those who have, more will be given, and they will have an abundance; but from those who have nothing, even what they have will be taken away" (Matthew 25:30).

Merton and Zuckerman applied the Matthew Effect to the sociology of science, specifically scholarly communication, to describe recognition among scholars. For example, citation of scholarly works tends to have a "snowball effect" in that once an item has been cited, the chance that it will be cited again increases significantly. The same is sometimes said for book circulation.

The Matthew Effect is similar in concept to the 80/20 rule, introduced to the library world in the late 1960s by Richard Trueswell, then head of the University of Massachusetts Department of Industrial Engineering. A maxim in Trueswell's home field, the 80/20 rule asserts that 20 percent of a business's stock accounts for 80 percent of its sales. Having developed an interest in library systems analysis, Trueswell suggested that 20 percent of a library's collection might, in fact, account for 80 percent of its circulation statistics.[3] Over the years, the 80/20 rule has also been applied to distribution of citations to previously-published work.

We can broaden the Matthew Effect to describe physical collections as well. Let's say an alumnus of a university in Kansas has developed a fairly significant collection of historical cookbooks from the American South, which she offers to sell to her alma mater at far below market value. Although the university and special collections library have no existing significant collection of this type of material, the offer is too good to pass up, and the purchase is made with the hope that it might yield benefits down the road. Suddenly, a special collections library in Kansas owns a fairly valuable collection of materials that have no significance to the parent institution beyond the personal interest of an alumna.

In subsequent years, however, an interesting thing happens: other collectors of historical Southern cookbooks hear about the "seed collection" at the Kansas university and, recognizing that a larger and more comprehensive collection is more useful than several smaller, disparate collections scattered among a number of special collections libraries, begin donating their collections to the Kansas university to add to the seed collection first donated by the university's graduate. The collection also begins to attract researchers from around the world interested in using the cookbook collection, and eventually the collection provides important support for the university's bid to host an important conference for a culinary studies scholarly society.

These are all benefits, some of which are financial. How, though, to comprehensively measure the collective benefit, accrued over a period of time, of acquiring the first seed collection of cookbooks?

Cost per Use

Cost per use (CPU) is, very simply, a calculation of the monetary cost of each use of an item (we will discuss the concept of use in the chapter 6). Typically, the proxy for use is an output measure like a book circulation or electronic item download; the cost to acquire and maintain access to a resource is divided by the number of times it is used over a period of time, the idea being that a resource with a lower CPU is more effective or of greater value. E-resources assessment is CPU's most common milieu, facilitated by tools like COUNTER-compliant reports of downloads.

Criticisms of Economic Approaches to Library Assessment

While these perspectives on assessment may make perfect sense for special libraries (and, indeed, originated in special library assessment), some consider it impossible to adapt them to measure resources and services provided by not-for-profit organizations like academic and public libraries. Some objections are practical: although we might add up the number of dollars we would have spent to purchase the books we've checked out from the library this year and determine a positive return on our investment via Tennessee's "wheel tax," there are a couple of big assumptions in play.

First, if we had to actually purchase those books in order to read them, we actually would have done so. Although we are voracious readers, the majority of the books we read are checked out from the library—we actually purchase very few pleasure-reading titles. We are far more likely to take a chance on a book that "sounds like it might be good" if we do not need to make a financial investment in it. If we had to purchase every book we read, there is no doubt our reading behavior would change significantly. How, exactly . . . we don't know.

Another shortcoming is that these approaches treat "value" as a proxy for quality. This is especially true in calculating cost per use; a very popular electronic resource, for example, is going to have a low cost per use, meaning it presents a good value to the institution and is more likely to be retained. In our opinion, this is sort of like saying a fast-food hamburger is superior to one prepared at a steakhouse because it is produced in greater volume, costs less, and is consumed by a larger number of people.

This leads to our final criticism of economic approaches to library assessment: they place an unhealthy emphasis on financial value incongruent with public and academic libraries' missions. We fundamentally object to assessing the value of information services, resources, facilities, and artifacts in a strictly financial sense. If we truly believe that libraries, and the resources and services they provide, have a role in helping patrons develop and share knowledge and skills in the short and longer term, we must reject the impulse to reduce the way we understand value and worth to solely monetary measures.

Standards-Based Assessment

Standards-based assessment is a term more typically used to describe an approach to measuring individual students' learning by designing lessons and assessments to address established standards of learning. At the institutional level, a standards-based approach to assessment calls for comparing your institution's measures of activity against an established standard of adequacy, or —for the more ambitious—excellence. Although not strictly an outcomes-based approach, standards-based assessment is not typically based on inputs and outputs. In "Staffing Chat Reference with Undergraduate Student Assistants at an Academic Library: A Standards-Based Assessment," Kelsey Keyes and Ellie Dworak offer an excellent example of the genre. To determine the level of quality student workers provided in chat reference transactions, the authors reviewed transcripts of sessions led by both reference librarians and student workers to determine how closely their behaviors comported with the Reference and User Services Association's Behavioral Guidelines for Reference and Information Services (often referred to as the "RUSA Guidelines").[4] The RUSA Guidelines outline the ideal behaviors, attitudes, and skills of those conducting reference work; in other words, they establish a standard for reference work against which real-life examples might be compared. Keyes and Dworak's study does not investigate the outcomes of these chat reference transactions—they don't, for example, attempt to determine the patrons' level of satisfaction with the service, or if the patrons were able to earn a higher grade on an assignment as a result of chatting—but the level of analysis is more sophisticated than simply counting how many chat reference transactions occurred during a specified period, or even the percentage of chat reference questions that were answered correctly.[5]

Standards-based assessment can be a powerful approach, but it's limited by a few important factors. First, there must be a relatively well-accepted standard to use as a point of assessment. As library work continually becomes more diverse and specialized, the likelihood of organizations developing standards similar to RUSA's guidelines decreases.

Second, because standards are likely to have been developed by a professional organization and tied to that profession's (hopefully) well-informed expectations, standards-based assessment might have less impact on stakeholders outside the library. Imagine trying to explain to one of the patrons on the other end of the chat reference sessions described in Keyes and Dworak's article that they shouldn't mind having been assisted by a college sophomore because they had ticked the boxes in the RUSA Guidelines. Would they even care how well the staff met the RUSA Guidelines? Unlikely. They are far more likely to be concerned with the outcome of their encounter.

Third, and perhaps most important: standards are developed by human beings and are, therefore, subjective regardless of the years of experience or study their creators have accumulated. They reflect the biases of their creators, who may not reflect the communities they serve.

Outcomes-Based Models

Rather than calculating inputs and outputs, outcomes-based assessment models focus on the end result of providing a resource or service. The purpose of outcomes-based assessment is to provide empirical evidence of a library initiative's positive impact. Outcomes-based assessment requires a shift in thinking. Where input-, output-, economic-, and even standards-based assessment center the library, its resources, and its services, outcomes-based assessment focuses primarily on the user. Rather than the book being checked out, or the electronic journal article being downloaded, outcomes-based assessment is concerned with changes to the individual checking out the book or downloading the journal article. The seeds of this change in thinking were planted in the late 1970s, when LIS authors like Douglas Zweizig began to advocate for stepping away from the longstanding approach of using statistical measures of library usage to demonstrate effectiveness in favor of a focus on user benefits from services provided by the library to document "the functional contribution of the library in terms of impact" and its "contribution to its supporting community."[6]

Outcomes-based assessment is considered by many to be the gold standard approach and is required by many regional and programmatic accreditors of K–12 and higher education, and by grant-making agencies such as the Institute of Museum and Library Services' model of outcomes-based assessment can be particularly meaningful and provide data that is especially useful for understanding impact and telling your library's story, but there are a number of circumstances that make executing this approach particularly complex.

In order to demonstrate an outcome, you have to know where you started: outcomes-based assessment requires a nuanced understanding of the state of affairs prior to implementing the service or resource being evaluated. Ideally, the introduction of any new service or resource is preceded by an environmental scan and robust planning process that will demonstrate the need for the initiative in question, but in reality, these decisions often seem to be made on the basis of intuition, availability, or, if we're being totally frank, a sense of competition. Think back to the time directly preceding your library's last big service or resource addition; whether the initiative had a positive or negative impact is not the point. Prior to installing that makerspace or combining your circulation, reference, and interlibrary loan service desks, did the library take the time and effort to establish the need and desire for such a large change and investment of person-power and other resources? How? Was the decision based on a large-scale inquiry of the relevant stakeholder groups, or on a few comments stuffed in the library's suggestion box, or on the fact that a certain peer institution had already done it?

In order to assess the outcome of introducing a resource or service, you need to have a clear sense of the following:

- the need or deficit to address
- the specific actions, resources, or services that might address the need
- the specific ways in which the resources or services under consideration would address that need
- the future (short-, mid-, and longer-term) impact of the change(s) under consideration
- the specific empirical evidence to demonstrate that impact
- how that evidence will be collected

A lot more complicated than downloading a COUNTER report, huh?

For example, let's say that you are looking for ways for your library to increase engagement with young adults and after an environmental scan and user study, you settle on installing a makerspace. First, you would need to figure out what "increasing engagement" means in this particular instance (i.e., operationalize it) and how you might measure this change. Before you could measure a change, you would need to get a snapshot of the current level of engagement among a group of young adults in the community. Then, you'd need to have them use the makerspace for a period of time (how long?), then assess their level of engagement to see if there's been a change.

1. How will you identify a group of young adults?

   a. Is it important to include young adults who are not current library users? (If you're measuring a change in engagement among your community's teens, yes.)

2. How will you measure engagement?

3. Will you design a survey instrument or conduct one-on-one interviews? Is there an existing instrument you can use?

4. How long do these young adults need to be involved with the makerspace?

5. How do you ensure that all the teenagers you're working with actually use the makerspace?

6. How do you assess the young adults' change in engagement?

Let's assume all of these questions are answered satisfactorily and findings indicate an increased level of engagement with the library. How do you prove that working with the makerspace is the cause? Attempts at outcomes-based assessment in particular are complicated by confounding factors. In research, a confounding factor is any element external to the phenomenon being studied that might have an influence on findings. In this case, perhaps the makerspace project coincided with a library initiative at the students' high school. Perhaps spending time with each other was the factor that increased engagement, not using the makerspace. Perhaps interacting with the librarians involved in teaching makerspace-based classes led to the change in attitude, and the young adults would have become more engaged with the library by attending any type of class. The school lesson, working with librarians—these are confounding factors. Did using the makerspace actually change the teens' attitudes? Probably, but we really can't say so definitively.

Social sciences research, because it centers on human beings, is messy. We are of the opinion that it's next to impossible to "prove" that A element caused B emotional, cognitive, or dispositional change in a group of people; our individual experiences, aptitudes, and inclinations create a unique context for each of us for which we cannot control. Sometimes, developing a preponderance of evidence must be sufficient. In chapter 4, we discussed the concept of triangulation—approaching an assessment-related research question with multiple data collection methods—which is especially important for outcomes-based assessment. Returning to our makerspace example:

in addition to gauging teenagers' attitudes about the library before and after makerspace installation by conducting surveys, it would be advisable to conduct one-on-one interviews or focus groups. Perhaps, too, it would be possible to compare the number of items specific teenagers checked out in a period of time before and after makerspace installation (note: we suggest quantifying numbers of items, not reviewing the specific titles the teenagers have checked out). Number and frequency of library visits might also help indicate changes to level of engagement or an increase in the number of library services each teen accesses.

> The question of patron privacy is particularly sticky in discussing how to approach outcomes-based assessment. Outcomes frequently must be understood individually before they can be aggregated to determine patterns and trends. This individual focus tends to make librarians uncomfortable when it bumps up against patron privacy, one of our profession's most closely guarded principles. We want to be clear that in no way do we advocate for violating patron privacy, however, we do ask careful consideration of whether data collection methods truly violate patron privacy before dismissing them.

It's difficult to claim that any of these individual data points conclusively indicate a change in isolation, but considered in aggregate, our argument grows more compelling.

Another complicating element of outcomes-based assessment is the fact that it is a longer-term endeavor than other approaches. The core of outcomes-based assessment is demonstrating change, and change takes time. Unfortunately, many of those who request evidence of the library's impact are unwilling to wait for that impact to develop.

Social Return on Investment

Social return on investment (SROI)—measuring the social benefits of investing in and providing specific resources or services—is an interesting twist on both outcomes-based and ROI approaches. Returning to the value of e-resources example discussed earlier, an SROI approach might consider the environmental benefits of allowing researchers to access academic materials from their homes or offices, thus eliminating the pollution created by driving to the campus library to access the resources in physical format. Reducing damage to the environment by forgoing automobile travel doesn't have a ready monetary value when considered on a smaller scale, but it does have collective, or societal, benefits.

Another type of social benefit we might consider is the library, its services and collections' contribution to the prestige, reputation, or cachet of its parent institution. For example, seemingly every college campus tour stops in the library. Why? Presumably, one purpose of the campus tour is to sell the institution to prospective students: how does visiting the library contribute to that goal?

The primary challenge presented by SROI is similar to that of many other approaches: isolating the facet of library resources or services of interest as the significant variable—the thing that tipped a donor or incoming scholar's opinion in favor of making a donation or accepting an offer.

Conclusion

There are a number of frameworks for conceptualizing library assessment, each of which has strengths and weaknesses. Input- and output-based assessment is the most common and longstanding; it relies on statistical measures of the elements that go into and come out of the system we call "the library." Although there are a number of characteristics that recommend this approach, including the automated nature of much of the reporting, ultimately, inputs and outputs only really tell us the what and provide no real information about the why, or, for that matter, the why not!

There are a number of economic models that rely on inputs and outputs as the basis for calculating the monetary value of specific resources, services, or facilities. These models were pioneered in special libraries, especially those serving for-profit organizations, but adapting them for public and academic libraries can present problems.

Standards-based assessment and benchmarking compare the resource or service being assessed to an established standard or another institution's measures of quality, respectively; both approaches provide more context than a strictly input/output-based approach, establishing that context can present a challenge.

Outcomes-based assessment measures the changes that result from accessing the library resources or services of interest. Although outcomes-based assessment can be tremendously compelling, designing and conducting it effectively consumes significant resources.

In chapters 6 through 8, we will discuss different approaches to gathering evidence within each of these frameworks.

NOTES

1. Carol Tenopir, "Measuring the Value of the Academic Library: Return on Investment and Other Value Measures," *Serials Librarian* 58 (2010): 43.
2. Robert K. Merton, "The Matthew Effect in Science," *Science* 159, no. 3810 (1968): 56–63.
3. Richard W. Trueswell, "Some Behavioral Patterns of Library Users: The 80/20 Rule," *Wilson Library Bulletin* 43 (January 1969): 458–61.
4. RSS Management of Reference Committee, *Behavioral Guidelines for Reference and Information Services* (Chicago: RUSA, revised 2011), http://www.ala.org/rusa/resources/guidelines/guidelinesbehavioral.
5. Kelsey Keyes and Ellie Dworak, "Staffing Chat Reference with Undergraduate Student Assistants at an Academic Library: A Standards-Based Assessment," *The Journal of Academic Librarianship* 43, no. 6 (2017): 469–78.
6. Douglas L. Zweizig, "Measuring Library Use," *Drexel Library Quarterly* 13, no. 3 (1977): 14.

Collecting Assessment Data

- Let's Talk about Use
- Use and the Survey
- Use and the User
- Conclusion

In chapter 5, we discussed some of the various frameworks for assessment. In this chapter, we will talk about some of the important principles underlying strategies for collecting assessment data. If we're thinking of a completed assessment project as a work of art, the analogy for the topics we'll discuss in this chapter would be the considerations an artist might take before deciding how to proceed. Drawing or painting? Oil or watercolor? Each has benefits and drawbacks, and some approaches will produce a superior result.

Let's Talk about Use

You might have noticed that *use* is a term that comes up a lot in discussing metrics-based and economic models for assessment. Indeed, a June 2020 search of the databases Library, Information Science, and Technology Abstracts (LISTA) and Library and Information Science Source (LISS) for items with "library" and "use" in the title and "evaluation OR assessment" as a subject generated a number of assessment-related articles. A quick perusal of just the first page of results reveals, however, that "use" is seldom defined. We will review three articles to illuminate this point:

- "Households' Public Library Use across the School Calendar," by Gregory Gilpin and Anton Bekkerman.[1]
- "Understanding User Experience in Bring Your Own Device Spaces in the Library: A Case Study of Space Planning and Use At a Large Research University," by Zoe Chao et al.[2]
- "Understanding Users' Continuance Intention to Use Online Library Resources Based on an Extended Expectation-Confirmation Model," by Soohyung Joo and Namjoo Choi.[3]

Gilpin and Bekkerman are the only authors to explicitly state which behavior (circulation) serves as a proxy for use in their study. In order to understand the meaning of use for Chao et al., one must extrapolate. Joo and Choi do not define use for readers; in their article, use refers to book circulation, patrons' physical presence in the library space, and some undefined behavior with online library resources. Neither Chao et al. nor Joo and Choi appear to have explained their interpretation of use for their interview and survey respondents. For example, Chao et al.'s interview protocol includes the question, "What do you typically use this space for?" While one item from Joo and Choi's survey asks respondents to assess their agreement with the statement: "Using online library resources improves my performance in completing my academic tasks."[4]

Why does this matter, and why, specifically, does this matter for our discussion of planning and assessment? So much of planning and assessment comes back to some notion of use. We plan for resources, spaces, and services that patrons "will use." We discuss whether or not a resource or service has been "used" when we make decisions about continuing our subscription or canceling it. We ask patrons what they use, why they (do or don't) use what they do, and what they would use if we were to provide it. If we lack a common understanding of what use refers to in any given planning or assessment scenario, our discussions cease to have meaning.

Use and the Survey

Joo and Choi and Chao et al. provide great examples of the problematic nature of relying on *use* as a primitive term (i.e., an idea that is so fundamental as to be indefinable) in assessment, which Abraham Bookstein brought to the library world's collective attention in 1982. Noting that "words, even simple words with seemingly absolute definitions, do vary in meaning from person to person," Bookstein pointed out that in surveys, or questionnaires, "we are subject to the same uncertainty of word use as we are in conversation."[5] To illustrate the point, Bookstein designed a study to explore how students in the Graduate Library School at the University of Chicago interpreted the concept of use. The students were asked their opinions about whether specific actions constituted use of the library. James Kidston replicated Bookstein's project a few years later with students from the University of Chicago's business program.[6] You may find the results of both studies surprising, especially when you consider that they were conducted before the introduction of remote access to library resources and services, so all of the actions described required visiting the library at some point.

Forty-seven percent of Bookstein's respondents considered *skimming a book—not finding it useful* to be an example of using it, but only 20 percent believed *skimming the introduction only before determining that the book was irrelevant* would be deemed a use.[7] Bookstein concluded that "to many people, it seems that a book is used provided it turns out to be 'useful,' and that use involves extended, immediate reading of it."[8] Kidston was unable to identify a similar theme for which actions his respondents considered "legitimate" library use, but it does seem like a larger percentage considered activities that were at that time confined to the physical space of the library, such as activities specific to the physical space of the library, consulting the reference collection, or browsing print journals, to be acceptable library uses.[9]

What's the point of revisiting these journal articles published more than thirty years ago? Well, survey authors still fail to operationalize the concept of use in their survey instruments, by default leaving it up to interpretation.

In Joo and Choi's survey, for example, respondents are asked to assess their agreement with statements like the previously referenced "using online library resources improves my performance in completing my academic tasks" without explaining what "using" means in this context.[10] As a result, one respondent might only consider an online resource to have been used if it was central to an argument they made in a major assignment, whereas another might consider having browsed their library's A–Z list of e-journals without actually reading or downloading any articles to be "using online library resources." Although there seems to be a growing awareness in library land that it's important to define our unique professional jargon for users, we sometimes overlook certain terms that are more generally pervasive in our language. For example, although Joo and Choi provide a definition for "online library resources" in the text of the article, it is not clear that the term was defined in the survey itself. In both instances, clear definitions are essential.

Use and the User

In our discussion of use, we should take an additional step further back and consider whether focusing on use is even the most appropriate approach to assessment. When we talk about use, we're most frequently discussing either (a) use as an abstract concept or (b) use as a transaction—an event captured in time that can be recorded numerically.[11] As we contemplate moving to outcomes-based approaches to assessment, we must think beyond use—which is typically attached to output-based measures—to the user, who is likely to experience the outcome we're trying to understand.

There have been several calls to abandon this focus on use in favor of shifting attention to users and how they employ the library, its resources, and services to meet their needs. Way back in 1977, Brenda Dervin called attention to the flawed assumptions inherent in approaching library assessment from the perspective of use rather than that of the user "the most obvious [of which] is that there is something of value to be obtained as a result of measuring library activities."[12] With co-author Douglas Zweizig, Dervin pushed for an approach to assessment that centered the user by interrogating the role of the library in resolving the user's individual need. The authors suggested we begin asking "What uses are made of the library? What uses could be made of the library?"[13] rather than just counting instances of use. In other words, how is the library *of use* to patrons? What are the *outcomes* of using the library, its resources, or services?

Conclusion

Taking a user-focused approach to assessment may not always be possible, but it's important to consider ways to center the user in your assessment efforts. As we discuss different approaches to collecting evidence for assessment, we will prioritize those that emphasize furthering our understanding of the user, their needs, and how well we're meeting them.

NOTES

1. Gregory Gilpin and Anton Bekkerman, "Households' Public Library Use across the School Calendar," *Library and Information Science Research* 42, no. 2 (2020).
2. Zoe Chao, Steve Borrelli, Bikalpa Neupane, and Joseph Fennewald, "Understanding User Experience in Bring Your Own Device Spaces in the Library: A Case Study of Space Planning and Use at a Large Research University," *Performance Measurement and Metrics* 20, no. 3 (2019): 201–12.
3. Soohyung Joo and Namjoo Choi, "Understanding Users' Continuance Intention to Use Online Library Resources Based on an Extended Expectation-Confirmation Model," *The Electronic Library* 34, no. 4 (2016): 554–71.
4. Chao et al., "Understanding User Experience," 205; Joo and Choi, "Understanding Users' Continuance Intention," 570.
5. Abraham Bookstein, "Sources of Error in Library Questionnaires," *Library Research* 4 (1982): 85–94.
6. James S. Kidston, "The Validity of Questionnaire Responses," *The Library Quarterly: Information, Community, Policy* 55, no. 2 (1985): 133–50.
7. Abraham Bookstein, "Questionnaire Research in a Library Setting," *Journal of Academic Librarianship* 11, no. 1 (1985): 24.
8. Bookstein, "Sources of Error," 89; 90.
9. Kidston, "Validity of Questionnaire Responses," 148.
10. Joo and Choi, "Understanding Users' Continuance Intention," 570.
11. Rachel A. Fleming-May, "What Is Library Use? Facets of Concept and a Typology of Its Application in the Literature of Library and Information Science," *The Library Quarterly* 81, no. 3 (2011): 297–320.
12. Brenda Dervin, "Useful Theory for Librarianship: Communication, Not Information," *Drexel Library Quarterly* 13, no. 3 (1977): 16.
13. Douglas L. Zweizig and Brenda Dervin. "Public Library Use, Users, Uses," *Advances in Librarianship* 7 (January 1977): 252.

Collecting Direct Evidence

- Quantitative Data
- Qualitative Approaches
- Conclusion

In this chapter, we will talk about the concept of direct evidence and best practices for collecting it, including quantitative and qualitative methods. specific approaches to collecting data, such as interviews, focus groups, surveys, and analysis of existing data sets, including usage statistics. We will also discuss established approaches to collecting data, such as the LibQUAL+, MISO, and MINES surveys. We will also briefly cover best practices and important considerations for storing and analyzing data.

We've talked about the distinction between direct and indirect evidence. Any holistic approach to assessment should include both types of data. Often, input- and output-based assessment are based on direct evidence that is also statistical in nature. Direct evidence, you'll recall, does not rely on users self-reporting their behavior. We can identify two subtypes of direct evidence: quantitative and qualitative.

> We typically dislike the distinction of quantitative versus qualitative, preferring instead to acknowledge that individual assessment projects differ from each other and require different types of—and therefore, approaches to—data collection. The *quantitative* versus *qualitative* construct is extremely pervasive, however, so we will discuss it briefly. Please forgive the over-generalizations inherent in such an abbreviated definition.
>
> > Quantitative data is "numbers-based." It can often be collected automatically and in large numbers. Think of circulation data, or the data generated in COUNTER-compliant reports of e-resource usage.
> >
> > Qualitative (many researchers who focus on qualitative approaches prefer the term *interpretive*) data is "words-based." It includes descriptions of activities generated through observation, and feedback generated through interviews, focus groups, and comments collected through surveys. Because qualitative data usually takes a longer time to collect and analyze than quantitative data, it is typically not possible to generate qualitative data from as large a number of participants as with quantitative projects.

Quantitative Data

There are a number of statistical measures, or metrics, that libraries collect as a matter of course. Typical proxies for use of materials include circulation statistics and table counts, while online resource activity is tracked through sessions, searches, instances of access, and downloads. This type of data continues to play an important role in library assessment; 78 percent of our survey respondents indicated they must be familiar with tools for analyzing input data such as material circulation, database log-ons and downloads, and website access logs.

Circulation

Perhaps the most common approach to library assessment is the humble circulation statistic. Rachel can attest that when she worked as a public librarian in a large city system, branches lived and died by their circulation statistics. This philosophy was made famous (and pushed to its extreme) by Charles Robinson, longtime director of the Baltimore County Public Library (BCPL). Robinson's philosophy of library collections and services was "Give 'em What They Want," which was gauged by circulation statistics. Under Robinson's leadership, BCPL was known for a very heavy emphasis on popular materials and boasted extremely high circulation numbers. In an interview with Nancy Pearl upon the occasion of his retirement, Robinson said, "I don't see any reason for keeping a book if it doesn't move." When pressed on the question of purchasing "classics" that may not circulate as heavily, Robinson said, "We buy books that have little circulation. But we insist they have some circulation. There are libraries even now who will hold onto an important book that never circulates. We don't."[1]

It's fascinating to note that in many discussions of Robinson's approach, high circulation is discussed as if it is the only meaningful measure of an item's quality. In a profile of Robinson published by the *Baltimore Sun*, BCPL is described as a "success" that has "thrived" under this philosophy.[2] Even Nancy Pearl, model for the librarian action figure, uses high circulation as a proxy for quality, asking Robinson if circulation figures are "still a valid way of judging a library's usefulness."[3]

The problem with equating a high rate of circulation with general high quality is that it's unclear what high circulation really means beyond a large number of books being checked out. As Rachel's mentor and former University of Alabama dean of libraries Dr. Charles Osburn once said, "Who knows why a particular book has been checked out once it leaves the building? Maybe it's precisely the right size to prop up an uneven dining room table?" Each of us can personally attest to having eyes bigger than our brain and checking out hundreds, if not thousands, of books over the years that went unread. In fact, Rachel's spouse returned one to the public library where he works just this morning.

We will share one more anecdote about the questionable wisdom of using circulation as your sole measure of quality: Rachel began her career working in a large public library system on the East Coast of the United States. At the time, the system included a very large main library, three "regional" libraries, and around fifty branch libraries. Unsurprisingly, these branches were located in all types of neighborhoods, some of which were extremely prosperous and others served communities with very little in the way of public support or private industry.

After working in the system for about six months, Rachel was temporarily assigned to the branch located in the most prosperous area of the city. This branch was renowned for its stats, which showed the highest circulation and door counts in the system. Indeed, patrons came into the library all day—but they were largely there to pick up new and bestselling titles they had placed on hold or to browse and check out new titles, after which they typically turned directly around and exited the library building. Beyond circulation and the turnstile, the level of activity in the branch was no higher than in any other of the ten or so branches she'd visited to that point.

A few months later, Rachel was permanently assigned to a branch in a far less prosperous area of the city with circulation and door counts on the lower end of the spectrum. As she got to know the staff and interacted with people served by that branch, she came to understand the systemic failures contributing to suppressed circulation rates, including

- The branch's collection of materials was less reflective of its community's interests than was the collection in the more prosperous neighborhood.
- Patrons were skeptical of making requests of the library such as placing holds or requesting material purchases, in part because their experience with city institutions were less likely to have been positive.
- Patrons were afraid to accumulate large fines they might have difficulty paying.
- Patrons were wary of their children acquiring library cards because they were afraid their children would check out books and lose them or forget to return them (as kids do).
- Patrons themselves had lost a book at some point and were unable to pay the (often astronomical) fee required to clear their records and begin checking out books again.

That branch's program attendance and other levels of engagement were relatively robust, but the system's assessment program was not organized to consider measures of activity beyond door counts and circulation statistics, the latter of which were stunted by the library system's own inflexible and punitive policies. Despite the branch serving as an essential community center and safe place, the larger system did not recognize any other measures of quality.

In-House Use

Measures of in-house use are more common in academic libraries and those public libraries with robust reference collections. Basically, the term *in-house use* applies to recording uses of materials within the library's confines. Measurement is often done as a matter of when materials left on tables were reshelved, but libraries sometimes make the more organized, systematic effort of conducting a *table study*, which is just what it sounds like: patrons are asked not to reshelve materials they've pulled and consulted and instead leave them out in a designated area on a worktable or book truck. Before reshelving by staff, these materials are, at the very least, counted, although more in-depth analysis of the types of materials consulted in-house can be illuminating.

Another anecdote: one of Rachel's areas of responsibility when she worked as an academic librarian was serving as liaison to the Classics department. As her library prepared to move a significant segment of the collection to off-site storage, Rachel met with her faculty counterpart (whom we'll call Dr. Augustus) to explain the system for identifying materials to move off-site: items published thirty or more years earlier that had not circulated within the last ten years would be pulled automatically. "That won't work for us," Dr. Augustus said, as it was very common for Classics students and faculty to visit the library and consult several translations of the same work, or several different Greek or Latin dictionaries, without checking out any of them. "We just stand right at the shelf," he said. He also pointed out that a resource that had been published thirty or more years ago wasn't really a relevant consideration for works published thousands of years earlier. In this case, conducting a table study would have provided helpful data to identify which books marked for off-site storage were actually consulted by faculty in-house.

e-Resource Usage

As library resources and services have moved online, e-resource usage measurement has become an important metric. Typically, usage refers to the number of database log-ons or sessions and the number of article downloads, kind of like the networked version of door counts and circulation statistics. Publishers reference high rates of usage to justify the cost of e-resource subscriptions. Chrispin Davis, then CEO of Reed Elsevier, gave this testimony to the United Kingdom House of Commons in 2004 when asked about the circumstances influencing increases to Elsevier's subscription rates: "The biggest single factor is usage. That is what librarians look at more than anything else and it is what they [use to] determine whether they renew, do not renew and so on."[4]

This analogy falls apart, however, when we consider that counting the number of people who walk through a door or the number of times a book is checked out is pretty straightforward, but in the early days of tracking e-resource usage, things weren't so well-defined. Enter SUSHI, or the Standardized Usage Statistics Harvesting Initiative and Project COUNTER (Counting Online Usage of NeTworked Electronic Resources) Code of Practice, now on Release 5. Launched in 2003, the purpose of COUNTER is to provide guidelines that standardize recording, format, and presentation of e-resource usage statistics, while also defining terms relevant to e-resources usage measurement. Vendors who wish to be deemed COUNTER-compliant agree to adhere to these guidelines. COUNTER-compliant reports are formatted similarly and present data fields with common definitions, making it easy for librarians to make apples-to-apples comparisons of the extent to which their patrons are accessing products provided by different vendors.

Notice that we say *accessing*, not *using*. As is the case with relying on circulation statistics to understand the quality of a print collection, a journal having high usage statistics is not the same as a journal being influential, rigorous, or of high quality. It merely means that the articles it publishes have been accessed a large number of times. Don't get us wrong—a frequently accessed journal can also be of high quality, but those two things don't always co-occur. Nevertheless, log-ons and downloads remain the most accepted metrics for gauging the quality of journals and other resources in the electronic format.

Counting Bodies: Door Count and Program Attendance

Another popular output in library assessment is—at the risk of sounding grim—counting bodies. Most public and academic libraries maintain turnstiles at their entrances to track the number of individuals entering the building. It is common practice to note the number of attendees at special events and programs and the number of students participating in scheduled classes. Many libraries, especially academic libraries, also track the number of patrons in the building at any given time. This count is frequently taken hourly. Again, these measures tell us nothing about the benefits those individuals derived from entering the library, attending a class, or sitting at a worktable.

Other Numeric Measures of Resources and Services

REFERENCE STATISTICS

It is also typical for libraries that provide reference and information services to track the number of questions patrons ask and they answer in a given period. Although a library's system of recording might be limited to a series of hash marks, many libraries have adopted a more nuanced approach, asking reference and information services staff to categorize the questions they're asked by type, degree of difficulty, and the amount of time consumed in formulating an answer. Of course, the busier an information services department is, the more difficult it is to find the time to make those categorizations, and in-person statistics tracking typically relies on staff rather than an automated system like an ILS. There are now a number of tools on the market to facilitate reference statistic recording, but ultimately, they still rely on the judgment and effort of staff members tasked with recording.

Qualitative Approaches

There are also a number of approaches that take a more nuanced approach to direct evidence of library resource and service utilization. Some of these have direct analogs among the quantitative measures we've discussed, but most represent a very different attitude about and approach to assessment.

Citation Studies

Citation is the act of formally referring to another text or resource, typically while providing the bibliographic information necessary for readers to locate that text. Citation is an important proxy for the concept of scholarly influence, the assumption being that if an author bothers to cite a work, that work must stand out in some way. Michael Kurtz et al. called citation "the primary bibliometric indicator of the usefulness of an academic article."[5] Citation assessment is a prominent qualitative approach to assessing the quality or impact of a collection.

> Eugene Garfield pioneered citation tracking with his Science, Social Sciences, and Arts & Humanities Citation Indexes (SCI, SSCI, and AHCI), which were subsequently converted to electronic format and renamed Web of Science. Journal Citation Reports (JCR) are an outgrowth of the citation indexes. JCR aggregates citations to specific journals and calculates an *impact factor* (IF) for each title. IF is a popular metric for assessing the influence of a specific journal.

For our purposes, we can think of citation as a step or two beyond checking out a book or downloading an article. Although it is still treated as a quantitative measure (citations are typically reported as counts), there is an implied qualitative aspect to the act of citing.

> Qualitative citation studies are less common, but very helpful, tools for collection assessment. A qualitative citation study looks beyond the fact that a work was cited to investigate the reasons for it to be cited. After all, even if you cite a work to disclaim it, you still have to cite it—the Web of Science does not place an asterisk next to the articles that were cited repeatedly because those scholars cited less frequently found them objectionable!

Although an individual title with high circulation and usage statistics may also be cited frequently, that is not always the case. Anita Coleman and Cheryl Malone sampled several articles published in the *Journal of Education for Library and Information Science* (JELIS), and compared the number of times they had been cited (as recorded in the Web of Science) to COUNTER-reported usage statistics and found that although the articles did not have an exceptionally strong record of citation compared articles published in other LIS titles, download numbers were comparable to or higher than those for articles published in more frequently cited journals.[6]

Observation

Observation is the act of surveilling the activities of library users to ascertain what they are doing and what they are using. Observation in the library can provide insight into user behavior and movement patterns within its space, services, or hours of operation. It can be tremendously helpful for collecting data prior to reimagining or reconfiguring spaces within the library or to determine usage patterns in order to reconceive service locations or hours of operation.

Observation is primarily structured one of a few different ways. Examples include:

> *Type of user:* When do senior citizens visit the library? What services do they use? What spaces do they visit? What spaces do they not visit? Do they visit alone, or are they accompanied?
>
> *Service:* Who is visiting your DVD collection? At what times and days of the week? How are they accessing the collection (browsing or pulling known items)? Do they request assistance? How many visitors leave empty-handed?
>
> *Space:* Who is visiting your local history collection? How much time do patrons spend there, on average? What are the busy days and times? What resources do they typically consult during their visits? Do patrons interact with each other or with library staff?
>
> *Wayfinding:* Do visitors consult your signage? Are they able to find their way to the various service points, or do you observe significant redirection? How many patrons appear to leave the building without having found what they were looking for?

Ideally, an observation project will be conducted over a period of time, at different times of the day and on different days of the week. It helps to enlist several staff members to take turns, if possible. A written guide to the observation and, if appropriate, a template for recording observations, will also make data collection easier, especially for those staff not involved with designing the project. See appendix C for an example.

Usability and User Experience Testing

We can think of usability/user experience (UX) testing as a digital form of observation. The most typical approach to UX testing involves providing a group of participants with a series of tasks to accomplish using a library resource. Libraries most frequently apply UX testing to their websites. The great thing about UX testing is that it can be designed and conducted on a wide spectrum of sophistication. One option would be to design and conduct a usability test with a pilot-tested, vetted selection of tasks to be completed by a carefully selected group of participants who proportionately represent your library's stakeholder groups, conducted in a UX lab with eye-tracking software that records user movement for later analysis, or to just pull a few students together and sit next to them while they try to use your library's website to find a specific journal article or place a book on hold. Jakob Nielsen, usability pioneer and co-founder of the Nielsen Norman Group, says running a usability test with just five participants is usually sufficient to identify problems.[7]

Pre- and Post-Tests and Rubrics

Pre- and post-testing and rubrics are two tools that are especially helpful for assessing learning. Both can be employed to assess library instruction; pre- and post-tests are frequently applied to this purpose.

PRE- AND POST-TESTS

Pre- and post-testing is probably the most common approach to assessing the effectiveness of library instruction. Ideally, the attendees-to-be would complete a pre-test far enough in advance to allow the librarian conducting the instruction to adjust their approach depending on students' existing skills and comfort. Then, the post-test would be administered later, after enough time has passed to determine if students had retained the knowledge shared in the session. Ideally.

Much more frequently, however, the pre- and post-test must be administered at the beginning and end of a one-shot session. For that reason, it's essential that the tests be brief, and that they employ different questions to address the same skills.

Let's imagine we'd like to create pre- and post-tests to assess the effectiveness of a library instruction session for a group of Political Science 101 students tasked with writing a paper. The instructor would like for them to properly cite "a few" scholarly sources in-text and in an end reference list. Because the course is in the social sciences, we'll assume that the references should be in APA style.

Pre-test:

1. What is a "scholarly" source?
2. In the following reference, what does 43(1) refer to?
3. When do you need to include a citation in the text of your paper?

Post-test:

1. What does "peer-reviewed" mean?
2. In the following reference, which item should be italicized?
3. Which of the following does not require an in-text citation?

It can also be helpful to provide an open space for comments. Whenever possible, pre- and post-tests should be administered using survey software to simplify data analysis and storage.

RUBRICS

Rubrics, which are more complex and difficult to develop, are less common tools of assessment.

A rubric provides a framework for assessing performance at different levels, typically by assigning a numeric score. Rubrics can make the subjective process of evaluation a little more objective and facilitate scoring by multiple graders.

Developing rubrics can be tricky; they are just as vulnerable to a creator's bias as any other assessment tool. Consulting with others knowledgeable about the topic of the rubric can be tremendously helpful, even essential.

As you begin constructing a rubric, consider the following:

1. What are the overall goals of the target of your assessment?
2. What are the overall objectives?

3. What are the most essential elements?

4. What might be some intermediate steps between not addressing those goals and meeting them perfectly?

Let's imagine we'd like to create a rubric to assess the effectiveness of our Political Science 101 class (students writing a paper that includes "a few" scholarly sources, properly cited in-text and end references). We'll use our professional judgment to quantify a few as three.

FIGURE 7.1
Rubric planning

What are the overall goals of the target of your assessment?	Teach students to find sources for a political science paper. Teach students to cite them properly.
What are the overall objectives?	Identify three topically appropriate items. Identify three peer-reviewed items. Integrate support into paper. Include properly formatted in-text citations (APA) for three items. Include three properly formatted references (APA).
What are the most essential elements?	Three relevant Three scholarly In-text citations for three End references for three Less essential: three fully integrated as support
What might be some intermediate steps between not addressing those goals and meeting them perfectly?	One or two relevant One or two scholarly One or two properly formatted in-text Three improperly formatted in-text One or two properly formatted references Three improperly formatted references

Using the planning worksheet shown in figure 7.1, we can create the rubric we will use to assign numeric scores for each of the areas we've identified (figure 7.2).

FIGURE 7.2

Sample rubric for evaluating paper

	Item:	0	1	2	3	Score
The Student ...	Identifies at least three peer-reviewed sources directly related to the topic.	Does not identify any peer-reviewed sources, or none of the sources identified are relevant to the topic.	Identifies one peer-reviewed, topic-appropriate source, or one peer-reviewed irrelevant source and one topical source.	Identifies two peer-reviewed, topic-appropriate sources, or two peer-reviewed sources and one topical source.	Identifies at least three peer-reviewed sources directly related to the topic.	
	Integrates support from three or more scholarly sources.	Does not integrate any sources, or none of the sources integrated are scholarly.	Integrates support from only one scholarly source or mentions two sources without integrating content.	Integrates support from only two scholarly sources or mentions three or more sources without integrating content.	Integrates support from three or more scholarly sources.	
	Correctly cites at least three peer-reviewed, relevant sources in-text.	Does not provide any in-text citations.	Includes at least one in-text citation, or two incorrectly formatted in-text citations.	Includes two in-text citations, or three incorrectly formatted in-text citations	Correctly cites at least three peer-reviewed, relevant sources in-text.	
	Includes APA-formatted references for at least three peer-reviewed, relevant resources.	Does not provide a reference list.	Includes at least one correctly formatted reference, or two incorrectly formatted references.	Includes two correctly formatted references, or three incorrectly formatted references.	Includes APA-formatted references for at least three peer-reviewed, relevant resources.	
TOTAL:						

A rubric like the one shown in figure 7.2 would make it easier (as an individual or part of a group) to review the papers submitted by the Political Science 101 students after the instruction session to see how well your instruction helped meet the instructor's goals for the paper. It is important, however, to avoid falling into the trap of thinking numbers = objectivity. Rubrics, although they assign numeric values, are full of concepts for which we each have our own individual interpretations. What, for example, is your threshold for "correctly formatted" APA references? Must every period and space be in the correct place? How would you interpret "scholarly" for the purposes of this assignment? A rubric can create the illusion of objectivity when the truth is more complicated.

Experimentation and Quasi-Experimentation

Experimentation may sound like a strange method for library assessment, but hear us out: at its essence, an experiment is simply an approach to evaluating the impact an intervention (*independent variable*) has on a population (*dependent variable*). A true experimental approach controls for as many variables as possible, whereas a quasi-experimental approach is less circumscribed. Although some consider "pure" experimentation to be the only scientifically sound approach, it's often outside a librarian's purview to control every aspect of an experiment. For example, let's say you're interested in assessing the impact a series of library instruction sessions has on undergraduate students' ability to create properly formatted citations. You identify two sections (A and B) of the same Political Science 101 course (controlled variable 1) taught by the same instructor (variable 2) with roughly the same student makeup in terms of number of credits earned, for example, distribution of first-, second-, and third-year students (variable 3). You administer a pre-test to both groups of students, then begin providing weekly instruction (1, 2, 3) to section A (don't worry—section B will receive the same instruction after the study's conclusion). After concluding section A's sessions, you administer a follow-up test to the students in sections A and B to see if the average score for students in section A is higher than that of students in section B. Figure 7.3 shows this progression.

FIGURE 7.3

Experimental design assessing effectiveness of instruction

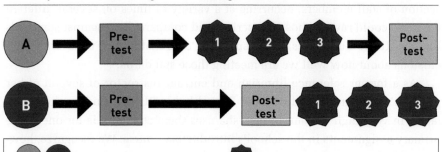

You have tried to control for as many possible confounding variables as possible (course, instructor, class composition), but is it really possible to control for everything? Not when human beings are involved! For example, what if section A meets first thing in the morning, while section B meets after lunch? Is it possible that students who choose to enroll in a class that meets at 8:00 a.m. are more motivated and diligent than those who elect to take the class at 1:00 p.m.? Or are the students in the afternoon class more likely to have enrolled in it because most honors courses are held in the mornings and this time slot would have conflicted with an earlier class. Do both sections meet in the same classroom, or does one face a particularly noisy street on campus, distracting the students?

Do either of these variables matter? Maybe? Possibly to some students, but not to others? It's difficult to say. Our best suggestion is to consider experimental design to be helpful, but don't overstate the conclusions generated by your experimental assessment.

Evaluation (Reference and Information Services)

We've discussed the standards-based approach to assessment, in which services or resources are compared to established criteria. We might consider the data generated by such an approach to be direct evidence, but with a grain of salt. Let's remember that standards are created by people, and however experienced and well-informed they may be, the humans who create standards have biases and blind spots, just like the rest of us. Nevertheless, if we were interested in gauging the quality of our reference chat service, we could collect transcripts from an assortment of sessions conducted by a cross-section of staff members, occurring at a variety of times on several different days. We could review those transcripts and compare them against standards like the RUSA Guidelines, thus generating data that allows us to draw conclusions about how well we are meeting those standards.

As a former reference librarian and current instructor of several of her program's reference-based courses, Rachel holds RUSA's guiding documentation in very high esteem. In fact, she uses them as the basis for one of the primary assignments in the school's introductory course. We recognize, however, that these documents were created by humans and reflect the collective experience of the members of the committee members who created them.

Conclusion

While collecting direct evidence is an essential part of any assessment project, it's important not to lose sight of the importance of listening to your users' lived experiences, which we might describe as *indirect evidence*. In our next chapter, we will discuss methods for collecting this important type of data.

NOTES

1. Nancy Pearl, "Gave 'em What They Wanted: LJ Interview with Charlie Robinson and Jean Barry Molz of the Baltimore County Public Library," *Library Journal* 121, no. 14 (1996): 136–38, https://www.baltimoresun.com/news/bs-xpm-1990-11-11-1990315186-story.html.
2. Pat van den Beemt, "Reading the Public: Charles Robinson Writes the Book on Luring People to the Library," *The Baltimore Sun*, November 11, 1990, https://www.baltimoresun.com/news/bs-xpm-1990-11-11-1990315186-story.html.
3. Pearl, "Gave 'em What They Wanted," 138.
4. Philip M. Davis and Jason S. Price, "e-Journal Interface Can Influence Usage Statistics: Implications for Libraries, Publishers, and Project COUNTER," *Journal of the American Society for Information Science and Technology* 57, no. 9 (2006).
5. Michael J. Kurtz, Guenther Eichhorn, Alberto Accomazzi, Carolyn Grant, Markus Demleitner, Edwin Henneken, and Stephen S. Murray, "The Effect of Use and Access on Citations," *Special Issue on Informatics: Information Processing and Management* 41, no. 6 (2005): 1396.

6. Anita Sundaram Coleman and Cheryl Knott Malone, "From the Editors: Scholarly Communication and the Matter of Use," *Journal of Education for Library and Information Science* 47, no. 1 (2006): 1–3.

7. Jakob Nielsen, "Usability 101: Introduction to Usability," Nielsen Norman Group, 2012, https://www.nngroup.com/articles/usability-101-introduction -to-usability/.

8

Collecting Indirect Evidence

- Surveys
- Standardized Surveys
- Interviews and Focus Groups
- Other Approaches: Case Studies and Mixed Methods
- Existing Data Sets
- Conclusion

In contrast to direct evidence of library user activity, which is gathered by employing systems and tools to record it, indirect evidence is a reported account of activity from the users themselves. It is conceptually more qualitative in nature, often asking respondents to assess and describe their opinions, feelings, or memories.

Surveys

The humble survey is one of the most common methods for collecting indirect evidence and is tremendously popular for gathering input from library users (and non-users). Designing and

123

distributing surveys are important assessment skills—79 percent of our survey respondents indicated these skills as job requirements.

We can think of surveys as kind of a hybrid of quantitative and qualitative because although they often ask respondents to make qualitative judgments ("how satisfied are you with your library's programming?"), feedback is often supplied ("please rate from 1–5, with 5 being the best") using numbers and analyzed (satisfaction of parents with children was higher than satisfaction of patrons without children by one standard deviation) using statistical formulas. Constructing effective surveys, distributing them appropriately, and analyzing the data they retrieve are all complex topics outside the scope of this text and for which there are a number of excellent guides. We would like to provide an overview of approaches, however, and a few suggestions we've gained from (sometimes painful) experience.

First, surveys can be great! They allow you to collect data effectively in a number of different circumstances:

- You need to gather data quickly and efficiently (after careful development of the survey, of course).
- You need data from a large number of people.
- You need data from geographically distributed people.
- You need to ask questions that might be sensitive or embarrassing to answer.
- You have limited resources for providing incentives for respondents.

What kinds of questions are surveys not appropriate for?

- Complex questions.
- Questions that might require follow-up or clarification.
- Questions for which the respondents may not really know the correct answer.

For these, the focus group or one-on-one interview might present a better option.

Creating Your Survey

Writing an effective survey is trickier than you might think! There are a number of terrific guides to creating surveys for library assessment, so we won't go into an extreme amount of detail here, but we do have some suggestions for proceeding in a way that will maximize your chances for success.

Presumably, you have already determined the area of interest for assessment and identified your respondent group(s) before settling on a survey as your method of choice. We would caution against trying to capture feedback from too many different types of users with a single survey, as each group will have different interests and needs. It can be difficult to capture the breadth of your stakeholders' interests with one instrument, and too much internal division and question segmenting within a survey instrument can make analysis extremely complicated.

TYPES OF QUESTIONS

There are a number of different types of questions to consider including in your survey; we will discuss the suitability of some of the most popular here, but it is by no means an exhaustive list.

Multiple Choice

Multiple-choice questions provide the answers for respondents, who are prompted to select a single option (figure 8.1).

FIGURE 8.1
Multiple-choice question, single answer

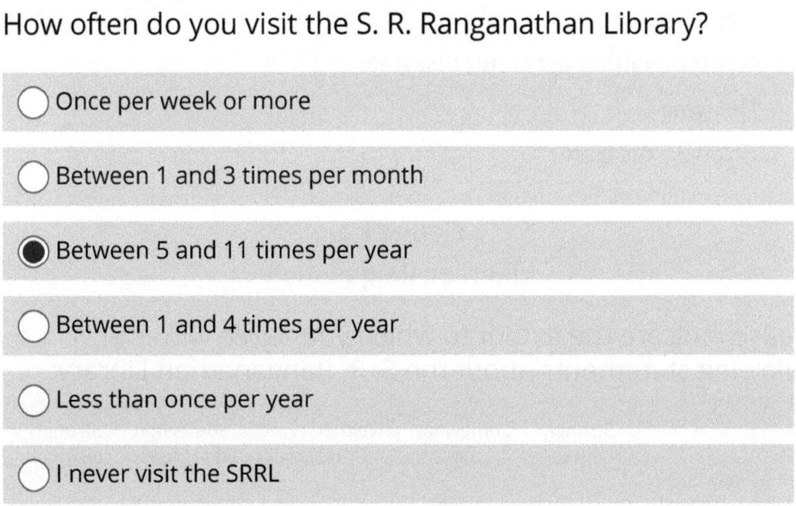

How often do you visit the S. R. Ranganathan Library?

- Once per week or more
- Between 1 and 3 times per month
- ● Between 5 and 11 times per year
- Between 1 and 4 times per year
- Less than once per year
- I never visit the SRRL

Some multiple-choice questions ask respondents to select all answers that apply, as shown in figure 8.2.

FIGURE 8.2
Multiple-choice question, multiple answer

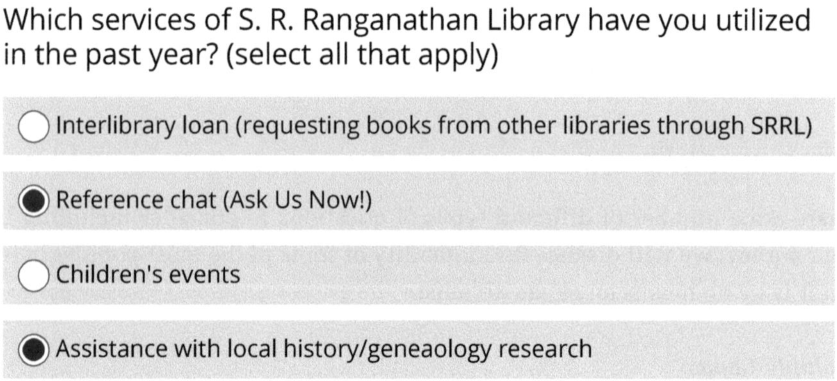

Which services of S. R. Ranganathan Library have you utilized in the past year? (select all that apply)

⭕ Interlibrary loan (requesting books from other libraries through SRRL)

🔘 Reference chat (Ask Us Now!)

⭕ Children's events

🔘 Assistance with local history/geneaology research

Likert Scale Questions

Likert scale questions ask respondents to select the degree to which they agree with statements. The classic model includes five choices (figure 8.3):

1. Strongly agree
2. Agree
3. Neutral/Neither agree nor disagree
4. Disagree
5. Strongly disagree

FIGURE 8.3
Likert scale question

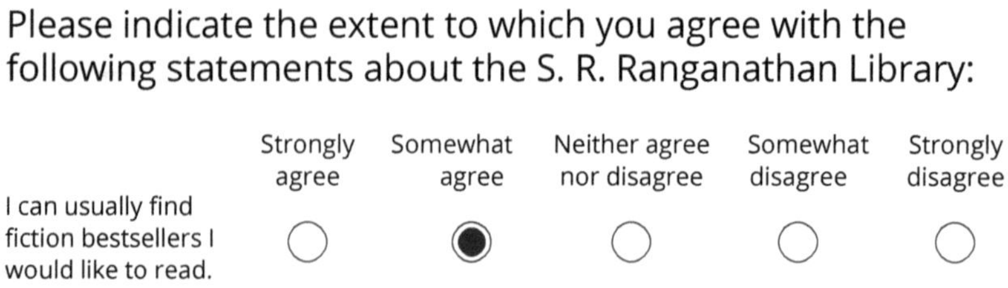

Please indicate the extent to which you agree with the following statements about the S. R. Ranganathan Library:

	Strongly agree	Somewhat agree	Neither agree nor disagree	Somewhat disagree	Strongly disagree
I can usually find fiction bestsellers I would like to read.	⭕	🔘	⭕	⭕	⭕

Each choice in figure 8.3 is assigned a numeric score from 1–5; responses are aggregated and calculated to develop an average score for each item.

The "neither agree nor disagree" option can be confusing for respondents; therefore, depending on the topic, it makes sense to include a "not applicable" option in addition to the numerical rating scale (figure 8.4). For example, what if the patron doesn't actually read fiction bestsellers and therefore doesn't look for them at the S. R. Ranganathan Library?

FIGURE 8.4
Likert scale question with "not applicable" option

Please indicate the extent to which you agree with the following statements about the S. R. Ranganathan Library:

	Strongly agree	Somewhat agree	Neither agree nor disagree	Somewhat disagree	Strongly disagree	Not applicable/ no answer
I can usually find fiction bestsellers I would like to read.	○	◉	○	○	○	○

If you add a "not applicable" option to some or all of your survey's numerically ranked questions, you will need to structure your analysis to exclude those scores. Most online survey platforms will allow you to exclude that option from analysis.

Although the ranked choices "strongly agree" to "strongly disagree" are the classic Likert scale options, it's possible to employ this model with different assessments (figure 8.5).

FIGURE 8.5
Likert scale question with alternative options

Please answer the following questions about your experience at the S. R. Ranganathan Library:

	Always	Sometimes	Half the time	Rarely	Never	Not applicable
How often does the library own the fiction bestsellers you would like to read.	○	◉	○	○	○	○

It's customary to aggregate a number of items in a single Likert-style matrix (figure 8.6). This is done less for philosophical reasons than as a space-saving measure.

FIGURE 8.6

Matrix of Likert scale items

Please indicate the extent to which you agree with the following statements about the S. R. Ranganathan Library:

	Strongly agree	Somewhat agree	Neither agree nor disagree	Somewhat disagree	Strongly disagree	Not applicable/ no answer
I can usually find fiction bestsellers I would like to read.	○	●	○	○	○	○
The SRRL hosts events that are of interest to me.	●	○	○	○	○	○
The SRRL serves the needs of every member of my family well.	●	○	○	○	○	○
The SRRL's weekend hours are sufficient for my needs.	○	●	○	○	○	○

A danger with questions styled in this manner is that respondents may stop reading the items and just answer options by buzzing through the matrix and selecting the same answer (e.g., "agree") for each item. A strategy for short-circuiting this phenomenon is to include a rephrased version of a question or item within the same survey (figure 8.7).

FIGURE 8.7

Likert scale matrix with two versions of single item

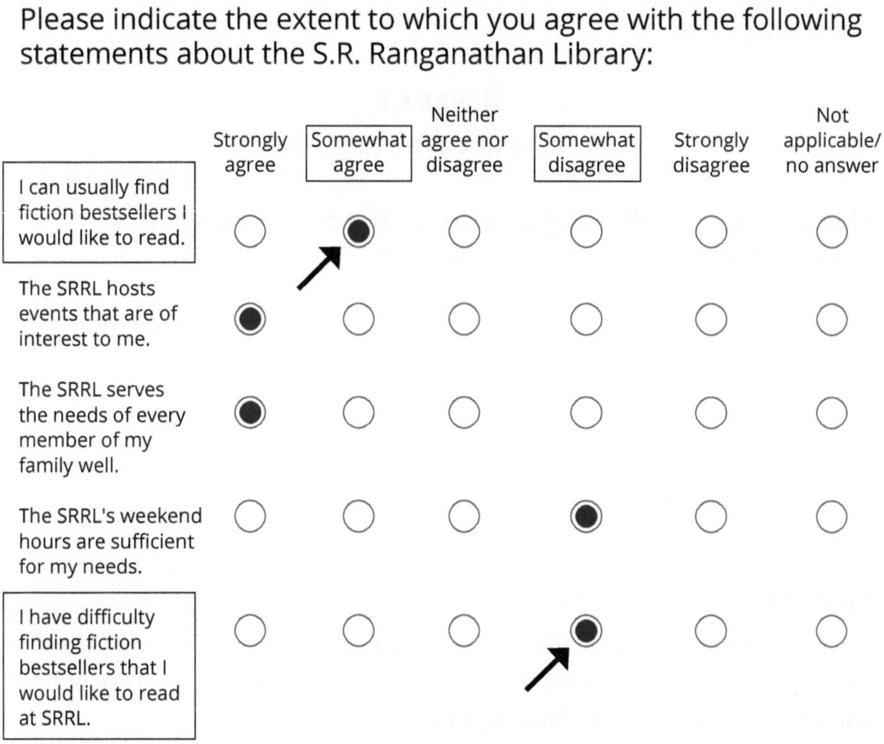

Please indicate the extent to which you agree with the following statements about the S.R. Ranganathan Library:

The first and final items in this section use opposing approaches that seek the same information (granted, this example is a little heavy-handed). If the respondent is paying attention to the items and the scale and answering thoughtfully, we would expect them to provide opposite answers for the first and final items in the matrix—for example, "strongly agree" and "strongly disagree." This type of agreement is called internal consistency and is a type of reliability.

This question also highlights a particular difficulty presented by surveys. Our respondent has indicated they "somewhat disagree" that "The SRRL's weekend hours are sufficient for my needs." This is helpful information, especially if a large number of respondents provide the same feedback. How, though, is it actionable? By opening earlier on Saturday or Sunday? Staying open later one or both days? Opening earlier and later? Without clarification, the information collected with this item is meaningless.

Ranking

Ranking questions present respondents with a list of like items and ask that they arrange them in order numerically, often in terms of importance or desirability (figure 8.8).

FIGURE 8.8
Ranking question (text box)

Please rank the following services of the S. R. Ranganathan Library in order of importance to you:

2	Interlibrary loan (requesting books from other libraries through SRRL)
1	Reference chat (Ask Us Now!)
3	Children's events
4	Assistance with local history/geneaology research

Open Text

Open text questions provide a space for respondents to write their own answers rather than choosing from preselected options as in the case of most other types of survey questions (figure 8.9).

FIGURE 8.9
Open-ended text entry question

What services would you like the S. R. Ranganathan Library to begin providing that it does not currently offer?

It would be great if you stocked DVDs at the branches as well as the main library.

Some questions include an open text box ("other: please describe") as one of the options for answering a question (figure 8.10).

FIGURE 8.10
Multiple choice with "other"

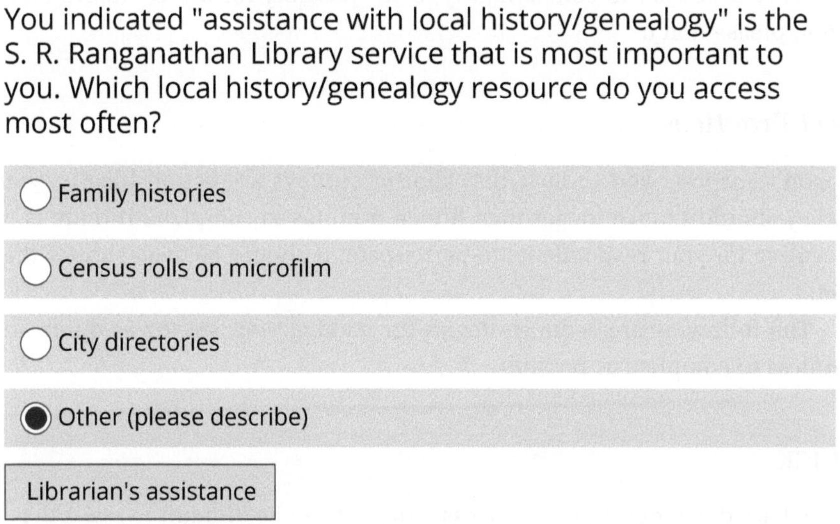

You indicated "assistance with local history/genealogy" is the S. R. Ranganathan Library service that is most important to you. Which local history/genealogy resource do you access most often?

○ Family histories

○ Census rolls on microfilm

○ City directories

◉ Other (please describe)

Librarian's assistance

There are a couple of reasons why it's advisable to limit the number of open text questions in your survey. First, the more open text questions a survey includes, the less likely respondents are to complete it. Thinking of an answer and then typing or writing it out is more time-consuming than checking a box or otherwise choosing a provide answer. Second, relying too heavily on open text questions renders moot one of the primary reasons for administering a survey: increased ease of aggregating answers and managing data. It is far more difficult to parse and categorize a written answer than to review a selected response.

If you can't figure out how to ask your survey questions in such a way that it's possible to provide answer options for your respondents, the topics might be too complex for a survey and you should consider conducting your assessment project as interviews or focus groups.

Demographic Questions

Demographic questions about the respondent's age, race, gender, marital status, and similar should be situated at the end of the survey and should be minimal in number. Many people include an extensive battery of demographic questions in their surveys as a matter of course, but please consider if it is truly necessary to collect that type of—possibly intrusive—information. If not, please don't.

Best Practices

It won't surprise you to hear that shorter surveys are better. Ideally, your survey shouldn't take longer than fifteen minutes to complete; if there is no incentive for your respondents to participate, it should be even shorter than that.

The following are some strategies for making your survey as quick and painless to complete as possible.

QUICK

- Pare down questions to the essentials. It can be difficult to resist the urge to ask every question you've ever had. After all, conducting a survey can be a tremendous undertaking, certainly not one you'd like to make super-often. It is better, however, to reduce the number of questions and survey once every year than to administer one extremely long survey every three years.
- Split your survey. If you can't bear to part with any of your questions and have a large enough pool of potential respondents, divide your respondent pool into two and split the survey questions into two surveys. Distribute Survey 1 to Group A and Survey 2 to Group B.
- Minimize open-ended questions. Although they allow respondents to provide answers written in their own words, they also take more time to complete. Analysis is more difficult, too.

PAINLESS

- Make questions easy to understand. Avoid overly sophisticated vocabulary and complex constructions. Read the questions aloud before you finalize them. Do they make sense?

- Make the survey itself easy to read and understand. In addition to writing the questions so they are easily understood, you need to make sure the way they are structured makes sense as well. Are the instructions comprehensible? Do the answer options fit? Most of us understand the conventions of multiple-choice and true/false questions, but survey tools have become more sophisticated in recent years and allow for much more creativity. If you are using more sophisticated question capabilities like heat maps (figure 8.11) and word associations (figure 8.12) that your respondents may not have seen on other surveys, clear instructions are key.

FIGURE 8.11

Heat map question, created in Qualtrics

Please select the area of the library where you are most likely to sit:

FIGURE 8.12

Word association/highlight question, created in Qualtrics

Please read the words listed below and identify which you associate with the S. R. Ranganathan Library, which you do not associate with the SRRL, and which you neither associate nor do not associate with the SRRL:

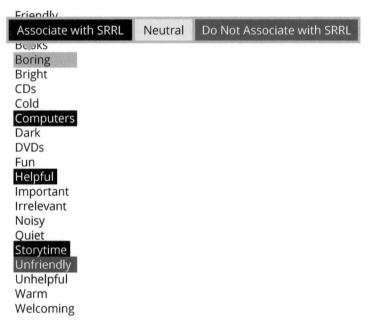

Avoid jargon. Use "real world" language. Several years ago, John Kupersmith launched "Library Terms That Users Understand," a project in which he aggregated and analyzed findings from fifty-one library usability studies. Among his findings was the revelation that library terminology is misinterpreted or just not understood by many patrons, including some terms that we might consider mainstream, like *library catalog, periodical,* and *database.*[1] Ask a non-library friend or relative to read your survey and flag any terms that might be unfamiliar.

Avoid absolutes. Respondents can find them difficult to answer! We know that if we are confronted by a question that asks about something like when was the last time we purchased a new mattress, we get a little anxious about our ability to recall specific feelings and actions. Unless it's extremely important that answers be ultra-specific, include phrases like "to your best recollection."

QUICK AND PAINLESS

Do you really need to ask that?

Before finalizing your survey, go through each question and ask yourself the following:

Do I really need the information this question will elicit?

Ask yourself this question twice if the question relates to anything your respondent might find particularly personal, including race or ethnicity, gender, marital status, or income. We find including these sorts of demographic questions is often done by rote. Be sure they're important. If they are, ask the following question.

Can I find this information elsewhere, or do I already have it?

For example, if you are surveying residents of the town in which your library is located, is it necessary to ask where they live? This brings us to the question of whether the most suitable survey format is print or online.

Is the most suitable survey format print or online?

There are benefits to both, and depending on your respondent group, one or the other approach might be of greater benefit (another reason to avoid surveying multiple user types simultaneously).

Web-Based Surveys

There are several online survey platforms with varying levels of sophistication and ease of use. Some platforms offer terrific flexibility for constructing the overall instrument; for example, some may include a large number of question templates and options like document upload. Others make it easy to download and analyze the data you collect, and perhaps even create graphics within the survey software, eliminating the need to import the data into a different program to create charts and graphs. If you are starting from scratch and need to select a platform, we encourage you to investigate several to determine which will best suit your needs.

Your parent institution might maintain paid access to one or more survey programs. If the platforms available don't provide features that you need and you plan to conduct a lot of surveys, it may be possible to secure an additional license on a much smaller scale. It's something to consider. It's also worth noting that the survey platforms' functionality also makes them a great option for hosting web-based forms, increasing their utility in the organization.

One of the most useful features of web-based surveys is their support for adjusting visibility of segments of the survey depending on a respondent's answer to a particular question. This feature is typically called *display logic* or *skip logic*. For example, your survey might ask respondents to indicate if they regularly visit your system's main library. You might set the logic to display questions about resources or services that are *only available* at the main branch if respondents answer in the affirmative. Skip logic jumps the respondent ahead in the survey depending on their response.

Skip and display logic makes it possible to branch your questions depending on a respondent's answer to a question about, say, their status or role, such as "what is your primary activity at the library?" but that approach can make the instrument unwieldy very quickly. The cleaner option is to create and distribute separate surveys for different groups.

Paper Surveys

You may be surprised that we're even mentioning the possibility of distributing paper surveys. After all, who can remember the last time they were asked to complete one? Indeed, there lies the primary strength of paper surveys: perhaps counterintuitively, they often elicit a better response rate than web-based surveys do. Take, for example, the ITHAKA S+R Faculty Survey, distributed in the United States every three years since 2000. The last print iteration of the survey was distributed by mail to a sample of 35,000 faculty members in 2009; 3,025 completed surveys were returned, for a response rate of 8.6 percent.[2] In 2012, the survey was distributed electronically for the first time; 5,261 responses were returned—an increase of 74 percent! Sounds great, until you consider that the 2012 sample was 160,008—which means the response rate of 3.3 percent.[3] In 2015 and 2018, the response rate improved, but 2018's (7.2 percent) was still not equal to the response rate for the last print survey in 2009.[4]

This is counterintuitive (to us, at least)! We would expect electronically distributed surveys to have a much higher rate of response than printed surveys. After all, you have to keep track of the envelope, put the completed survey inside, seal it, put it in a mailbox—and many of us don't mail a lot of stuff anymore. Could that be why response rates for printed surveys tend to be better? The novelty? Depending on your target population, mode of distribution may have a more or less significant impact; studies across populations have shown that younger respondents tend to prefer online surveys more than do older respondents.[5] So, if you're surveying undergraduate students, online should be fine. If you're getting feedback from patrons who participate in those programs more likely to be populated by older patrons, paper is probably a better bet.

At any rate, web-based surveys are superior to printed surveys in every way except the possibility that response rate might not be as strong. They are easier to customize, edit on the fly, distribute, collect, analyze, and use as a basis for reports. Depending on the cost of subscribing to the platform you use, online surveys are also probably significantly less expensive—paper-based surveys will require you to print all of those pages, and you should expect to cover the postage required to send the surveys out *and* return them.

Distributing Your Survey and Collecting Data

There are two important, interconnected considerations in distributing a survey and collecting responses: the *sample* and *response rates*. The sample is the group who receives the survey. Depending on the size of the group you're hoping to survey, you may or may not need a sample. For example, if you would like to survey your city's population about their satisfaction with the library and you live in a city of 500,000 residents, you will want to use a sample rather than trying to administer a survey of such a large number of people. On the other hand, if your population of interest is the seventy-five doctoral students in your university's college of business, a sample is probably not necessary.

If, however, you do need to create a sample, you first must establish your sampling frame, or the characteristics of the overall population being surveyed that you want to maintain in your sample. For example, if you want to survey your city's residents about their satisfaction with the library, you'll want to be sure your sample reflects the city's overall demographics so that your findings will be generalizable to the overall population.

In both cases, the response rate is relevant. A survey's response rate is essentially the percentage of the people who received the survey and completed it. The higher your response rate, the lower your *margin of error,* or the greater the likelihood your survey responses represent the community you sampled. If your survey was distributed to a representative sample, you will need to calculate a more finely grained response rate depending on the demographics of the people in the returned surveys.

For example, let's say you are interested in assessing which age groups are most interested in a variety of services your library offers. Your city demographics break down like figure 8.13. (We are using Urbana, Illinois, as the source for these numbers.)

FIGURE 8.13

Urbana, Illinois: population by age group

Age	Number (30,972 over 18)
18–24 (42.5%)	13,175
25–44 (31.0%)	9,608
45–64 (15.5%)	4,804
65+ (10.9%)	3,385

We want to distribute the survey to 10 percent of the adults in town, maintaining the age demographic breakdown within our sample. A representative sample of adults by age group would resemble figure 8.14.

FIGURE 8.14

Urbana, Illinois: 10 percent sample, representative by age group

Age	Number (3,097)
18–24 (42.5%)	1,317
25–44 (31.0%)	961
45–64 (15.5%)	480
65+ (10.9%)	339

RESPONSE RATE

Opinions vary on the minimum response rate that is acceptable. Suffice to say, higher is better! In our opinion, it really depends on your purposes for conducting a survey and what conclusions you hope to be able to draw from it. Survey findings are more generalizable when the response rate is higher and the sample is larger. On the other hand, if your survey was intended to be more of a tool for gathering input, the representativeness of your sample and responses is less important.

If it's important that you track the representativeness of your sample in your responses, you'll need to put measures in place to track it whether it's in print or online. For example, if your survey is distributed in print, you can include a code on the survey that corresponds to the individual recipient's characteristics such as age group or zip code of residence. Tracking online survey responses can be trickier, especially if you're relying on a broad distribution approach such as an e-mail list. If your survey is being sent to specific participants, many online survey platforms allow you to create a unique URL for each survey recipient, allowing you to track individual responses.

For the sake of discussion, figure 8.15 shows a 25 percent response rate.

FIGURE 8.15

Urbana, Illinois, survey: 25 percent response rate, representative by age group

Age	Sample (3,097)	25% Response Rate
18–24 (42.5%)	1,317	329
25–44 (31.0%)	961	240
45–64 (15.5%)	480	120
65+ (10.9%)	339	85

Just like every other type of human-involved assessment, securing responses is the most challenging part of conducting a survey. Here are some tips for encouraging responses:

- Incentives can be helpful. Interestingly, studies have shown that offering a chance to win a more significant incentive ("Five of the people who complete this survey will win a $25 Amazon gift card!") is more effective for increasing responses than offering a small incentive ("You will receive a $1 Amazon credit") to each respondent![6]
- Personalized, rather than generic, invitations can increase response rate, especially if the invitation makes what is referred to as an "egotistic appeal," such as "your viewpoint is essential to the success of this survey."[7]
- Reminders can increase response rate, and the format of both invitations and reminders can have an impact on responses. A recent experimental study tested response rates for a variety of approaches to distributing invitations and reminders. Each model included an invitation with log-on information, followed by a reminder for those who hadn't completed the survey. Of the four models tested (paper invitation/paper reminder, e-mail invitation/e-mail reminder, e-mail/paper, paper/e-mail), the paper/paper approach had the highest response rate, closely followed by e-mail/paper.[8]

Standardized Surveys

There are a number of proprietary surveys on the market for assessing library resources and services. These have a number of benefits:

- They do not require your library to create its own survey.
- They have been vetted.
- They are easier to administer.
- They allow for comparison with other institutions.
- They are often longitudinal, allowing trends to be tracked over time.

They also have some drawbacks:
- They are (typically) minimally customizable.
- The framework and methods used to create and test the instrument are out of your control.

- You may have less control over administering the survey.
- Your institution's data is often shared with other institutions.
- Creators may be reluctant to adjust the questions or format, making the survey slow to adapt to changes in library resources and services.
- And a big one—cost.

Participating in standardized, large-scale surveys can be very expensive. Costs for the three discussed here are as follows for 2020–21:

- LibQUAL+: $3,200 up, depending on services and products selected (https://www.libqual.org/about/about_lq/fee_schedule).
- MISO: $2,200 to 3,400, depending on survey structure, audiences, and distribution (https://www.misosurvey.org/choosing/pricing-and-registration).
- MINES: $7,000 to 15,000, depending on survey length and deliverables (www.minesforlibraries.org/about/conducted).

LibQUAL+

The most well-known of the standardized surveys is LibQUAL+, a product launched in 2000 by the Association for Research Libraries (ARL). Based on the SERVQUAL+ protocol for assessing impressions of customer service, LibQUAL+ covers library facilities, services, and resources using twenty-two items and a comments box.

LibQUAL+ takes the unique approach of measuring the gap between patrons' expectations of a service, resource, or facility, and their perception of the reality. Each of the twenty-two items asks the respondent to gauge, on a scale of 1–9, the minimum acceptable level of provision, the desired level, and the actual level. For example, for an item like "When it comes to readiness to respond to users' questions," you might determine that your minimum service level is 6, your desired service level is 9, and the perceived service performance is 7.

Ideally, the perceived level of service should be equal to or greater than the desired level of service. An item with a perceived level of service lower than the minimum acceptable level of service indicates improvement is needed, or at least that patrons believe improvement is needed.

It is important to note that LibQUAL+ is not without critics. For one thing, the instrument is based on SERVQUAL+, a tool created to measure

FIGURE 8.16
LibQUAL+ item visualization

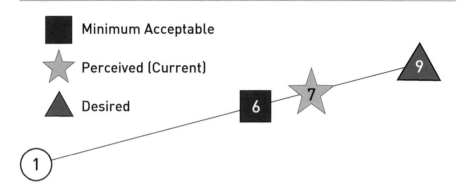

satisfaction with customer service. William Edgar makes the point that adopting an approach from the private sector ignores important aspects of the library's mission, including education, preservation, and knowledge organization.[9] Although a customer's frustration with how a department store organizes its housewares may be reason enough for the store to change its layout, should a library begin shelving books alphabetically because patrons are dissatisfied with the classification system? Anyone who's worked at a library's public services desk knows that our profession's commitment to patron privacy can be frustrating for a parent who would like to know which books their child has checked out in order to conduct an expedition for lost items. Is parent dissatisfaction reason enough to abandon those principles?

MISO

In 2004, Measuring Information Service Outcomes (MISO) was created for Bryn Mawr College after staff were unable to identify a survey that would capture the breadth of services provided to their faculty, staff, and students. MISO markets its survey as being more customizable than other (read: LibQUAL+) standardized surveys; institutions can include or omit any of the questions the survey team makes available. To abbreviate the survey, it is also possible to divide questions into two shorter surveys, which will then be distributed to two different groups of respondents.

MINES for Libraries

Another ARL product, MINES for Libraries, is the abbreviated name for the Measuring the Impact of Networked Electronic Services survey program. MINES takes e-resources assessment beyond recording usage statistics to asking randomly selected patrons logging on to a library-provided electronic resource or OPAC three to five questions in a pop-up box. Typically, the MINES survey asks respondents to identify their status and affiliation, the location from which they are accessing the e-resource in question, their broad purpose for selecting the e-resource, and the more specific reason for accessing it. Some institutions choose to include an open text box in the pop-up.

Interviews and Focus Groups

Although a smaller percentage (62 percent) of our survey respondents indicated designing and conducting focus groups and interviews were a required skill, both are powerful tools for generating assessment data. These two approaches involve asking respondents (who are typically preidentified) questions in real time. We're going to discuss interviews and focus groups together because (a) there are some similarities between the two methods, and (b) we want to very clearly describe the differences between the two and the type of circumstances for which each is appropriate.

> A note about terminology in this section: we will refer to interview and focus group methods collectively as *real-time dialogue.* Interview by telephone has always been relatively common, but online meeting platforms have now made it feasible to conduct many focus groups at a distance. *Real-time* is meant to include face-to-face and remote approaches to these two techniques.

Real-time dialogue methods are helpful for eliciting answers to questions that:

- are complex
- may require follow-up
- may not be understood by the respondent

Both approaches are time- and effort-intensive when executed properly, making them inappropriate for collecting data from large numbers of respondents or in a short period of time. In the appropriate circumstances, however, interviews and focus groups can provide wonderfully rich, nuanced, deep data in a way that other methods really can't touch.

Let's walk through the steps of conducting an assessment project that uses one of the real-time dialogue approaches:

Interviews and Focus Groups: Conceptualizing and Planning

Preparation is the watchword in any type of assessment; real-time dialogue approaches are no different. After you've identified the questions you'd like to answer and determined that a real-time dialogue method is most appropriate, it's time to choose which.

Each approach has distinct benefits and drawbacks: although both offer the opportunity to follow up on respondents' statements and gain a deeper understanding of their needs, feelings, and behavior, one-on-one interviews are more personal in nature, and focus groups leverage the group dynamic to enhance data generation.

One-on-one interviews are more appropriate when

- you need to collect data about individuals' experiences or opinions, and you prefer that they not be influenced by others
- your questions might be sensitive
- you are not concerned with identifying the needs, priorities, and feelings of a specific, or multiple specific, user types. In other words, you don't expect any of your respondents' demographic or other characteristics to have an effect on their answers or have an impact on your analysis *but* you think power differentials between different types of respondents might have a chilling effect if they participate together
- you are interested in how very specific user characteristics, needs, and behaviors relate to their behavior and opinions

A focus group makes more sense if

- you have a focus: on a particular type of user, type of behavior, or type of resource or service
- your topic and questions are not overly personal in nature

- you believe the collective atmosphere will enhance discussion
- you are not concerned with identifying the needs, priorities, and feelings of a specific, or multiple specific, user types *and* believe potential power differentials among respondents (e.g., professors and students) will not have a chilling effect

There's nothing wrong with practical considerations as long as they don't short-circuit your ability to generate and collect meaningful data. While both approaches consume significant resources, focus groups make it possible to speak with a larger number of respondents in a shorter amount of time than in one-on-one interviews. That being said, it would be a mistake to think hosting three focus groups of seven people is an easy way to collect data from twenty-one people; data collected in a focus group is different from data collected from an individual. If your subject, participants, or protocol aren't appropriate for a focus group format, you could end up without usable data.

After choosing your approach, you'll need to start thinking about identifying participants and how you will entice them to participate. Real-time dialogue approaches ask more of your participants than surveys do, and your ability to collect feedback depends on at least one person (other than you) showing up when and where they say they will. Although participant "leakage" is a reality, there are a couple of strategies we can offer to help secure participation.

> *Cast a wide net:* Undoubtedly, this is the most challenging aspect of any assessment project, but especially interviews and focus groups. This is a great time to seek help from your network within and outside the library!
>
> In the case of an academic library, that includes
>
> - faculty in academic departments
> - administrators, especially those in audience-facing roles (e.g., office of dean of students)
> - library student workers
> - library staff in public-facing roles.
>
> For public libraries, seek assistance from
>
> - Friends and advisory groups
> - volunteers

- Board of Trustees or equivalent
- community partners, (e.g., Boys and Girls Clubs)
- library staff in public-facing roles

Offer incentives: Because you're asking people to share their time and experience with you, we believe offering them some kind of compensation is only fair. Money is great, if you have it—over the years, we have offered both gift cards and cold hard cash. You're probably doing math in your head right now (24 x $20 = $480, ouch) and cringing, but we're not advocating you open your own wallet. Explore potential sources of funding such as a research incentive fund, a budget line for marketing, a grant from your institution or municipality—be creative. Also, it's important to be aware that many institutions have limits and prohibitions on gifts and cash awards—be sure you can actually deliver what you're planning to promise. Keep in mind that although one type of gift (e.g., cash) might be verboten, another (gift cards) might be acceptable.

Whether or not you can offer an incentive of cash or goods, refreshments are always welcome—and we also think it's just polite.

Make the location convenient: Take the conversation to them. Offer to meet them at their office, home, or favorite coffee shop, or reserve a conveniently located facility that has ample parking or convenient access to public transportation. If you don't think the data will suffer much by doing so, conduct the interview or focus group using a web-conferencing platform. This has the added benefit of allowing easy recording of the dialogue.

We will note here that this also serves the purpose of satisfying another area of best practice for assessment-related real-time dialogues: avoiding the library building. There is a school of thought that participants are more likely to be forthcoming with honest, negative feedback if the focus group or interview is not held in the location being assessed. Maybe it's kind of like feeling uncomfortable criticizing someone in their own home?

Make the time work for your respondents: You may be at your best first thing in the morning but, depending on your respondents, scheduling interviews at 9:00 a.m. may result in a whole lot of unanswered texts and phone calls. Similarly, late afternoon might work for you, but your respondents may need to be home to meet their children's school bus when it arrives. This may require a little investigation on your part, but if you work around your respondents' commitments and the preferences they are likely to have concerning time of day and day of the week, you'll be glad you did.

Be transparent: Unless you have a good reason for being vague or secretive about the topic of your assessment, be up front when soliciting participants. People are more likely to agree to participate and then follow through if they know what they'll be talking about and with whom. You will need to share this information anyway if you've sought IRB approval for your project.

It's also important to let participants know how much time you're asking them to commit. Don't just let them know the start time; tell them when they can expect to be done. An hour is about the maximum length of time you can reasonably ask participants to commit.

Send reminders: But don't be too overbearing. E-mail, text, call at reasonable intervals after they've agreed to participate. Ten days, three days, and the night or morning before are good benchmarks. If you ask how they'd prefer you send reminders, honor that; otherwise, try to match the approach with your participant group's preferences when possible.

Over-solicit participants: If you want to complete twenty-five interviews, secure commitments from thirty potential respondents. At worst, you will end up with five more responses than you'd initially planned on, which is not a bad thing! For focus groups, it's a little trickier because a too-large group presents as much of a problem as one that is too small. You could have a couple of participants in reserve with the understanding that you will provide whatever incentive your participants have been promised, or schedule one focus group more than the number you originally selected in case you need to throw out data from one of the sessions.

Real-Time Dialogue: Structure

Now that you have a broad area of inquiry and people to talk to, how should the actual session proceed? The next step is figuring out what, specifically, you'd like to ask.

Both focus groups and interviews employ what's called a *protocol*. This is basically a list of questions to be asked. There are a few approaches to constructing a protocol and conducting the sessions. Interviews, especially, are typically categorized in one of three ways:

> *Structured:* The interviewer follows the protocol very closely and does not deviate or follow up on respondent comments. This approach is essentially a survey in real time, which, in our opinion, obviates the benefits of speaking with respondents. When we receive a phone call inviting us to participate in a poll, we often participate because we often learn something from the way the questions are constructed. Many, many times we have frustrated the pollster by asking what a specific word means, or if we can answer "not applicable" even though it wasn't one of the options presented. They always say no! Of course, this is because the pollster wasn't involved in writing the poll but works for a company contracted to tap into its data bank and call dummies like us (reader excluded, of course) who are willing to answer and speak with them. The primary purpose of the structured interview is gathering data that can be aggregated and reconstituted in some way, usually more effectively accomplished in assessment by conducting a survey. One exception might be collecting information from potential users who do not currently visit the library with any regularity and are therefore less accessible for a survey.
>
> *Semi-structured:* The interviewer begins with a protocol, but allows for clarification, tangents, discussion, and follow-up questions. This is the most typical approach to assessment-related interviewing. The main challenge is being sure to return to the protocol and complete the questions before expending your allotted time.

Unstructured: The interviewer may begin with a few questions, but the session is primarily led by the respondent. This is not a typical approach for assessment, although it could be useful if you were interested in a more in-depth exploration of the library-use habits of a small number of patrons.

Focus groups are more likely to resemble a semi-structured approach. We've already established that the unstructured model is not a great choice for meeting most assessment-related goals; maintaining strict adherence to a specific list of questions is even more difficult when working with a group of respondents. Because the semi-structured model is the most common for interviews and focus groups, you can assume we are discussing that approach unless we state otherwise.

PILOT TESTING

Regardless of your protocol's level of structure, we implore you to *pilot test* your questions, preferably with a person who would realistically participate in your assessment. A pilot test is a small-scale run-through of the study to ensure the questions make sense, don't take too long to answer, and cover everything you'd like without getting too far off topic. We would never, ever start an interview or focus group project without pilot testing; we always discover that some questions are confusing or can be misinterpreted, or that we have neglected to include a question that we really need answered. Your pilot test needn't be extensive, but it is absolutely essential. This is also true of surveys.

FOCUS GROUP COMPOSITION

The quality of data generated in a focus group depends as much on its composition as on the questions asked. The group dynamic is an unacknowledged variable in focus group research that can really make or break the experience for everyone.

Although the focus group method, which comes from market research, traditionally focuses on participants' feelings and opinions about a product or brand, in library assessment the "focus" in focus group can refer to a few things, alone or in combination.

Focusing Your Participant List

The three main approaches to focusing your research are on participants who are

- focused on a single topic, for example. a resource or service such as the library's interlibrary loan service
- stakeholders with a specific concern or interest, such as genealogical research
- a specific type of user, such as history graduate students

In our experience, it's best to focus as narrowly as possible in terms of focus group topic or participant type without shrinking your pool of potential participants so much that you're scrambling for volunteers. For example, several years ago, Rachel and a colleague decided to conduct a series of focus groups to learn more about how doctoral students viewed the role of the library, its resources, and services in their research. Rachel was a doctoral student herself at the time and had come to understand that doctoral students' concerns, behaviors, responsibilities, and commitments could vary dramatically depending on the nature and discipline of their program. Rather than speaking with any group of doctoral students, they decided it made more sense to invite PhD students from the social sciences departments. They understood that political science students would approach research differently than would anthropology students, but figured political science and anthropology students would have more in common in terms of research behavior and needs than either would with biology or English doctoral students. They will never know if they were correct, but Rachel can tell you that they neglected to consider that psychology students in the research-focused PhD program would approach research differently from those pursuing a PhD in clinical practice. That seemingly small difference disrupted the progress of one focus group sufficiently to indicate this was the right call!

Who Should Participate?

It's also important to anticipate your group's internal dynamics before finalizing its composition. Yes, both undergraduate history majors and full professors of history probably both access primary sources in your special collections, maybe even for some of the same purposes. Do you think a nineteen-year-old undergraduate student is likely to be fully forthcoming with their sixty-year-old faculty advisor in the room? They're much more likely to sit quietly until the session concludes. Also be aware of reporting relationships and avoid inviting anyone who might supervise or be supervised by another invited participant.

Securing the appropriate number of participants is tricky. Just *determining* the appropriate number can be tricky! It really depends on the topic(s) being discussed and the type(s) of participants. In our experience, focus groups should have six to ten participants. Some recommendations indicate twelve participants as the upper threshold, but we think that's so large that some won't have a chance to speak.

Keeping Track of What's Said

Whether you choose to conduct interviews or focus groups, you will need to decide how to record the sessions. It's not at all uncommon to rely on notetaking as the method of recording comments from participants during interviews and focus groups, but we are not a fan of that practice, especially if the topic of discussion is not excessively controversial or personal. A much more reliable, albeit more effort-intensive, approach is to create an audio or video recording of the sessions *in addition to* taking written notes.

Of course, this means the recordings will need to be transcribed before they can be analyzed and written up, but we promise that in the process of transcription (or reading the transcript if you're lucky enough to have someone else transcribe it for you!), you will rediscover comments you'd missed the first time or forgotten. We don't make this statement lightly! We know from first-hand experience that transcription is extremely time-consuming and not especially fun. Having an accurate record of your participants' comments is essential. They gave you a gift of their time and opinions (even if you remunerated them in some way) and deserve to have their statements represented accurately.

There are programs and apps for speech-to-text recognition that might get you partway there, but you'll need to transcribe some of it by hand. Be sure to take advantage of one or more of the programs available to support transcription—it really is amazing how helpful it is to just slow down the rate of the playback—and consider investing in a foot pedal to start and stop playback hands-free.

As far as video recording is concerned—it's not necessarily a bad idea, but we wouldn't do it unless it was absolutely necessary for the assessment.

Although it's possible to maintain respondents' anonymity to a large extent with audio recordings, video just eliminates it entirely. Also, if you're seeking IRB approval for your project, requesting video recording permission will slow down the process. Limiting your respondents to those who are willing to be video recorded is likely to shrink the pool even further.

Staffing Your Interview or Focus Group

Back to note-taking: it's very difficult (for us, anyway) to take notes and ask questions at the same time. For that reason, we recommend interviews be staffed by the interviewer and a note-taker who also might be able to help with recording equipment, and that focus groups teams include at least one moderator (who asks the questions and directs discussion), a technical support person (for the recording equipment), and a note-taker. It's not necessary in either model for the note-taker to try and record comments verbatim, but it is helpful for them to indicate especially salient comments or threads of discussion so they're not lost in the volume of material.

Speaking of moderators, best practice is for that person to be as impartial as possible, and thus preferably not employed by the library. There are a couple of reasons for this: participants may be more willing to be forthcoming about ways in which they find library resources or services lacking if they know the person asking the questions doesn't work for the library. It can also be difficult for a library employee moderating a session to resist responding to negative comments or correcting misconceptions about the library, and you can be sure you'll encounter at least a few! Consider partnering with an experienced moderator from a local college or university, if possible. They may be willing to moderate your sessions and collaborate with you on an academic paper or presentation. If you can pay them, that's okay, too. There may also be graduate students in the area who might be interested in working with you.

An ideal moderator should be:

- welcoming to participants and respectful of their opinions
- able to direct the conversation without being overbearing
- able to gently redirect focus from any participants who begin to dominate the conversation

Having a good moderator is essential to the success of any focus group. If the best candidate for moderator works in the library, so be it.

At the end of your data collection phase for an assessment project using real-time dialogue approaches, you should have a collection of written transcriptions, ready for analysis. We will discuss our approach to that process in chapter 9.

Other Approaches: Case Studies and Mixed Methods

As discussed in chapter 4, fully exploring an assessment-related question often requires approaching it from multiple data points. A project that leverages multiple data collection mechanisms to explore the manifestation of a phenomenon in one or more specific settings is called a *case study*. For example, if you were interested in exploring the impact of your public library system's new summer reading program, you might conduct a survey of school-age children during the school year; compare children's book circulation statistics for two periods of time; interview participants, parents, or teachers; administer reading-level assessments before and after the summer reading program conclusion—or any other of a number of data collection strategies. You would then compile the data you'd collected and use it to create a portrait of your library's summer reading program—not to compare it to other libraries' summer reading programs—but to describe *your* system's experience and impact. It is possible to conduct multiple case studies simultaneously, but it is important to note that even if data is collected from multiple sites, it is not aggregated and treated collectively. For example, you might expand your summer reading program assessment to include two other systems in your area and decide to collect data through observation; interviews with stakeholders; and review of circulation, door count, and event attendance statistics. Rather than aggregating, for example, survey data from all three systems and analyzing it collectively, if you were using a case study approach, you would treat each system separately and use individual data points to help each system create a distinct portrait of its summer reading program.

Mixed methods projects employ multiple data collection methods as a means of triangulating findings; case studies are mixed methods projects by definition. Typically, a project that is classified as mixed methods includes at least one qualitative and one quantitative approach to collecting data. Depending on a project's goals, the qualitative or quantitative segment(s) of a project might be conducted sequentially, with findings from one segment informing the structure of others. In other instances, segments are conducted concurrently.

Existing Data Sets

One of our big rules for designing any type of research or assessment project is "don't reinvent the wheel." With so many assessment-related questions to answer, there is no honor in collecting data that already exists! Although not as useful for assessment as for less-applied research, it can be helpful to explore preexisting data sets collected at different levels of remove from your library. For example, data from surveys, collections of demographic information, or expenditures can provide important context for your own assessment efforts. In the United States, examples include NSSE (the National Survey of Student Engagement) for higher education, the surveys conducted by the United States Census Bureau, such as the American Community Survey, and data collected by the US Department of Education. The Pew Research Center is also an excellent source for unique insights into life in the United States and (to a limited extent) elsewhere.[10]

Conclusion

So, you've closed your survey, finished transcribing your interview recordings, or downloaded all your usage reports. What now?

In the next chapter, we will discuss some tips for reviewing and analyzing your data.

NOTES

1. John Kupersmith, "Library Terms That Users Understand," e-Scholarship, University of California, Berkeley, 2012, https://escholarship.org/uc/item/3qq499w7.

2. Roger C. Schonfeld and Ross Housewright, "US Faculty Survey 2009," *Ithaka S+R* (blog), April 27, 2010, https://sr.ithaka.org/publications/us-faculty -survey-2009/.

3. Ross Housewright, Roger C. Schonfeld, and Kate Wulfson, "Ithaka S+R US Faculty Survey 2012," 2013, 9–10, https://apo.org.au/sites/default/files/ resource-files/2013-04/apo-nid34295.pdf.

4. Melissa Blankstein and Christine Wolff-Eisenberg, "Ithaka S+R US Faculty Survey 2018," Ithaka S+R (blog), April 12, 2019, https://sr.ithaka.org/ publications/2018-us-faculty-survey/.

5. Tamara Taylor and Anthony Scott, "Do Physicians Prefer to Complete Online or Mail Surveys? Findings from a National Longitudinal Survey," *Evaluation and the Health Professions* 42, no. 1 (2019): 45.

6. Mogens Jin Pedersen and Christian Videbæk Nielsen, "Improving Survey Response Rates in Online Panels: Effects of Low-Cost Incentives and Cost-Free Text Appeal Interventions," *Social Science Computer Review* 34, no. 2 (2016): 229–43.

7. Pedersen and Videbæk Nielsen, "Improving Survey Response Rates."

8. Joseph W. Sakshaug, Basha Vicari, and Mick P. Couper, "Paper, E-Mail, or Both? Effects of Contact Mode on Participation in a Web Survey of Establishments," *Social Science Computer Review* 37, no. 6 (2019): 750–65.

9. William B. Edgar, "Questioning LibQUAL+TM: Expanding Its Assessment of Academic Library Effectiveness," *Libraries and the Academy* 6, no. 4 (2006): 445–65.

10. "Evidence-Based Improvement in Higher Education," National Survey of Student Engagement, https://nsse.indiana.edu; "American Community Survey (ACS)," United States Census Bureau, https://www.census.gov/programs-surveys/acs; National Center for Education Statistics, https://nces .ed.gov; Pew Research Center, https://www.pewresearch.org.

Analyzing Data

- Types of Assessment Data
- A Word about Statistical Analysis
- Resources Usage: e-Resources and Print Materials
- User and Stakeholder Surveys
- Interviews, Focus Groups, and Open-Ended Survey Questions
- Services and Facilities Usage
- Data Hygiene
- Conclusion

This chapter will cover best practices and important considerations for storing and analyzing data.

Like anything else worth doing, data analysis is a skill that can be improved upon with study and practice. Although it is beyond the scope of this text to address anything beyond very basic principles, we do think it's important to provide a little guidance to help get you started. There are a number of excellent guides to each of the particulars of analyzing data, not to mention countless continuing education opportunities for learning about quantitative and qualitative data analysis. Some suggestions are listed at the end of the chapter.

Types of Assessment Data

Generally speaking, library-related assessment will generate three types of data: quantitative, or statistical; qualitative, or textual; and . . . everything else. We realize this probably sounds glib, but that's not our intention—it's just impossible to characterize each type of data generated by assessment into the "quant/qual" binary.

As we've already discussed (ad nauseum? We have no regrets!), the assessment question you've settled on should have determined your method of collecting assessment-related data. The type of data you've collected should, in turn, determine your method of analysis. This is a bit of an over-simplification, considering it's very common for library assessment projects to generate several different types of data (remember triangulation?); in this case, you'll simply need to analyze each type of data appropriately.

It may be tempting to rely on the data collection and analysis techniques that you find most comfortable regardless of the question being asked, but try to resist this urge. Remember the old adage about what happens if you lack any tool other than a hammer? Everything looks like a nail. You can't (or so we assume) build a house with only a hammer and nails.

A Word about Statistical Analysis

A crash course in statistics is (thankfully) far beyond the scope of this text, but it is helpful to establish a few basic concepts for discussion.

Taking you back to fifth-grade math class, the mean (average), median (central data point in a collection), and mode (most frequently selected option) are examples of measures of central tendency that are all frequently referenced in assessment data analysis. A central tendency is the "typical" score distribution for a collection of data, while the range establishes its full scope from highest to lowest score. Standard deviation is the amount of variation among responses.

Generally speaking, there are two types of statistical analysis, descriptive and inferential. Descriptive statistics describe a situation: how many people from each age group visit the library weekly, how many books circulate per week by patron age group, and so on. Inferential approaches to statistical analysis allow the researcher to make inferences, or draw conclusions, about relationships between variables. For example, are senior citizens more or less likely to visit the library weekly than are patrons under the age of twenty? Inferential approaches to statistical analysis can be illuminating and are often worth working out, but for most reporting purposes, descriptive statistical analysis is perfectly adequate.

So, what do you use, and when? Our goal for this text is that it be practical, so rather than centering our discussion on approaches to analyzing data, it might be more instructive to consider the types of data generated by specific (common) areas of library assessment.

Resources Usage: e-Resources and Print Materials

Much of the data surrounding resources usage remains input- and output-based: circulation counts, database log-ons, article downloads, and so on. Much of the analysis of this type of data is descriptive by necessity; this type of data doesn't lend itself easily to more fine-grained analysis. As we discussed in our examination of the concept of use, relying solely on this type of data for decisions about budgeting, purchasing, deaccessioning, or other important questions is not advisable because so much of the user behavior for which these measures are proxy is obscured. Remember: a book might circulate a lot simply because it's just the right height to prop up a wobbly dining room table. It's fine to use this data as a starting point for decisions, but it should always be explored through other assessments before it's acted upon.

That being said, the best predictor of future behavior is past behavior. This type of data is important to consider when allocating future resources. If a specific subscription database has been accessed and searched more frequently than any others consistently over the past several years, it's probably a good bet that you should maintain that subscription. For those items about which you are on the fence, it's best to consult colleagues who use that resource regularly or the end users who rely upon it.

This topic reminds Rachel of a story that illustrates why it's so important to gather different types of data when making decisions about eliminating a resource or service. The academic library where she worked had the very common policy that it didn't maintain subscriptions to journals in both print and electronic formats—when it secured electronic access to a journal title, it canceled the print subscription. One of Rachel's duties as an academic department liaison was notifying faculty about impending cancellations.

One of Rachel's counterparts in an academic department was a wonderful patron—they knew several librarians by name, attended events, always responded to our requests for input, and so on. Rachel let them know the library was about to cancel its subscription to a print journal in their area and they'd have newly established electronic access! Wasn't that great?

No, it wasn't great. The professor found the print format of that particular journal, which included some art reproductions, far preferable to the electronic version. Could the library maintain the print subscription?

Rachel spoke with our acquisitions department: the print subscription was relatively inexpensive and maintaining it would make this faculty member very happy. Rachel met some resistance but was able to secure an exception to the policy. The price of a fraction of a percent of the library's overall budget generated significant goodwill with an important and influential user.

User and Stakeholder Surveys

It is very common for surveys to include several different types of questions, which require different approaches to analysis (see chapter 6 for a fuller discussion). Typically, these questions can be sorted into two buckets: those that generate numeric (statistical) data, and those that generate textual data. Somewhat confusingly, there can be several different question types that can be used to gather data about one type of information, and determining which type is most appropriate can be challenging. See figure 9.1 for guidance.

Most of the time, statistical library assessment data will require little inferential analysis. Note the use of *require* here—we're certainly not saying that library assessment data can't or shouldn't be put through more sophisticated statistical analysis, just that it's generally not necessary to do much more than cross-tabulation. Cross-tabulation, or contingency table analysis, allows the researcher to analyze the relationship between multiple variables. Figure 9.2 is an example.

FIGURE 9.1
Survey question types and data analysis

Question Type	Example	Data Generated	Analysis
Multiple choice: specific options listed	"Which of the following S. R. Ranganathan Library services is most important to you?"	Nominal: answer options are named; no value assigned to individual options.	Percentage: ratio of respondents who selected each answer option. Mode: answer selected most frequently.
Multiple choice: numeric options listed	"How many times did you utilize this SRRL service last month?"	Ratio scale: answer options have numeric value with "absolute zero."	Mean/mode/median; regression analysis to identify other characteristics of respondents.
Scale (Likert or otherwise)	"Please tell us how important each of the SRRL services is to you on a scale of 1: not at all important, to 5: extremely important."	Interval: answer options have a logical order with numeric value attached; "interval" between options is uniform, e.g., "agree" versus "strongly agree."	Percentage (typically) of respondents who selected each option. Average "score" if using a numeric scale.
Ranking	"Please rank the following SRRL services in order of importance . . ."	Ordinal: answer options have a logical order with a numeric value assigned to each. Differs from interval data in that "spaces" between options may not be uniform, i.e., a respondent may consider a service ranked of greater importance than another to be only slightly so.	Percentage/number of respondents who selected each option, more sophisticated approaches to compare ordinal groups.
Open text	"Please explain why this SRRL service is most important to you."	Textual: respondent generates answer in own words rather than selecting from pre-established list.	Interpretive: typically by coding responses to identify themes (see interview/ focus group data analysis).

Crosstabs are described by the number of rows (R) by the number of columns (C). The example below is a 4 × 5 crosstab. If one of the library service options were eliminated, it would be a "square" table because the number of rows and columns would be the same (4 × 4).

FIGURE 9.2
Cross-tabulation of academic library user survey responses

		What library service or resource do you use most frequently?					
		Study space	Computers	e-Resources	Popular reading collection	Research assistance	Total
Which best describes you?	Undergraduate	21	16	5	3	7	52
	Graduate	23	9	12	2	14	60
	Faculty	4	2	43	1	4	54
	Staff	2	5	15	18	12	52
	Total	50	32	75	24	37	218

Let's think practically about the kind of analysis we might like to run on this data. Perhaps, before distributing this survey, we developed a hypothesis that graduate students would value the library for study space more than any other user group. If we collected this data for a research project we planned to submit for publication, we would want to test our data to determine the extent to which our hypothesis was correct.

In real-life assessment, however, would we actually need to determine the extent to which our hypothesis was correct? Probably not. A more useful test would be calculating the extent to which our two variables of interest—being a graduate student and making extensive use of the library as a study space—are likely to go together or be correlated (this is called a *correlation coefficient*, and tests to calculate it include Pearson's r and Spearman's ρ). For most assessment-related purposes, however, simply presenting the data as collected is sufficiently informative. The number of respondents in our study is small enough that such a calculation might not be accurate or informative.

Interviews, Focus Groups, and Open-Ended Survey Questions

Understanding how to analyze qualitative data was identified as essential knowledge by 80.7 percent of our survey respondents. Because interviews and focus groups, along with open-ended survey questions, generate textual data in the respondent's own words, it is especially important that this type of data collection and presentation be meticulous. You don't want to rely on your own memory of what an interview participant had to say. Recordings of interviews and focus groups should be transcribed, and survey responses should be transferred to a document for analysis.

The most common approach to textual data analysis is referred to as coding, a process through which researchers review the text for concepts and common themes. Researchers handle coding differently. There are a number of tools to support textual data analysis; some researchers prefer hand-coding. Regardless, the conceptual model is the same.

How does it work? We will provide a couple of examples of one approach to coding textual data.

Let's say we conducted a series of interviews with parents of young children who are not currently regular users of the library. In response to the question: "what barriers are there to your bringing your child to the library?" a parent provided this answer:

> Storytime always seems to fall during naptime. It's also difficult to find a place to park nearby without having to park in a pay lot. Even if I can park relatively close, I'll need to use the stroller and carry it up the front steps of the library.

First, we'd create a table and paste the statement into it, dividing the text among several lines, as shown in figure 9.3.

FIGURE 9.3
Interview question answer in table format

Storytime always seems to fall during naptime.
It's also difficult to find a place to park nearby
without having to park in a pay lot.
Even if I can park relatively close
I'll need to use the stroller
and it's difficult to get it up the front steps of the library.

Then we'd add a column for individual codes. This next step, shown in figure 9.4, is where researchers' real quirks and preferences show up: developing codes. We like to use three-letter codes.

FIGURE 9.4
Interview question answer in table format, with concept codes

Statement	Code
Storytime always seems to fall during naptime.	SCD
It's also difficult to find a place to park nearby	DFC/PRK
without having to park in a pay lot.	EXP/PRK
Even if I can park relatively close	DST/PRK
I'll need to use the stroller	EQP
and it's difficult to get it up the front steps of the library.	BRR/ETR

We add the concept code to a master list (figure 9.5) as we go.

FIGURE 9.5
Code/concept master list (interview)

Code	Description
SCD	Schedule, Scheduling
DFC	Difficulty
PRK	Parking (auto)
EXP	Expense
DST	Distance
EQP	Equipment
BRR	Barrier
ETR	Entry/Entrance

We would complete the same process with the rest of this interview and the others we'd transcribed. Then, we'd review the coded transcripts for themes and see what kinds of conclusions we can draw from the data.

Of course, "coding for themes" makes the process sound very simple. It's not. Typically, a researcher reviews and refines their coded materials several times, grouping similar or related codes and refining codes for greater nuance while condensing codes that are very similar. It is best practice for multiple researchers to code the same collection of text to see if they identify similar codes and themes (remember inter-rater reliability from chapter 4?).

Other Textual Analysis

Other types of text can be coded as well. For example, we might want to analyze the University of Tennessee Libraries' mission statement for themes:

> The University of Tennessee Libraries enrich and advance our community, the nation, and the world by providing expertise and leadership in accessing, creating, disseminating, and preserving knowledge.[1]

Just as we did with our interview example, we'd divide the statement among cells of a table, as shown in figure 9.6.

FIGURE 9.6

Mission statement in table format for coding

The University of Tennessee Libraries
enrich and
advance
our community
the nation
and the world
by providing expertise
and leadership
in accessing
creating
disseminating
and preserving
knowledge.

We would then create codes for each idea (figure 9.7).

FIGURE 9.7

Mission statement in table format, with codes

Statement	Code
The University of Tennessee Libraries	UTK/LIB
enrich and	FNC
advance	ADV
our community	LCM
the nation	NTN
and the world	GLB
by providing expertise	UTK/LIB/EXP
and leadership	UTK/LDP
in accessing	ACS
creating	CRT
disseminating	DSM
and preserving	PRV
knowledge.	KNW

We would add these codes to a master list as we worked (figure 9.8).

FIGURE 9.8
Code/concept master list (Mission Statement)

Code	Meaning
UTK	University of Tennessee
LIB	Library
FNC	Financial mission
ADV	Advance
LCM	Locals community
NTN	Nation
GLB	World/Global
EXP	Expertise
LDP	Leadership
ACS	Access
CRT	Create
DSM	Disseminate
PRV	Preserve
KNW	Knowledge

We might want to compare our coded mission statement to another document—a key difference from the parent interviews in our first example, which were coded as a comprehensive body of data. Perhaps we are interested in how closely UTK Libraries' mission statement compares to that of the larger University of Tennessee, or to the mission statement of a peer institution's library. The same principles of analysis would apply.

Figure 9.9 gives you an idea of what the process looks like when using a software package to organize the process (which 34 percent of our survey respondents indicated was a requirement of their position). This product is NVIVO.

FIGURE 9.9

Interface for NVIVO qualitative research analysis software

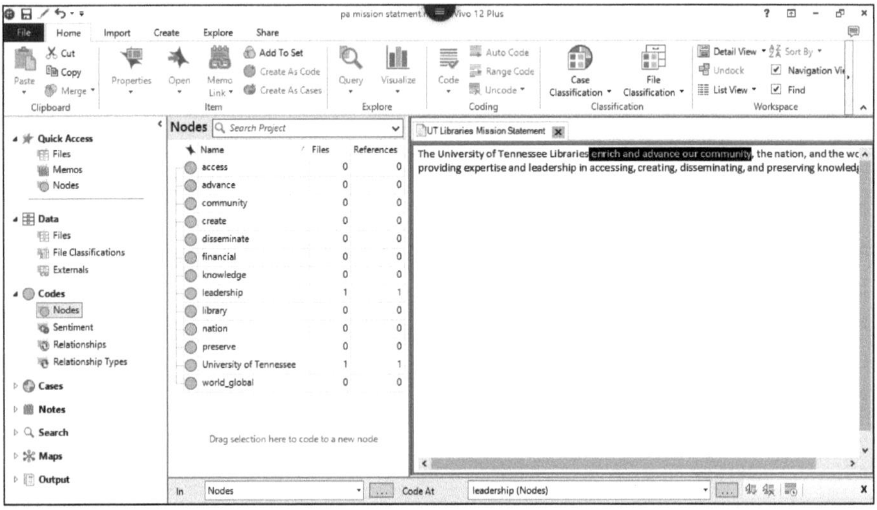

Services and Facilities Usage

Although much of services and facilities usage is recorded as inputs (number of hours of operation) and outputs (number of reference questions asked), there are some approaches with more nuance, such as observation.

Observation Data

As discussed in chapter 7, observation can provide helpful insight into how a physical space—as small as a room or as large as the library—meets users' needs and how they interact with it. Observation data analysis can be as simple as comparing recorded notations on a template or in written notes (see appendix C for an observation template), or it can employ more sophisticated tools like geographic information system (GIS) tracking, or movement and heat sensors. If the purpose of the assessment is identifying problem spots where signage or flow could be improved, it should be possible to identify those within a relatively short period of time.

Usability Testing

We also might consider usability testing to be a kind of observation, but rather than finding their way through a physical space to locate services and resources, patrons navigate a library's electronic resources to address their needs. As we've discussed, usability testing can be conducted with little more than a laptop and a session guide, or the tester can employ more sophisticated tools that track and record participants' keystrokes as well as cursor, mouse, and eye movement.

FIGURE 9.10

Simulation of sequenced eye-movement tracking on UTK Libraries' website (each line corresponds to an individual participant)

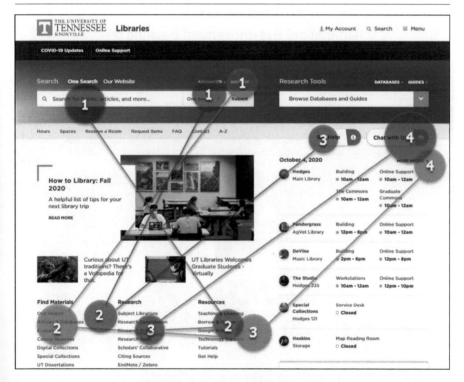

Figure 9.10 represents the moves of three different usability test participants. The numbers within the circles represent the sequence of moves (i.e.,
those labeled "1" were the first point) and the size of the circle indicates
the length of time the participant spent at that particular spot on the page
(larger circles = more time). We can observe that all three participants began
their test focused on the upper-left or upper-center part of the page, so we
might consider that a good spot for most-sought information or resources.
The dense collection of links on the lower left generated a good deal of interest, but without hearing participants' thought process, it's difficult to know
why: did they linger there because they found the links confusing? We should
also note that only one participant visited the upper right-hand corner of the
screen, and then only late in the session (third of four "stops").

FIGURE 9.11

**(simulation) Eye-movement tracking on
UTK Libraries' website: Heat map**

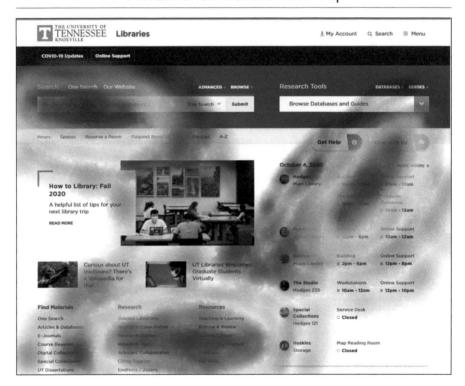

You can think of the heat map in figure 9.11 as a slightly more nuanced presentation of the data presented in figure 9.10, but with a dimmer rather than an on-off switch. The length of the usability test participant's attention is indicated on a "ROYGBIV" spectrum, with red being the most intense.

Data Hygiene

Regardless of the type of data you're working with, it's very easy to become overwhelmed. Practicing good data hygiene is essential, especially if you're collaborating with anyone. Here are some suggestions from (hard-won) experience:

- Set up your data recording mechanisms so they're easy to understand and remember. Develop a system of file naming and stick with it.
- Don't make data recording more complex than it needs to be. Microsoft Excel is great and very powerful, but if you're not planning to use its functions, why not just create a table in Word? Use the simplest tool that will get the job done.
- This goes for mechanisms of analysis, too. Do you really need to slice and dice your data six different ways? Does your analytical approach really serve your question?
- Keep a separate record of your data analysis process. While you're working and immersed in the project, it might seem inconceivable that you'd have difficulty resuming your work into it after stepping away for a few days, but you'd be surprised.

Conclusion

Finally, data analysis can be really rewarding and fun. It encourages you to make connections and see things differently. It can help you answer long-held questions about the nature of your work and the people you work with. It allows you to use your imagination and develop solutions in a way that may be a little different from your typical work.

NOTE

1. University of Tennessee Libraries, "Mission and Vision," https://www.lib.utk
.edu/about/mission-and-vision/.

FURTHER READINGS

Chun Tie, Ylona, Melanie Birks, and Karen Francis. "Grounded Theory Research:
A Design Framework for Novice Researchers." *SAGE Open Medicine* 7 (2019).

> A great, recent overview of qualitative data analysis with an eye toward
> grounded theory development. Very accessible.

Corbin, Juliet M., and Anselm L. Strauss. *Basics of Qualitative Research: Techniques
and Procedures for Developing Grounded Theory.* Thousand Oaks, CA: SAGE
Publications, 2014.

> This is one of the classic texts for learning interpretive (qualitative) data
> analysis. The authors walk through the steps of processing, analyzing,
> and writing up non-numeric data for concepts and themes.

Gonick, Larry, and Woollcott Smith. *The Cartoon Guide to Statistics.* New York, NY:
HarperPerennial, 1993.

> A fun introduction to some pretty sophisticated statistical analysis.
> Especially helpful for more visual learners.

SAGE Little Green Books: *Quantitative Methods*, and SAGE Little Blue Books:
Qualitative Methods.

> Each slim volume of SAGE's long-running series provides a concise over-
> view of a single research method. The complete run is available through
> some of SAGE's e-resource products, and individual titles are very
> inexpensive.

Reporting and Presenting Data

- Assessment Data Management

- Data Privacy

- Preservation and Storage of Data

- Performing a Library Data Inventory

- Reporting

- Data Definitions

- Reporting Periods and Deadlines

- Managing Your Stats

- Managing Relationships

- Other Considerations

- Communicating Results— Designing Effective Reports and Communications

- Data Visualization

- Conclusion

Managing data may be one of the greatest challenges you will face as an assessment professional. Even if you are very fortunate and a predecessor has tackled the organization and management of all of your organization's data, you will still have to familiarize yourself with it and hold in mind all of the vast number of data sources, systems, and people that make up an information organization's data ecosystem, as well as constantly integrate new data and data sources. It's a lot. And that's before you consider the fact that if you cannot analyze and present this data in meaningful and compelling ways (indicated as a job requirement by 90 percent of our survey respondents), then it's all for naught. In this chapter, we will first discuss the management and organization of library data as relevant to assessment and planning, including performing a data inventory and issues relevant to data privacy, preservation, and storage. The second part of this chapter will cover reporting basics and some general best practices for data visualization. Although each of these topics could be an entire book in itself, the goal here is to give you a general overview to use as a starting point for deeper investigation.

Assessment Data Management

It may be best to begin with some clarifications of terminology. While there is much literature in the field on the topic of the data management plan (DMP), this is a term that is usually used very specifically to refer to

> a written document that describes the data you expect to acquire or generate during the course of a research project, how you will manage, describe, analyze, and store those data, and what mechanisms you will use at the end of your project to share and preserve your data.[1]

Such plans are often required by agencies that fund research, and each agency may have specific requirements for what its plan entails. Many academic libraries advise and consult on the development of such plans with their faculty researchers, and there is a growing body of literature in this area. Although there may be some things we can learn from DMPs that would apply to managing library data, it is important to be clear that for the purposes of our discussion, data management in libraries refers to the management of library data, for example circulation statistics, collection statistics, and reference statistics. While some of the data you use in assessment and planning may come from your own assessment projects, much of it will be automatically generated in the course of a library's daily operations. This produces a number of special concerns and considerations that you may encounter as you pursue your assessment and planning goals.

Managing library assessment data intersects with the general library data management policies and procedures in place at your particular organization. Because every organization tends to be unique, as we've said before, there is no one-size-fits-all explanation or approach. Working with existing library data, as well as managing the data you create through assessment projects, can include "identifying, selecting and preparing data to be deposited into a repository; creating or transforming metadata; and [being involved in the development of] policies and the strategic planning process."[2] Managing this data also includes considering various aspects, such as "file naming; access to data; data documentation; creation of metadata and vocabularies; data storage; data archiving and data preservation; data sharing and data reuse; privacy of the data; intellectual property, and data publication."[3]

As your library develops assessment programs for its departments and services, the amount of data available and collected will continually increase. This is true of all types of library data collection and storage. Transparency and availability of library assessment data are crucial to developing a culture of assessment (see chapter 11), as well as to facilitating assessment and planning activities throughout the organization. In addition, the data must be stored and preserved in such a way that it remains accessible in the future, both for the sake of longitudinal comparisons and general comparative evaluations and to ensure it is preserved in the face of changing staff and data storage systems and policies. Being as proactive as possible in leading your organization in developing effective policies and procedures is advised, but you will probably encounter some challenges as well.

There has been little research into developing best practices for library data management, perhaps partly because modern libraries tend to be so individual in their structures and operations. The best practices that have been outlined for scientific researchers and related institutions may sometimes be applicable in libraries but often simply do not apply.[4] And where data management policies or best practices have been identified in a particular institution, it's not uncommon for them to be ignored, for staff to be uninformed about them, and for staff to modify policies and procedures to suit their needs or preferences.[5]

But perhaps the biggest barrier to effective data organization and management for libraries is the siloed nature of library data. The sheer number of different types of data, data systems, and departments that collect and manage data make it difficult to create an effective plan with appropriate practices for an entire institution.[6] And there is, of course, the human factor as well. As we've discussed, there are many data gatekeepers in the average mid- to large-sized library who, for a variety of reasons, may be resistant to changing, or sometimes even sharing, their practices. As you approach the herculean task of understanding and integrating library data into your assessment and planning, it's important to keep in mind that what may appear as an individual or department's arbitrary (or questionable) approach to collecting or storing data may actually have been based on the basis of real-world experience. In fact, there is usually a good reason lost in the mists of time for most practices or policies that at first glance seem nonsensical. As always, it is better to ask gently probing questions and listen with an open mind before coming in with a pronouncement about the best way to do things. In general, it is wise to look upon your assessment data management efforts as more of a marathon than a sprint. Below, we will discuss some concrete steps you can take to start this process.

It is also worth noting here that in recent years there has been an effort in the industry to develop products explicitly intended to integrate all of the siloed data into one system. One of the better-known among the current contenders at the time of writing is SpringShare's LibInsight, which is intended to "organize and consolidate all library statistics in one place to run cross-dataset analysis and make data-driven decisions."[7] An evaluation of these products is beyond the scope of this book, but they certainly offer promise for the future. If your library is considering such a product, a very important question to ask is how many working hours will be required to import your data into the system and get it up and running, and also what sort of ongoing support will be provided. Keep in mind that software tends to become obsolete rather quickly these days and companies often discontinue support for older products unless you purchase new updates.

Migrating and integrating data from multiple platforms can be a very time-intensive process, so it is best to make sure that your organization is prepared to put in the work required to make any new product functional and to support that product for the long term.

Data Privacy

An issue that has sometimes been a perceived or actual barrier to library assessment efforts is the library field's deep and historical support of patron privacy.[8] The American Library Association's position on privacy is very clear:

> The right to privacy—the right to read, consider, and develop ideas and
> beliefs free from observation or unwanted surveillance by the govern-
> ment or others—is the bedrock foundation for intellectual freedom. It is
> essential to the exercise of free speech, free thought, and free association.[9]

The issue is so central to the practice of librarianship that it is included in
ALA's Library Bill of Rights, first drafted in 1939.[10]

We agree that it is an absolute necessity to maintain patron privacy at all
costs. But it's worth noting here that other disciplines have well-developed
practices for handling sensitive data related to human subjects and have created policies that respect the privacy of those individuals while still storing,
preserving, and sharing that data.[11] It is possible to collect data that includes
data points which can be invaluable to your assessment efforts in such a way
that you retain crucial information, such as demographic data, while ano-
nymizing the data before use or storage. Although a thorough discussion of
patron privacy is beyond the scope of this book, there are many discussions
of the ethics of patron privacy available. Jason's Vaughan's "Library Privacy
Policies" is a particularly thorough resource on privacy policies.[12]

Preservation and Storage of Data

Chances are that your library already has practices and policies in place for
the storage and preservation of library data. But it's helpful to understand a
little about the data life cycle and some basic best practices for handling both
library-generated data and assessment-generated data. The typical research
data life cycle begins with a planning stage, before moving on to the collection and description phases. The cycle continues with the process and
analysis phase, before transitioning to the publication phase and ending with
the preservation stage.[13] This process is relevant to assessment data created
through a specific assessment project, for instance, a user survey (though you
may or may not formally publish such data, you will share it internally in
your organization, which for our purposes is an analogous stage). We refer to
this as *assessment-generated data*. But there is a great deal of data that is generated automatically through the normal daily operations of the organization,
such as circulation data or gate counts. We refer to this as *library-generated
data*. The life cycle for this type of data is a bit different and may best be
reflected by the practice of data life cycle management (DLM). The stages of

DLM are:

1. Data acquisition and capture

2. Data backup and recovery

3. Data management and maintenance

4. Data retention or destruction

If you are in a medium-size or large organization, it's likely that someone else will be responsible for these stages for library-generated data. For the assessment-generated data that you create through your activities, you will generally follow the overarching practices of your organization for steps 2 through 4.

Although it is unlikely that you will be tasked with immediately revamping your organization's DLM practices, it's still important for you to be aware of the most important elements of data management and to understand how to apply them to any data collection you personally undertake. Those elements include:

1. A data backup policy for all data (including digital and non-digital data)

2. The assignment of responsibilities for data collection and data management upkeep through the entire data cycle

3. Discussion of and provision for storage, with an eye toward security, especially for sensitive data

4. Discussion of the length of time that data should be stored or preserved, with a focus on storage considerations that meet funding, institutional, and potential governmental requirements

5. An estimated budget for the entire data cycle, from data collection to processing and storage, as well as maintenance[14]

Any data management plan needs to be a collaborative effort between those collecting data, those using the data, those storing the data, and those protecting or sharing the data. In a library context, this could mean administration or senior staff, specific departments and individuals, and IT departments.

For any data that you do collect or manage, be aware of specific considerations related to appropriate naming, saving, and storage. Starting early and being consistent with file naming, for instance, will be a gift to your future self that you will always be grateful for.

The list below is drawn from a variety of sources that outline general best practices.

Name and Format

- Use consistent, descriptive, and informative file names that contain information which identifies the data file but is flexible enough that it can be used across different data management platforms.
- Save files in sustainable, non-proprietary or open file formats that are in common usage by the designated community that ensure long-term access.
- Track different version of the files by including version numbers, information about the status of the file, and what changes were made.

Metadata

- Determine the metadata standard for the repository or storage system the file will be stored in.
- Create and maintain metadata for all files.
- Create and maintain metadata when the file is created.

Preservation

- Designate a central storage system where participants can save and store information.
- Determine an appropriate saving interval, whether it is daily, weekly, or monthly.[15]

Two further considerations are important to keep in mind when working with library assessment data (which, again, is potentially all library data). First, it is very important that outgoing staff make their data and data policies available after they depart the institution or department.[16] Because staff departures can sometimes be sudden, ideally, data would be stored in a shared drive where more than one person has access to it, and any procedures for accessing data in library systems should be documented and that documentation shared in a central location as a matter of policy. A second consideration, related to the first, is the desirability of keeping all library assessment data as transparent and accessible as possible. As mentioned earlier in this chapter, access to data is an important element of developing a culture of assessment. Transparency of data builds trust. Both are necessary for a robust assessment culture in any organization.

Performing a Library Data Inventory

Because libraries and information centers tend to generate massive amounts of different types of data, your first step in getting a handle on it all may be to simply understand what data your organization collects. This may sound like it should be simple, but there are some common pitfalls you may encounter, such as there being no central list of what data is collected, no documentation on how to access various data, and data "gatekeepers" who may be reluctant to share access to the data under their purview. If there is no clear listing of what data your organization collects, we suggest you perform a data inventory as your first step.

Terminology connected with data can have many different and specific meanings, depending on who is using it and how. What we are calling a data inventory may also be referred to elsewhere as a data audit, data dictionary, data matrix, or data framework.[17] For our purposes, the most basic definition of a library data inventory as used here is a list of what data the library collects and where to find that data (i.e., how to access it). Understanding those two things about your organization's data might be thought of as a quick-start guide to understanding your organization's data. If you have the time and resources to go deeper, there are other types of metadata that may be helpful for you to collect, document, and share about your organization's data.

Why perform a data inventory? The most compelling reason is that as you perform assessment in your organization, you will constantly need to access your organization's data. Also, knowing what data is already collected may prevent you from wasting time and duplicating work that is already being done elsewhere. To do your job, you will need to know not just what data exists but also where to find it and how to access it. You may think some types of data are not relevant, but eventually you will probably need to access all sorts of data for reasons you cannot foresee. Assessment has a way of being far reaching and unpredictable. Another important reason to perform a data inventory and share it with your organization is that lack of access to data is reported by library staff as one of their main barriers to performing assessment.

A good first step in any assessment project is to explore what has been done before. Try to determine if anyone else in your organization has done any work to document data. Start with the obvious suspects, those responsible for IT and administrators, but don't assume that others haven't done work in the area. It is always best to cast a wide net to determine who may consider themselves a stakeholder in a project before you begin. It is also a good idea to communicate with the entire organization about what you are doing and why. If you make it clear that what you are collecting will be a resource that will be available for the entire organization to use, it may encourage buy-in and cooperation with your project.

When you are ready to start your data inventory, determine how much information you want to collect and what your must-haves, as opposed to nice-to-haves, are. Again, the bare minimum of data points to collect are what data exists and where to find it. But if time and resources allow, it is useful to collect some other information while you are investigating. If time doesn't allow a more thorough project, however, don't let that stop you from making a start. You can always build on it later and over time.

We recommend using a spreadsheet to collect and store your data inventory; set it up so each row is a separate data point and each column represents a separate descriptor. It may be helpful to format your inventory as a table and add filters so that it is easier to navigate. It is also good practice to have a unique ID for each data point, which can be helpful if you later decide to create a database or use visualization software to make interfacing with the inventory more user-friendly. Other basic data descriptors you may or may not want to collect, based on your needs, include data category and subcategory, reporting department, responsible party, data collection frequency, data collection procedure, platform and login information, data requestor(s), how the data is used, and any other miscellaneous notes that may be helpful in locating, accessing, and understanding the data point.[18]

Once you have your initial data inventory completed, it's a good idea to review and update it annually, ideally as part of your annual reporting process.

Reporting

Reporting your assessment results is arguably the most important part of the entire process. After all, if your assessment activities have no effect, then even the best data collection and analysis in the world are a waste of time you might better spend elsewhere. The perennial mystery applies here: if library assessment takes place but no one hears about it, does it make a sound? In this section, we will cover the essential basics of reporting, from routine reporting of statistics to developing reports and other communications for best results.

Statistics Collecting and Reporting

For many librarians working in the area of assessment, a routine but important part of the job is to collect and report statistics regularly to various bodies. Some of the most common reporting surveys are below.

PUBLIC LIBRARIES

Public Libraries Survey (PLS)—This survey is administered annually by the Institute of Museum and Library Services.

Public libraries may also be accountable to various local, state, and federal legislating bodies and may report statistics in various individualized ways.

ACADEMIC LIBRARIES

Integrated Postsecondary Education Data System (IPEDS)—This is a series of surveys conducted each year by the National Center for Education Statistics (NCES), which has a library component. Completing these surveys is mandatory for any institution that participates in federal financial assistance programs. These surveys have a hard deadline.

Association of College and Research Libraries Academic Library Trends and Statistics Survey—This survey is administered annually by ACRL and is the largest survey of academic libraries in the country.

Association of Research Libraries (ARL) Statistics Survey—This survey is conducted annually, collecting data only from ARL's 124 member institutions. While a relatively small number of libraries contribute data to this survey, it has historically been very influential in the field of academic library assessment. (See chapter 2 for information on its history.)

SCHOOL LIBRARIES

National Teacher and Principal Survey (NTPS) —This survey is also conducted by NCES and replaced the former Schools and Staffing Survey (SASS). It is currently conducted every two years.

School libraries may also receive a number of local or state surveys or be required to report to various individualized local or state bodies, often on a random, as opposed to annual, basis.

SPECIAL LIBRARIES

Although there is no universal survey for special libraries, they may be required to report data to or through a parent institution or as part of a larger library system.

This section has been written for those new to coordinating the collecting and reporting of statistics, but it may be useful for those who have been doing it for a while. Likewise, your institution may have procedures in place for collecting and reporting these statistics, but it may be worth reviewing those procedures with a view to possible improvements.

Data Definitions

Data definitions are the starting point for collecting statistics. For every data point you are expected to collect and report, there should be a written definition of what is and is not included in that number and how specifically it is defined. This is important because the reporting organization may not be using specific data labels in the same way your organization uses them; therefore, a label may not mean what you think it means. Following the data definitions closely from the beginning may save you time and heartache in the end.

It's a good idea to review the data definitions used by a specific survey every year (or every time you report them) because they can change from year to year. Also, if you are reporting to multiple surveys, there may be overlap between what the various surveys ask for. Being aware of this may save you time and also allow you to only request or calculate that data point once per year, even though you are reporting it in multiple places.

If you are new to coordinating your institution's response, it is a good idea to walk through the survey definitions with those who have been providing data, as well as how they have calculated their responses in the past. It's useful to have a general understanding of where the data for each data point is stored, who has access to it, and how they have pulled and calculated the data in the past. If you find that their procedures have not followed the data definitions provided by the reporting organization, don't panic. The first thing to do is to understand why they have deviated from the definitions. It may be simply because they were not aware of them, but it's also possible that they may have a good reason for any deviations and it's important to fully understand the situation before attempting to make changes.

If you do find that you need to make changes to how any data point is calculated, be sure to note exactly what changes you are making, both in your own documentation and in your reporting. If numbers deviate widely enough from the previous year, it may trigger a review and justification, but all that is required is to make a note of why the deviation has occurred (e.g., you changed the way you calculated the numbers). In some cases, there may be external reasons for a great deviation (e.g., a one-time infusion of funds causing expenditures to increase drastically for one year). As time goes on, you will find that you are grateful for any notes from previous years because it can be hard to remember a few years later what was going to make the numbers swing up or down. You can't predict how you may use this data going forward or who may look at it and have questions, so documenting unusual circumstances is something you will thank yourself for later.

Reporting Periods and Deadlines

Most surveys should define the period for which you are reporting. This will generally either be the calendar year or the fiscal year, but it's a good idea to always verify and pay close attention to such details. The surveys will also set deadlines for reporting. Some deadlines are hard deadlines and simply cannot be missed, such as with IPEDs. In other cases, you may be able to ask for an extension if you find you need one. It is a good idea to note the reporting deadlines far in advance and also verify these deadlines each year, as they are also prone to being changed.

Managing Your Stats

Our suggestion for best practices for statistics collection is to mock up a survey form in Excel for each survey to which you will report. It doesn't have to exactly mirror the survey in appearance, but it should just follow the order in which the data points are collected on the survey. This makes it easy for you to fill out the survey and provides you with a back-up copy of all the statistics you report. It also gives you a place to keep your own personal notes. Your notes may include data definitions, details of how the data point was calculated, who in your organization provides the data, which systems produce the data, and any local details such as circumstances that affected the data and helpful notes about good workflows or other efficiencies in securing the data.

Store these spreadsheets in a shared document drive or folder, if possible, and make sure that someone other than you—or ideally multiple people—has access to it. If you are comfortable with this, based on your assessment of those you are working with, you may want to give those providing data direct access to the spreadsheet so that they can enter the data they are providing directly into it. They would also be able to see the data definitions in the spreadsheet, which would be an added bonus and an easy way of making that information easily accessible to them.

You may want to include the last three years' responses on the same spreadsheet as the current year's data collection. This will make it easy to check the current year's data for consistency. One would expect data to change a little from year to year, but if it changes greatly or in a direction you wouldn't expect (such as having fewer volumes when you haven't weeded the collection), it may be a sign that there might be an error in the calculations or something as simple as a transcription error. It's a good idea to check your data two to three times before reporting it, and, if possible, have another pair of eyes look at it too.

Managing Relationships

We've assumed that you will have to rely on others to provide at least some of the statistics that you will need. This is because of the siloed nature of library data and the large number of different systems of generating and recording data that are used in the average library. While we do suggest that you gain access to as many of these different systems as possible over time, it's unlikely that you will ever be able to collect and report all the stats you need without consulting someone else in your library (unless you work in a one-person shop, which some librarians do!). So, working effectively with others in your organization is once again key to your success.

As mentioned above, note deadlines well in advance and plan to collect your data internally a little before they are actually due. In other words, plan for those providing data to miss deadlines. Also, give yourself a cushion of time to check over the data they provide for consistency with previous years' returns and follow up if necessary. If your data is due to the reporting agency on October 15, you may want to ask your reporting partners to have it to you by October 1. You don't necessarily need to tell them when the real deadline is, as some people will only hit the drop-dead deadline. If you have a hard deadline that you know cannot be extended for any reason, you may want to give yourself even more of a cushion. Because you generally have a few months between the end of the reporting period and the reporting deadline, you can usually give others several weeks or even months to respond and still have space for a cushion.

If you encounter an unwillingness to collect statistics, focus on the administrative value of the surveys and make sure that data from past surveys is available to your colleagues as well as to library or institutional administrators. Hesitant colleagues may be more willing to contribute to data collection efforts if they can see the value in benchmarking as a source of data to support their own requests or reporting efforts. Following up with those who provide data to let them know the ways in which that data is used can also be very effective in encouraging them to collaborate with you and strengthen that relationship for future requests. You might be surprised at how meaningful it can be for those who contribute the data to know how it is used and to see the value of their work and effort.

Other Considerations

The statistics you are providing may be used in a number of ways by a number of different people, so accuracy and integrity are very important. There are a few areas that experience has shown us can be a bit tricky, particularly for those new to this.

New assessment professionals may be obsessing over accuracy and fretting over those stats that pose difficulties in that regard. It can be helpful to note that not every question in the survey is widely used for comparison, ranking, or other decision-making purposes. So, for instance, for most libraries, it is far more important to ensure that budget and staffing information is accurate than that the collection is counted down to the last vertical file or that reference transactions are completely filtered to remove somewhat "directional" queries. Perfect accuracy can be difficult or impossible to achieve for some types of questions. What is most important in those cases is consistency in how you are counting and calculating your answers so that changes over time are still meaningful, even if not exact down to the last decimal point.

This is particularly true in electronic resource usage statistics, which remain a challenge for the field as a whole. You should take any and all electronic resource stats with a large grain of salt, regardless of who is reporting them. Over the years, there have been, and will continue to be, constant changes to vendors, platforms, and standard statistics. It's good to note that some surveys will specify which reports should be used to answer these questions, while others are more open-ended. Every library's reporting tends to interpret, collect, and report these stats in its own way, so even with standard data definitions, direct peer comparisons may not be very meaningful. Also, you should not spend an excess of time calculating these stats yourself to try to achieve perfection. This is an area where 85 percent good enough should be your goal, or you will likely drive yourself crazy. Again, consistency in how you arrive at your data and documenting for yourself what you've done are key. We recommend only reporting statistics from vendors that provide up-to-standard COUNTER reports and excluding (with a footnote) usage statistics from platforms that do not provide these reports. It is much better to say exactly what you are counting, even if it is not complete, than to layer several estimates together and have no way of knowing, year to year, if you are counting the same things in the same ways. And if a vendor's data is not COUNTER-compliant, it is suspect at best.

Communicating Results—Designing Effective Reports and Communications

Effectively communicating the results of your planning and assessment efforts is arguably the most important step and is a job requirement for an astonishing 93.4 percent of our survey respondents. Simply put, if no one knows or understands what you've done, and no one is moved to action by your efforts, then the sad truth is you have wasted your time. This is also a step that is often overlooked in the library assessment literature. There are, however, a few simple best practices that can make all the difference in your communication efforts.

Know Your Audience

The cardinal commandment for all types of communication is "know your audience." There is a reason that advertising and marketing firms still conduct focus groups on a regular basis. They understand not only that their target audience may think differently than they do, but also that they cannot accurately know how their audience thinks or what may be important to them without asking them. They conduct repeated focus groups because they realize that their audience's opinions and concerns may change over time or in the face of new circumstances.

Knowing your audience means, wherever possible, not just guessing at what matters to them, but gathering any evidence you have access to. You may not be able to do focus groups with your state legislators, for instance, but you can be familiar with their public statements and their legislative agenda. Likewise, if you work in an academic library, you may not be able to interview the chancellor of your university, but you can review the university's published strategic plans and goals, as well as talk to your library director to get a sense of any unstated priorities that may be important to your chancellor at the moment. Understand that the concerns of all your stakeholders will change over time, so make it a priority to be plugged in on a regular and ongoing basis.

When it comes to sharing the results of library assessment, you will probably have many different audiences for the same data. Over time, you will probably need to design reports and data visualizations for every category of stakeholder that we've listed below. Potential library stakeholders include:

- faculty, other instructors, and research staff
- undergraduate and graduate students
- library and institutional administrators
- federal, state, and local legislators
- alumni, donors, vendors, accrediting bodies, library staff, and community members

Take the time to customize reports and visualizations for different audiences. The suggestions below are drawn from a number of sources that discuss best practices for communication.

For each type of audience, ask yourself:

- What is most important to these stakeholders?
- What are their goals, interests, and needs? In other words, why would they or should they care about what I want to communicate? (Hint: the reason you care about it is probably not the same reason they care about it, unless it's your coworkers—and sometimes not even then.)
- What types of decisions do these stakeholders make?
- What type of data would help them make those decisions? What is the best way to present the data to help them make those decisions? What do I most need to highlight to facilitate their decision-making?
- What type of communication and content are most likely to appeal to these individuals?
- How much time are they likely to spend looking at this? How long is their attention span, particularly for the information I want to communicate? What level of detail do they want? Would they prefer a longer, more in-depth report, or do they want something they can understand in a glance? You could potentially communicate via e-mail, in a meeting, through a presentation, through a long report, through a poster, or even through a bookmark. The content of your message could be nothing but statistics and charts or it could include quotes and graphics and tell a story. Which is best for your target audience? Or would a combination of approaches be best for your goals?
- What is your audience's area of expertise?
- Are they technical or non-technical? Will they understand any jargon you are using? A highly technical audience may actually want more

detail and distrust anything that is too simplified, but a non-technical audience will glaze over at your first use of jargon. Don't talk down to your audience, but when in doubt, make sure you define anything that could be confusing (or just don't include it, if it is not necessary).[19]

Keep It Simple

Although you never want to oversimplify your reports, in general, it is always best to reduce "noise" in your communications. Use of library jargon is generally the number one offender in library communications. As a rule, you should never use jargon in a communication not meant solely for librarians. And even if your communication is meant solely for librarians, reconsider any jargon you use and make sure it really is appropriate for your audience and that you have reasonable confidence that everyone who might be in that audience will understand it.

Librarians also tend to be verbose—and to use words like *verbose*. In general, try to avoid both. You don't have to dumb down your message but writing clearly and concisely will also avoid ambiguity and make it more likely that your core message gets through. Studying best practices for writing for the web and for business writing is worth your time. Both focus on using clear and concise language, an active voice, and a conversational tone, and emphasize the importance of formatting your message in easy-to-digest bites. This is the best approach for the majority of communications and reports you design.

Make It Aesthetically Pleasing

You don't have to be an artist to use the basics of good design in your documents. Symmetry and balance are key to any good design, including documents and communications. Make sure to balance text with graphics and leave plenty of white space between paragraphs and around graphics. Use normal margins in documents. This will improve reading comprehension for many readers. Also be aware that, for some readers, contrast between text and background is essential. This is true not only for readers with various reading challenges, but also for older readers. Choose a color scheme for your message and stick with it. Where appropriate, using the color palette of your organization is a good idea and helps to brand your message. And, it goes without saying, make sure that your communications have been proofread and are grammatically correct.

Repetition Is Key

Communication is often cited as a problem in large organizations, and libraries are no exception. In Regina's early days as an assessment librarian, when she asked about areas for possible assessment, the issue of communication came up more than any other. And yet, when Regina mentioned this to a colleague, she said, "We communicate just fine; they just don't like what they heard." The fact is sometimes people won't like your message or may have a hard time digesting it, but that is not the same thing as not hearing it at all. And the attitude that there is nothing you can do to improve communication gives your power away and puts the responsibility for communicating solely on the shoulders of your audience.

But there is an approach used by practitioners of neurolinguistic programming that can change the way you think about communication forever and give you back the power to communicate effectively. *The meaning of the communication is its effect.* This means that it doesn't matter what you intended to communicate, whatever the effect your communication had is what you actually communicated, regardless of your intention And if people don't receive your message, the effect is the same as if there was no communication at all. It doesn't matter that you sent them an e-mail. If they didn't read it or it didn't register, then you didn't communicate.

We've noticed that when we first share this approach with people, it tends to make them mad. "I can't control whether or not they read my e-mails!" Nope, you can't. But you can investigate what's going on. Are they inundated with too many e-mails? Would a different subject line catch their attention? Would formatting your e-mail a different way make a difference? Should you have a meeting instead? Do you need to have several meetings and e-mails? Taking this approach seems hard at first, but if you look at it as an adventure in discovery, it can truly empower you. And the alternative is throwing up your hands and saying there is nothing you can do about it.

John Kotter listed one of the key errors made by businesses when trying to implement change is "under-communicating the vision by a factor of ten."[20] This means that in most cases you probably need to communicate ten times more than you think you do. Not twice as much. Ten times more. Of course, knowing your audience is the cardinal rule and there are some cases where communicating that much would not be appropriate at all. Use your common sense. But in general, when it comes to communicating with your colleagues or with your users, more is more.

> When they are sick of hearing it, they've heard it for the first time.

Regina once gave a presentation on a website usability test at several meetings, tailored to each audience, in addition to sharing the results in a report and via e-mail. A colleague who had attended several of these meetings joked with her after the last one that Regina should come to his house for Thanksgiving because his parents were the only ones who hadn't heard it yet. That is when she knew her work was done. And if you think we just stated our basic premise—communicate more than you think you need to in four different ways—you are absolutely correct. See what we did there?

Finally, remember that true communication is always two-way. One definition of communication is "exchange of information." We live in a world where people talk at us a lot. In fact, it sometimes seems that we call communication is really just one person narrating the events of their day, or thoughts, or whatever, into the void. Remember that listening is also a part of communication, perhaps the most important part. In all of your communications and reporting, try to build in opportunities for feedback, whether it be on the content of your communication or its format. Audience feedback that you listen to and learn from will be far more valuable to you than anything we can say here.

Data Visualization

Now that we've outlined some basics for communications in general, let's go a little deeper and focus on some best practices for data visualization.

A simple definition of data visualization is "the graphical display of data." According to Michael Mahoney:

> The main goal of data visualization is to communicate information clearly and effectively through graphical means. It doesn't mean that data

visualization needs to look boring to be functional or extremely sophisticated to look beautiful. To convey ideas effectively, both aesthetic form and functionality need to go hand in hand, providing insights into a rather sparse and complex data set by communicating its key aspects in a more intuitive way. Yet designers often fail to achieve a balance between form and function, creating gorgeous data visualizations which fail to serve their main purpose — to communicate information.[21]

It bears emphasizing that "visualizations are often the main way complicated problems are explained to decision makers."[22] As discussed above, we often have only moments of someone's attention in which to get our point across. Decision-makers at all levels tend to be busy people. Realistically, you are lucky if you have their undivided attention for five minutes at a time. Learning to communicate complex ideas clearly, accurately, and quickly may be the best investment of your time you could make in life. Not just for library planning and assessment, but for every area of your life.

Data visualization is the art and science of the visual representation of data. It is a science because there are clear rules anyone can follow and an art because there is always at least a bit of serendipity, for lack of a better word, involved in the development of a truly inspired data visualization. But anyone can improve their data visualization by following a few basic tips.

"The purpose of visualization is insight, not pictures."—Ben Shneiderman[23]

Edward Tufte, a pioneer in the field of data visualization, defined some characteristics of good graphics. Good graphics:

1. Show the data
2. Induce the viewer to think about the substance rather than methodology or graphic design
3. Avoid distorting the data
4. Make large data sets coherent
5. Serve a reasonably clear purpose: description, exploration, tabulation, or decoration[24]

Tools for Data Visualization

When it comes to tools for creating data visualizations, our primary recommendation would be to focus on mastering Microsoft Excel first. In general, if you could only have one tool for all of your assessment and data needs, Excel is the one. Although more specialized tools exist, you can do everything you would ever need to do in assessment with nothing more than Excel. Taking the time to master it will pay the greatest dividends over the long term of anything you could learn. What's more, Excel is a tool that has been around for a long time and will probably persist into the future. There are also similar open source spreadsheet tools that anyone can use for free, although it's likely that if your organization can afford any tools at all, it will provide Excel.

Programs designed specifically for statistical analysis can be helpful. They allow you to do some things much more easily than you can in Excel, with the caveat that there can be a steeper learning curve with these programs. Some examples are SAS, SPSS, and R. For a freely available option, R is a good choice. We've found these programs to be more helpful for statistical analysis than for data visualization, but the two naturally go hand in hand.

Some relatively newer products created specifically for data visualization include Tableau, PowerBI, and, for a free option, Google Charts. Each of these is a bit different, but they were each created specifically for data visualization and in particular to create interactive visualizations or combine data to create dashboards. Interactive data visualizations can be a very powerful tool for supporting assessment in your organization. They can allow people without the data analysis skills of an assessment professional to interact with the data in a meaningful way and see trends and indicators that might otherwise be missed. The flipside of all of this is that these tools are generally more challenging to master. These tools are also spreadsheet-based, so again, mastering a spreadsheet program is still the best place to start.

Data guru Ann K. Emery contends that you can do beautiful, professional, data visualizations with nothing more than Excel and PowerPoint, which we have found to be the case. What's more, by using tools that most people are already somewhat familiar with, this approach is much simpler to master. Excel can produce a variety of wonderful visualizations, and PowerPoint can be used in lieu of more complex document design software. Simply format your PowerPoint slide to be the size of a normal document, create normal margins, and begin designing your document. PowerPoint is preferable to Word for this sort of document creation because it easier to precisely place text and graphics in PowerPoint than in Word.

If your tool doesn't let you create the visualization you want, use a different tool. Start first with what you want to convey and what you think the best way to do that for your target audience is. Sketch things out with a paper and pen first, if that's the only way to get your concept out. Then you can consider how best to represent it in a more formal way.

Ann K. Emery suggests three main rules for good data visualizations:

1. Know your audience.
2. Design graphics that can stand alone outside the context of a report or presentation.
3. Design graphics that communicate key messages.

KNOW YOUR AUDIENCE REDUX

We've already discussed the importance of knowing your audience in the context of general communications, and all of that still holds true when it comes to data visualizations. But there are a few more specific points to keep in mind when it comes to communicating data. Again, consider how technically minded your audience is when you consider specific choices such as whether viewers want aggregated or disaggregated data, how many decimal places are useful, how many points in time viewers need to see, and what types of comparisons are useful.

Some other specific suggestions from Emery are simple but powerful:

1. Avoid 3-D charts, diagonal text, and other hard-to-read/interpret effects.
2. Eliminate visual noise—grid lines, border lines, unnecessary tick marks on axes, redundant legends, etc.
3. Use font and color to brand your visualizations.
4. Use color to highlight key patterns.
5. Label data directly.
6. Use labels sparingly.
7. Visualizations should highlight significant findings or conclusions.
8. Use an appropriate level of precision.

9. Give viewers context and comparison data.

10. Use correct proportions to avoid distorting data.

11. Ensure data are intentionally ordered.[25]

An example, presented in the figures below, will illustrate the difference that these tips can make. Both present the same data—results from a user survey question about effective outreach mechanisms—and could make a very significant difference in a library's outreach efforts. But the first chart (figure 10.1) is unlikely to reach library staff or influence them to change their practices.

FIGURE 10.1

Column chart, presentation 1

The creator of this chart seems to have forgotten the primary purpose of graphically representing information: to promote its maximal impact on the viewer. Of course, data can't make an impact if it can't be absorbed and processed effectively. The disorienting three-dimensional representation and superfluous gridlines introduce unnecessary visual noise into a chart that should offer a clearer presentation of data than would be possible in text. When possible, data points should be presented in a way that makes sense either visually (e.g., in descending order), or by some other organizing mechanism (e.g., alphabetically). While there may be a principle at play here, it is not obvious, defeating one of the primary objectives of visual presentation of data.

The chart's two most egregious shortcomings, however, have to do with its labeling elements. First, presenting the percentages along the y-axis requires the viewer to constantly shift their focus back and forth between the columns and the labels to the left while trying to remember which data point each column represents. And that's assuming the viewer can decipher what, exactly, each data point is. Because the chart creator declined to edit the item descriptions in favor of presenting them in shortened form on the x-axis, they are largely useless. For goodness' sake, three different items read "news stories in/on the . . ." What? On the radio? On the web? In the newspaper? On television? Delivered by morse code? As a result, the findings as presented are not actionable. To be blunt, the time spent creating this chart was largely wasted.

The second chart (figure 10.2), however, conveys the exact same data in a way that is much more likely to have an impact.

FIGURE 10.2

Column chart, presentation 2

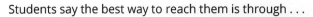

Students say the best way to reach them is through . . .

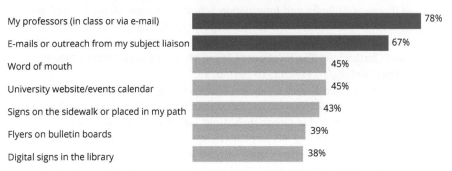

My professors (in class or via e-mail)	78%
E-mails or outreach from my subject liaison	67%
Word of mouth	45%
University website/events calendar	45%
Signs on the sidewalk or placed in my path	43%
Flyers on bulletin boards	39%
Digital signs in the library	38%

As you can see, removing unnecessary grid lines and legends, avoiding diagonal and hard-to-read text, directly labeling data, intentionally ordering the data, and presenting only the most actionable data can make a huge difference—you can do it all without using anything more than Excel (really, you *could* even do it in Word)!

Conclusion

Effective data visualization does not have to be difficult or mysterious, and these very simple principles can seem like magic to the uninitiated. We highly recommend checking out Ann K. Emery's website (https://depict datastudio.com/), which has much free information and many how-tos. If you can afford her workshops, they are excellent and well worth it.

> Perfection is finally attained not when there is no longer anything to add, but when there is no longer anything to take away.
>
> —Antoine de Saint-Exupéry, *Terre des Hommes* (1939)

NOTES

1. Stanford University, "Data Management Plans," Stanford Libraries, https://library.stanford.edu/research/data-management-services/data-management-plans.
2. Carol Tenopir, Robert J. Sandusky, Suzie Allard, and Ben Birch, "Research Data Management Services in Academic Research Libraries and Perceptions of Librarians," *Library and Information Science Research* 36, no. 2 (April 2014): 84–90, https://doi.org/10.1016/j.lisr.2013.11.003; Holly H. Yu, "The Role of Academic Libraries in Research Data Service (RDS) Provision: Opportunities and Challenges," *The Electronic Library* 35, no. 4 (August 2017): 783–97, https://doi.org/10.1108/EL-10-2016-0233.
3. Alexandre Ribas Semeler, Adilson Luiz Pinto, and Helen Beatriz Frota Rozados, "Data Science in Data Librarianship: Core Competencies of a Data Librarian," *Journal of Librarianship and Information Science* 51, no. 3 (November 2017): 771–80, https://doi.org/10.1177/0961000617742465.
4. Gareth Knight, "A Digital Curate's Egg: A Risk Management Approach to Enhancing Data Management Practices," *Journal of Web Librarianship* 6, no. 4 (2012): 228–50, https://doi.org/10.1080/19322909.2012.729992.
5. Tibor Kálmán, Danah Tonne, and Oliver Schmitt, "Sustainable Preservation for the Arts and Humanities," *New Review of Information Networking* 20, no. 1/2 (2015): 123–36, https://doi.org/10.1080/13614576.2015.1114831.
6. Knight, "A Digital Curate's Egg."
7. "LibInsight—Analyze Library Services and Make More Informed Service Decisions," SpringShare, https://www.springshare.com/libinsight/.
8. "ACRL Proficiencies for Assessment Librarians and Coordinators," Association of College and Research Libraries, January 23, 2017, www.ala.org/acrl/standards/assessment_proficiencies.

9. "Privacy," Advocacy, Legislation and Issues, American Library Association, June 13, 2008. www.ala.org/advocacy/privacy.

10. "Library Bill of Rights," Advocacy, Legislation and Issues, American Library Association, June 30, 2006, www.ala.org/advocacy/intfreedom/librarybill.

11. Laura B. Palumbo, Ron Jantz, Yu-Hung Lin, Aletia Morgan, Minglu Wang, Krista White, Ryan Womack, Yingting Zhang, and Yini Zhu, "Preparing to Accept Research Data: Creating Guidelines for Librarians," *Journal of EScience Librarianship* 4, no. 2 (2015): 1–11, https://doi.org/10.7191/jeslib.2015.1080; Yu, "Role of Academic Libraries in RDS."

12. Jason Vaughan, "Library Privacy Policies," *Library Technology Reports* 56, no. 6 (2020): 1–53.

13. Margaret E. Henderson, *Data Management: A Practical Guide for Librarians* (Lanham, MD: Rowman and Littlefield, 2017).

14. Henderson, *Data Management.*

15. Susan Hickson, Maria Connor, Kylie Ann Poulton, Joanna Richardson, and Malcolm Wolski, "Modifying Researchers' Data Management Practices," *IFLA Journal* 42, no. 4 (2016): 253–65; Robert B. Cook, Yaxing Wei, Leslie A. Hook, Suresh K. S. Vannan, and John J. McNelis, "Preserve: Protecting Data for Long-Term Use," in *Ecological Informatics: Data Management and Knowledge Discovery,* edited by Friedrich Recknagel and William K. Michener (Cham: Springer International Publishing, 2018), 89–113, https://doi.org/10.1007/978-3-319-59928-1_6; Stanford University Libraries, "Data Management Plans," https://library.stanford.edu/research/data-management-services/data-management-plans.

16. Knight, "A Digital Curate's Egg."

17. Starr Hoffman, "Creating an Assessment Plan and Data Inventory: Aligning and Managing Success Metrics," presented at the 2019 ACRL Conference, Cleveland, OH. https://docs.google.com/presentation/d/1qhU8UcMvwFzkZMauZYHdlnqvgWi9UtstuOexFyCETc4/edit#slide=id.p.

18. Hoffman, "Creating an Assessment Plan and Data Inventory."

19. Ann K. Emery, *Great Graphs,* Depict Data Studio, https://depictdatastudio.com; Evelyn Jenkinson, "Communication Best Practices: Or 'Everything I Know about Communications I Learned the Hard Way,'" presented at the Western Connecticut Health Network, February 2013, https://www.slideshare.net/ejenkinson/communication-best-practices-west-conn-presentation; Megan Oakleaf, *Academic Library Value: The Impact Starter Kit* (Chicago: American Library Association, 2017).

20. John P. Kotter, "Leading Change: Why Transformation Efforts Fail," *Harvard Business Review* 73, no. 2 (1995): 63.

21. Michael Mahoney, "The Art and Science of Data Visualization," *Medium,* October 14, 2019, https://towardsdatascience.com/the-art-and-science-of-data-visualization-6f9d706d673e.

22. Mahoney, "Art and Science of Data Visualization."

23. Jessica Hullman, "'The Purpose of Visualization Is Insight, Not Pictures': An Interview with Ben Shneiderman," *ACM Interactions*, https://interactions .acm.org/blog/view/the-purpose-of-visualization-is-insight-not-pictures-an -interview-with-ben; Ben Shneiderman, "Encounters with HCI Pioneers: A Personal History and Photo Journal," *Synthesis Lectures on Human-Centered Informatics* 12, no. 1 (2019): i–187, https://doi.org/10.2200/ S00889ED1V01Y201812HCI041.
24. Edward R. Tufte, *The Visual Display of Quantitative Information*, 2nd ed. (Cheshire, CT: Graphics Press, 2001).
25. Emery, *Great Graphs*.

Collaboration and Relationship Management

- Culture of Assessment
- Organizational Structure of Assessment
- General Strategies for Effective Collaboration
- Conclusion

Effective planning and assessment in libraries and information centers require a certain combination of so-called "hard" and "soft" skills. Although the hard skills, such as performing qualitative and quantitative research, data analysis, and statistical reporting, are often the focus of literature and education in this area, none of those such skills will ultimately have much of an impact without an even greater grounding in the so-called soft skills of communication, collaboration, leadership, management, and administration. As figure 11.1 makes clear, our survey respondents indicated that these skills are tremendously important.

FIGURE 11.1

FIGURE 11.1

Survey of assessment librarians. "In my
position, I must know how to…"

In my position, I must know how to . . .

Manage team-based projects	91.2%
Plan and lead meetings	89.2%
Mentor (staff, colleagues, students, etc.)	73.0%
Manage group dynamics	72.3%
Resolve conflict	68.2%
Supervise staff	48.6%

In this chapter, we will focus on these elements, which might be loosely grouped under the heading of creating and maintaining an organizational culture of assessment. First, we must explore how to define a culture of assessment, how to recognize if your organization has one, and how to go about creating one if it doesn't. We'll follow this with a discussion of where assessment "lives" in the organizational structure of a library, including the most common models and how organizational assessment structures tend to evolve over time. This will lead naturally into a discussion of the use of matrix leadership by assessment professionals as well as strategies for effective collaboration and some good practices for working with assessment committees and groups.

Culture of Assessment

A foundational goal for any organization that wants to operate by an evidence-based decision-making model is to create a culture of assessment. As an assessment professional, working in an organization with a robust culture of assessment greatly expands the scope of what you can accomplish. This may take some time to establish, but once it takes hold in your organization, your job will suddenly become much easier. It's a goal worth pursuing and one whose accomplishment can sneak up on you.

What is a culture of assessment?

"A Culture of Assessment is an organizational environment in which decisions are based on facts, research, and analysis, and where services are planned and delivered in ways that maximize positive outcomes and impacts for customers and stakeholders. A Culture of Assessment exists in organizations where staff care to know what results they produce and how those results relate to customers' expectations. Organizational mission, values, structures, and systems support behavior that is performance and learning focused."[1]

"In a culture of assessment, assessment becomes the norm and a valued part of planning and teaching. New services are planned for with consideration for how they will be assessed. The library doesn't just collect data; it acts on and learns from that data."[2]

"'Assessment culture' is code for not just doing assessment but liking it."[3]

Wendy Weiner describes an organization with a culture of assessment as having "a set of mindsets that help create a positive response to the wider call for accountability."[4] In definitions of the phrase "culture of assessment," the word *mindset* recurs frequently; Greg MacAyeal defines it as "a set of attitudes, approaches, and understandings."[5] As you work to establish a culture of assessment in your organization, what you are really trying to accomplish in concrete terms is to change the attitudes, behavior, and shared vocabulary of your staff. As noted above, none of these are things that change overnight. And changing attitudes and behavior is not as clear-cut an activity as, say, calculating statistical significance. The latter has an established set of steps and a clear right or wrong answer. The former is more of an art than a science, but there is also a budding consensus on some ways to begin to successfully make the necessary shifts.

Signs of a Culture of Assessment

The above definitions are still somewhat amorphous in trying to pin down what a culture of assessment looks like in the real world. Weiner has identified the following elements that are more concrete evidence of a culture of assessment:

- clear general goals
- common use of assessment-related terms

- staff ownership of assessment programs
- ongoing professional development in assessment skills
- administrative encouragement of assessment
- practical assessment plans
- systematic assessment
- inclusion of assessment in plans and budgets
- consistent use of assessment data
- celebration of successes[6]

Organizational culture in general is set from the top down. Hence the repeated emphasis on administrative support and buy-in throughout this chapter. Although you may not have control over what your administrators do (assuming you are not an administrator yourself), you can track their activity and provide feedback. While the research in this area is still emerging, Meredith Farkas et al. conducted a survey of academic libraries at four-year institutions in the United States and found the following elements to be most likely to be associated with a perceived culture of assessment in an organization:

- Library has clear expectations for assessment.
- Library has an assessment plan.
- Library leadership uses assessment data systematically in decision-making.
- Librarians, staff, and administrators have a shared understanding of the purpose of assessment in the library.
- Library staff and faculty are adequately supported in their assessment work.
- Librarians use assessment data to improve practice.[7]

In addition, written comments from this survey suggested that "access to professional development/training/education" were key to developing a culture of assessment. Another important element suggested by these findings is the availability and transparency of assessment data (and, as we've discussed, any library data is potentially assessment data). The following section breaks down these findings into actionable steps you can take toward establishing a culture of assessment in your organization.

Practical Steps Toward a Culture of Assessment

Establishing a culture of assessment involves making a significant change to your organizational culture. Such a major change can present quite a challenge, and there are some well-defined pitfalls. In 1995, John Kotter wrote a piece called "Leading Change: Why Transformation Efforts Fail" that became one of *Harvard Business Review*'s most requested articles. If you have any experience of organizational change efforts, the eight most common errors that Kotter identified may be all too familiar. They are:

- not establishing a great enough sense of urgency
- not creating a powerful enough guiding coalition
- lacking a vision
- under-communicating the vision by a factor of ten
- not removing obstacles to the new vision
- not systematically planning for and creating short-term wins
- declaring victory too soon
- not anchoring changes in the corporation's culture[8]

As we detail suggestions for establishing a culture of assessment, you will notice that each of them addresses at least one, if not several, of these common errors.

1. Include assessment in annual planning and strategic planning documents and reports.

   We've never encountered a group of librarians more motivated to embrace assessment than those working at a university in danger of losing its accreditation due to not complying with assessment requirements. Although the library had done nothing wrong in this case, nevertheless they had a true sense of urgency around getting up and running with assessment as fast as possible. That organization had already skipped over the bulk of resistance to change because everyone in the entire organization had a very good understanding of why it mattered and a palpable deadline looming.

   While you don't need to be in a situation as extreme as this in order to establish a culture of assessment, you do need a clear and shared understanding that assessment is immediately important. Often, an organization may have similar, if less extreme, external pressures spurring change, but one simple way to create a sense of urgency is simply for your administrators and upper management to embrace and set expectations for assessment activities by including it in annual and strategic planning documents and reports.

Building assessment into reporting is a very effective way to incorporate it into the daily routines of an organization. If staff know that they will be expected to include not just a report of what they have accomplished, but also measures of how effective or efficient those accomplishments were, or other established metrics, they will automatically build it into their workflows. This will take time, and obviously you shouldn't expect them to include these items without plenty of advance notice. But over time, if assessment reporting is a consistent expectation, it will become a natural and assumed part of most processes.

Tracking progress toward strategic goals can also be a powerful experience for the entire organization. If this is done in a regular and systematic way, it can transform an organization and make your strategic plans truly effective. But you can't wait to assess your successes or challenges until your strategic plan expires three to five years later. This is perhaps the most common mistake organizations make when it comes to strategic planning. If everyone is expected to regularly report on progress toward strategic goals, however, those goals themselves will become energized for the entire organization.

Although staff may balk at this type of reporting at first, you may be surprised to find that over time they embrace it, particularly if their accomplishments and progress are appropriately celebrated.

2. Assign ownership of assessment.

   If your organization has hired you as an assessment librarian, obviously it has already made great strides on this step. But in organizations that cannot afford a position dedicated solely or even partly to assessment as a formal part of the job description, there are other approaches to assigning ownership. This might be in the form of establishing a formal standing assessment committee or establishing more temporary working groups to perform specific assessments. In either scenario, assessment should also have an official home in the organization's administration, either by being part of administration or reporting to a specified administrator and being accountable to them for results.

In addition, in larger organizations, it can be a good strategy to develop assessment "reps" in each department or throughout the organization in a way that makes sense for your particular environment. This can be a formal or informal assignment. These individuals can serve on an assessment committee or simply be the designated assessment contacts for their area, taking on responsibility for collecting data from their departments, ensuring assessment is included in planning and reporting documents, and providing feedback in the assessment planning process. Over time, some individuals may express a natural interest in assessment, particularly if you arrange organizational trainings on assessment methods and tools periodically. Keep an eye out for these folks, as they can become valuable resources and welcome allies.

3. Develop a shared vocabulary, understanding, and expectations around assessment.

This goal will take time and should happen organically through incorporating assessment into planning and reporting processes, offering assessment-related training, and presenting assessment findings at meetings and through widely shared reports. Help it along by being consistent in the terminology and phrasing you use and through often repeating the basic concepts around why assessment is important for your organization. This sort of repetition reinforces these concepts in those who have heard them before, but also introduces them to new staff and gives them a chance to get on the same page. Incorporating information about assessment and about your strategic plan into any onboarding procedures you have for new staff is another way to make sure everyone is exposed to these concepts and has an understanding of their importance in your organization.

4. Create an assessment plan and communicate regularly about assessment efforts and outcomes.

We wrote in an earlier chapter about the elements of an assessment plan and how to create one based on and guided by your organization's mission and strategic goals. But creating the plan is just the first step. Once you have your plan in hand, you must not only follow the plan, but also share your goals and progress regularly. Some options for doing this include sending regular e-mails to the whole organization to share your progress, including updates on progress at key meetings, publicizing any meetings to the whole organization, and scheduling open meetings to present findings and outcomes of assessment activities. Include not only the results, but also the context for why the assessment activities are important, why you chose to use a particular approach, and any outcomes, changes, or realizations that result from assessment activities.

5. Offer regular opportunities for staff to access professional development, training, and education in assessment methods and techniques.

You can do this in a number of ways, depending on the resources available to you and what makes sense for your organization. If your budget allows, arranging workshops on key tools for library staff and funding travel to conferences or other trainings that are assessment-related are impactful. But if that's not possible, you can create trainings as you master tools and methods or point staff to freely available resources and arrange study groups or debriefings to help carve out time for learning. This is also a good way to foster an assessment community of practice in your organization, an informal network of those with a shared interest who learn from and teach each other.

6. Work toward making data accessible, transparent, and usable.

This action is phrased purposefully. It would be easy to say, "make data accessible." But you may find that this is easier said than done. If your organization has a formal data management plan or even an existing data management system, and it all works well and is easily accessible and usable by all in the organization, then you should seriously thank your lucky stars. This situation is the exception more than the rule. Library data tends to be heavily siloed, that is, it exists in many different systems, and different people throughout the organization are gatekeepers for different types of data. If your organization is in the early stages of making assessment data widely available, start small and build on your successes. For instance, the first place to start would be to make sure that any statistical data your organization reports regularly (e.g., to ACRL, ARL, IPEDS surveys, etc.) is easily available to your staff and users.

7. Celebrate success.

This is perhaps the most overlooked and yet most important element in creating a culture of assessment. Indeed, all too often organizations never stop to reflect on their accomplishments, but rather focus on what still needs to be done, or on what didn't go well. Although that sort of reflection is important and has its place, we've found that little is more powerful in motivating future behavior than recognizing and rewarding the behavior that you want to encourage. Often the best reward is simply acknowledgment and sincere appreciation. Giving staff an opportunity and creating forums for sharing their accomplishments can also be surprisingly effective. In general, staff are proud of their hard work and may welcome a chance to share it with others if given an opportunity to do so in a way that doesn't add to their workloads excessively. For instance, one of the most surprisingly successful things we did in tracking progress toward strategic goals was to have an annual party to celebrate our accomplishments and putting a brief sentence about each accomplishment that had been achieved on a rotating slide deck that played on a couple of TVs in the party room. Staff were unexpectedly mesmerized by this display and got very excited when they saw their own accomplishments come up. Don't assume staff are too cynical to appreciate this sort of basic acknowledge. Of course, providing free food always helps! Experiment and see what your staff respond to.

Organizational Structure of Assessment

Because assessment is still an emerging field and a relatively new practice in many organizations, there is no one cookie-cutter way that assessment shows up in an organization. Who does assessment and how it's done varies according to many factors, particularly the size and type of organization. But there is some research and some anecdotal observation that give us an idea of how assessment structures and practices evolve in larger organizations.

Typically, assessment may start as a special project and, as such, a group or committee may be formed to perform a particular assessment. This group may then evolve into a standing committee or working group. Eventually, an individual may be given assessment as a formal part of their duties, either part or full time. In larger organizations, this may eventually give way to an entire assessment department, with specific positions such as assessment data analyst, assessment librarian, user experience librarian, and others.

> However, because assessment is structured in an organization, it is crucial that librarians and staff performing assessment have strong ties and communication with the organization's administrators.

Ideally, assessment positions would live in administration and report directly to higher-level administrators. This makes sense if you consider assessment to be fundamentally an administrative practice. The two main purposes of assessment support this view: to demonstrate the value of an organization, and to facilitate evidence-based decision-making. Both of these broad categories are fundamentally administrative activities, although they can also be used by anyone at any level.

We've discussed in previous chapters the importance of strategic assessment and of tying your assessment activities to the mission and goals of your organization. If you are lucky, your organization has a well-articulated strategic plan that is current and reflects the real goals of your library. But as we've also discussed previously, this is not always the case. This is another reason why close ties to administration are so important for assessment professionals. Wherever your position lives in your organization, it's advisable to make every effort to form a good working relationship with your library leaders.

The results of assessment may have multiple audiences: internal library staff and administrators, library users (members of the community, students, faculty, etc.), parents, university administrators, accrediting bodies, state and federal legislators, donors, alumni, other funders, library board members, members of Friends of the library groups, and so on. In some cases, you can communicate directly with an audience, such as internal staff or your users, in order to better understand their priorities and how best to structure assessment and report your results. But in other cases, such as with board members or university administrators, it may not be possible for you to survey them or conduct focus groups to better understand their concerns and what types of data are compelling for them. This is where a close relationship with your library leaders comes in. It can be easy to think of stakeholders as a monolith or to not really think about them at all when planning and reporting assessment. But the truth is every administrator, board member, and legislator is also a human being. They have individual quirks and preferences. The library leaders who interact with them personally are in the best position to help you understand the individual personalities that are making decisions about funding and other crucial elements affecting your organization. If these individuals are going to be the audience for some of your assessment efforts, you need to understand their true priorities, as well as what types of data and reporting are compelling to them. Sometimes, these things are clearly spelled out in strategic plans, but there are also unspoken priorities that only your library administrators may know.

Assessment Committees

Because of the way assessment tends to evolve in organizations, many new assessment professionals inherit standing assessment committees and may face challenges and uncertainty as to how to best utilize these groups. A few good practices have been suggested, based on preliminary research:

1. Develop clear goals for the group, including a stated charge or mission.

2. Put together a team that is representative, inclusive, and the right size. (Between three and twelve is generally the best size for an effective team.)

3. Set regular meeting times and share the group's agendas and meeting minutes.

4. Cultivate crucial organizational support (and feedback) at the highest level.

5. Establish how the group will work and define each member's role.

6. Give members real work, not busywork.

7. Aim for small sustainable projects with easily measurable impacts. Break down larger projects into steps with measurable impacts.

8. Communicate results consistently.[9]

These practices are definitely a good starting point for working with assessment committees. As with any group, having clearly defined goals and a clear scope for the team is important. For any standing group, it is advisable to have a written charge that clearly states what the purpose of the group is, how membership is determined and how long a membership term lasts, to whom the group is accountable, who ultimately directs and evaluates the group's efforts, and other administrative information, such as where the group's minutes and other shared documents will be stored. For groups with revolving membership, it's particularly important to make a plan for document sharing. For groups that are formed for the short term, a written charge may be enough. Standing groups should consider creating new goals on an annual basis and reviewing and, if needed, revising their charge from time to time.

Who should be on your team? That very much depends on the purpose and scope of the team. If you are forming a working group to complete a specific project, such as a team charged with testing the library's website, you would want to include members who could perform the technical aspects of this project, as well as representatives of the various stakeholders who will be concerned with the contents and functioning of the library's site. If you are forming a standing group that will act as an advisory and planning group instead of or in addition to performing assessment projects, you may want to take a different approach and include a representative from each major department or area of function in your organization.

Keep in mind that studies show a group is best kept between three and twelve individuals for optimal functioning. If you must have a group larger than this for political or administrative reasons, consider forming smaller working teams to actually accomplish any important tasks, such as drafting plans or working on assessment projects, and then vet their products with the larger group.

Obviously, it's important to consider inclusivity and representation in all of our activities. Making a team as diverse as possible is especially important when it comes to assessment. One of your greatest challenges is being aware of your assumptions. This is true for absolutely everyone. Assumptions are arguably a main reason we even need to perform formal assessment. We assume we know what users want and how they are going to behave and design our services and choose our resources based on those assumptions. Perhaps most damagingly of all, we tend to assume that all our users are alike and that they are all like us. A diverse team can help you be aware of your own blind spots and see things that you would otherwise never notice. It's particularly desirable that your team be diverse and inclusive, not only in terms of representing different functions in the library, but also in terms of representing cultural, racial, and religious diversity; gender and sexual orientation; and generational diversity. Generational diversity, in particular, is frequently overlooked but often represents a significant divergence in outlook, preference, and approach.

A word here about choosing team members. All things being equal, if you have the choice, choose individuals with whom you work well and who work well together—especially if you are new to the job or if you are attempting to get an assessment program off the ground. Small, consistent wins will be important in gaining ground and eventually creating the culture of assessment that is the ultimate goal for your organization. Often, individuals who are known to be difficult to work with may be suggested to serve on a team, sometimes with an eye toward getting their cooperation or heading off anticipated objections. This can be a good strategy in some cases, but again, unless you have a compelling or strategic reason to do otherwise, do yourself a favor and choose to work with people who are known to be team players and who deliver.

General best practices for successful meetings should be followed when working by committee or in teams. The basics are not new but bear repeating here:

- Have a set agenda for every meeting and share it ahead of the meeting so that attendees can appropriately prepare.
- Set a recurring meeting time, if possible, at the same time each week, month, or at whatever interval makes sense for your group and project.
- Take minutes at each meeting and share them, ideally not only with those at the meeting, but also with your whole organization.

- Determine a document-sharing protocol if your organization does not already have one in place. Storing all documents related to the committee in the same place, ideally in a drive that can be accessed by all the members, if not everyone in the organization, will save lots of trouble in the long run and also make transitions in the group easier. Google Docs, Sharepoint, or other document-sharing options can work well.
- Establish a website or even a LibGuide with some basic information about the group and links to appropriate documents, especially if your document-sharing system doesn't have a landing page to make navigation easier.
- Establish central document sharing for assessment reports and information about past projects, such as project plans, IRB approvals, and other administrative documents. Ideally, all your assessment information should live in one place, including information about assessment that was done by others in your organization. This can be an invaluable source of information for future projects and save time for everyone, as well as being a record of what you have done in the past. (You should, of course, have secure storage for all your data, but keep in mind that raw data should not be stored in a public place.)

It's very important that your group has the full support of your organization's administrators and leaders. What does this mean, exactly? First of all, it means that the group is formed at the direction of or with the express approval of administrators, and the charge of the group has been approved at this level. Ideally, the goals and aims of the group have been thoroughly discussed with and approved by leadership. It's also important to clearly establish who has ultimate oversight of the group and to whom the group is ultimately accountable. If your administrators are skeptical of the group, or worse, openly critical or unsupportive, or even just indifferent, you probably won't accomplish much. The support of administration and leadership also extends to practical support, which includes fully funding equipment and activities and encouraging and supporting staff to take time to participate in the group and the group's activities. Depending on the nature of the group's charge, especially if it is a working group, the activities could take a significant amount of its members' time. Unless there is full, explicit support at the highest level, it's unlikely that managers will support their staff spending time serving on the group. Without administrative support, it's also unlikely that the outcomes of the group's activities will be acted upon. Administrative support will also ensure that the group's goals are strategically aligned with the mission and goals of the organization as a whole. Yet again, close relationships with administration are key.

A good strategy, especially when trying to get a group, or even an entire assessment program, off the ground, is to aim for manageable, sustainable, realistic goals that can still make an impact, perhaps in small but key or measurable ways. In general, change is hard in large, historically successful organizations. Change is hard for humans in general, for that matter. But a study of behavior change science can give us a few good principles to start with. When the goal is to make a large change, it is, ironically, best to start small. For one thing, a large change is more likely to fail. If a change is too big, requires too much of a shift in behavior, processes and procedures, and mindset, there are too many places where it can go wrong. One failure can turn people off from investing more time and effort into it. But on the other hand, people like to invest in a winner. If you can demonstrate small early successes, others may be more likely to get on board for your next project. Also, it's easier to scale up from something that is already successful and well-established. As an example, let's say that your administrators would like staff to include assessment outcomes and stats in their annual reports. Giving people one clear and achievable piece to include the first year makes it part of the workflow. Once that is established, you can scale up over time to include the full data that you would like to have there. Likewise, if you have one short user survey that gets a very wide response, which allows you to make a change based on that feedback, staff will be more likely to work with you on your next survey and users will be more likely to respond to your next survey.

Matrix Leadership

Unless you are an administrator who is also charged with performing and leading assessment efforts, chances are you have few, if any, direct reports. Many assessment librarians start off with a department of one—themselves. But even if you are working within or leading an assessment department, the reality is that you will not be supervising everyone you need to work with. Assessment eventually requires the participation and collaboration of nearly everyone in your organization. The job of an assessment professional is to be

an expert on assessment. But assessment touches every function in the organization, and you cannot possibly be an expert on every single job, service,
and resource in the library. At the same time, it is necessary to have access to
expertise in the things you want to assess. Ergo, you will have to collaborate
with those who are experts on what they do in order to apply your expertise
at assessment.

This is why assessment positions are often considered matrix leadership
positions. When Regina first began as an assessment librarian, as a department of one, it occurred to her that she needed everyone's cooperation but
was no one's boss. This is the reality many assessment professionals face. You
must lead the organization in assessment efforts and you must lead across the
organization. Sometimes, you must even lead your own leaders. This can be
tricky, to say the least.

General Strategies for Effective Collaboration

When working within your organization, the importance of building and nur-
turing good relationships cannot be overstated. Key to these relationships
is trust and communication. Trust, as in all healthy relationships, will take
time to build. This is why it is a good practice to build social capital before
you need it. In other words, begin establishing those trusting relationships
with as many throughout your organization as possible, well before you need
to collaborate with them. The fact is that there is very little in the realm of
library assessment that you can do completely on your own. You will need
the cooperation of others in your organization to gain access to necessary
data, to understand the details of what you are trying to assess, and to implement the insights gained through assessment.

A first step to building strong relationships is to put yourself in the shoes
of those you are working with. Try to see things from their perspective. Informal polls of those we've worked with over the years suggest that the greatest
perceived barriers to assessment are lack of knowledge or skills, too little
time, lack of clear expectations, and lack of trust. And the often-unspoken
barrier is the fear of being judged and found wanting. Those unfamiliar with
assessment can feel very threatened by it. They may also interpret assessment
that shows something is no longer working as being a criticism of years of

work and ways of doing things, without considering that what once worked very well can change over time. In all your interactions, begin to address the issue of trust first because you won't make much headway on anything else if you don't. Following are some suggestions for building trust that we have found effective over the years.

Guard Your Integrity at All Costs

As we've discussed in previous chapters, there are many opportunities to be purposely or inadvertently unethical with assessment data. And it's possible that you could face pressure from your peers or superiors to knowingly misrepresent data or findings to satisfy their agenda. So, start early practicing being Switzerland. Be as neutral as possible in your organization by being scrupulously faithful to the data. To do this well, you will have to examine and understand your own inherent biases, which can be a difficult and ongoing process. If you make a mistake, own it. Admit you were wrong and do what you can to correct it. Be open to others' opinions and ideas, even if your first instinct is to say no. Be a true scientist: observe, question, test, and iterate. Be ready to change your ideas based on what you find. Try new things and take calculated risks and be honest about the outcomes, even, and especially, if they aren't what you expected. If you do these things consistently, over time, people will come to think of you as being a person of integrity. This will be perhaps your greatest asset. Your colleagues will trust and value what you say because they will know it is evidence-based and non-partisan.

Speak Openly to People's Fears and Reassure Them

If assessment is a new practice in your organization, or if you are new to the organization, assume that people may have misgivings. One thing Regina likes to do at the beginning of any talk with folks new to assessment, or new to her, is to say:

> *You* are the expert on your job. It's my job to be an expert at assessment. I can't be an expert on everything that is done in this library, so therefore I can't effectively perform assessment in your area without your help. In all our work together, your expertise on what you do will always take precedence.

Likewise, at the very beginning of a project, it may be helpful to affirm that how things were done in the past was likely the right way to do it, at that time.

Get to Know People, Be Friendly, but Be Authentic

This speaks to the concept of building social capital before you need it. In brief: make friends. Get to know people, smile, say hello and call them by name when you see them, stop and chat from time to time. Having strong collegial relationships with people throughout your organization can smooth over a lot of potentially difficult patches. It sounds simplistic, but if people like you or just have generally positive associations with you, chances are that they will be more willing to do you a favor, get that old data from that outdated system that you need, take your survey, and, again, trust you. But there is a caveat here: the most important thing is to do what feels authentic to you. Because if you are not authentic, people will sense it and your efforts will backfire. So take this advice with a grain of salt and do what feels natural to you. If you are someone who is reserved or would like to increase your social skills, a good place to start is the book *First Impressions: What You Don't Know about How Others See You* by Ann Demarais and Valerie White. Give it a try and you may be surprised at the results.

Cultivate the "There Is No Failure, Only Feedback" Attitude

Another barrier to assessment is that people fear doing things wrong, making mistakes, not being perfect. This is a somewhat universal human trait. No one likes to fail, and many people are afraid to try something new for fear of looking foolish or failing. The reality is that assessment is always an iterative process. No matter how long you've been doing it, invariably as soon as you launch a study, you will notice three things you wish you'd done differently. And when you start looking at your data, you will likewise notice areas for improvement in your design, things you left out, new avenues of inquiry. Cultivate the attitude for yourself and for others that this is perfectly normal. It's part of the process. Regina believes she hasn't really even done an assessment until she learns something that surprises her. Relish those surprises, seek them, and welcome them. If you discover that your whole project is worthless because of a mistake (which will probably never happen, there is always something to be gained), celebrate what you learned and how you will never ever make that same mistake again. And you won't. You will make totally new mistakes every time. And it will still be okay. Regina personally makes a practice of taking exaggerated notice of when she's wrong about something as a way of modeling for others that it is okay to be wrong and okay to make a mistake, as long as you take responsibility for your mistake and do what you can to fix it and not make the same mistake again. We read the phrase "there is no failure, only feedback" in a management book some years ago and started saying it almost as a joke, but we were surprised at how people responded to that concept and thrived in an atmosphere where it wasn't really possible to fail because the concept of failure was transformed into something most librarians feel very positive about: information.[10] Over time, this has become the motto of Regina's assessment department and committee. Now, they genuinely approach assessment as an exciting journey of discovery so that individuals throughout the organization are at the least not threatened by it and in many cases downright enthusiastic about it.

Conclusion

In closing, it is our hope that this book provides practical information and support for those with an interest in the planning and assessment journey. We hope we've achieved our goals in this text: to provide a solid foundation, suggest avenues for further study, and communicate our own enthusiasm for and enjoyment of planning and assessment. Although this might at first seem like an intimidating subject, being interested and curious are the most important qualifications for success in this field. You can learn everything else (we're still learning all the time)! In fact, that's our most important suggestion: keep learning.

NOTES

1. Amos Lakos and Shelley Phipps, "Creating a Culture of Assessment: A Catalyst for Organizational Change," *portal: Libraries and the Academy* 4, no. 3 (July 1, 2004): 352.
2. Meredith Gorran Farkas, "Building and Sustaining a Culture of Assessment: Best Practices for Change Leadership," *Reference Services Review* 41, no. 1 (2013): 15.

3. Daniel Ennis, "Contra Assessment Culture," *Assessment Update* 22, no. 2 (April 2010): 2; 15.

4. Wendy F. Weiner, "Establishing a Culture of Assessment," *Academe* 95, no. 4 (2009): 28–32.

5. Greg MacAyeal, "A Culture of Assessment: Five Mindsets," *College and Research Libraries News* 75, no. 6 (2014): 311.

6. Weiner, "Establishing a Culture of Assessment," 29–31.

7. Meredith Gorran Farkas, Lisa Janicke Hinchliffe, and Amy Harris Houk, "Bridges and Barriers: Factors Influencing a Culture of Assessment in Academic Libraries," *College and Research Libraries* 76, no. 2 (March 2015): 162–64.

8. John P. Kotter, "Leading Change: Why Transformation Efforts Fail," *Harvard Business Review* 73, no. 2 (April 1995): 59–67.

9. Michelle Brannen, Sojourna Cunningham, and Regina Mays, "Assessment Committees: Good Practices from ARL Libraries," *Performance Measurement and Metrics* 17, no. 3 (January 1, 2016): 233–34.

10. Sue Knight, *NLP at Work: Neuro Linguistic Programming: The Difference That Makes a Difference in Business*, 2nd ed. (Boston: Nicholas Brealey Publishing, 2002), 245.

FURTHER READING

Demarais, Ann, and Valerie White. *First Impressions: What You Don't Know about How Others See You*. New York: Bantam, 2005.

Sample Library Assessment Plan

Library Assessment Plan FY21–23

Introduction

The mission of the assessment program at the XYZ Library is to foster continual improvement in the Library's services and resources and to support the Library in fulfilling its mission. Well-designed and well-executed assessment will identify areas for improvement and track progress toward our goals, as well as help illustrate the value of the Library to the community we serve.

Since it is not possible to assess everything, priorities for assessment must be decided strategically. The assessment program will be guided by the following guiding principles:

Meaningful—Assessment activities should look at areas that matter, in ways that will yield meaningful evidence.

Necessary—Assessment activities should be necessary, focusing on areas where improvement or information is needed and will make a difference.

Actionable—Assessment should focus on areas where action can actually be taken based on the results.

Simplicity—Although research and solutions should be as complex as necessary to adequately address issues, the simplest approaches and solutions that meet all needs are best.

Evidence-based—All our activities should begin and end with well conducted research. Our activities should be guided at all times by evidence.

Inclusiveness—Our activities rely on participation by all members of the Library staff and should include and value the input of departments and staff throughout the Library, as well as the input of our users.

User-centered—Our ultimate goal is to improve the user experience and help the Library to constantly improve at meeting their needs.

Integrity—Assessment activities should be guided by ethical behavior, accountability, and honesty. At all times, the program will be faithful to methods and evidence considered scientifically rigorous and accurate.

Structure and Roles for Library Assessment

Assessment Librarian

With advice from the Library Director and Library Leadership Team, the Assessment Librarian manages the Library's assessment program through leadership of the Assessment Committee, working with project teams to implement assessment research, and providing statistical analysis and reporting of project results.

In addition, the Assessment Librarian is available as a consultant to any Library staff in need of support for assessment project design, implementation, analysis, and reporting. The Assessment Librarian also determines the need for assessment-related training for staff and provides it.

Assessment Committee

The mission of the Assessment Committee is to provide support for the achievement of the Library's strategic goals and to facilitate continual improvement in meeting user needs by identifying assessment priorities, planning data-driven assessment activities, and communicating and acting on assessment results.

Members: Group members participate on project teams or may be assigned other assessment tasks, such as statistics work, environmental scanning, organizational communication, or training.

Chair: Assessment Librarian

Meetings: Regular meetings occur on a monthly basis.

Project Teams

Project Teams are formed to plan and implement specific projects, to interact with the project advisory group, and to report results. Teams will provide presentations and discussions of assessment results that are open to all in the organization. It is important to include librarians and staff from throughout the Library in assessment projects to spread knowledge and understanding of assessment processes, to focus assessment in directions having high priority for the organization, and to provide staff to implement the projects.

Members: The Project Teams include members of the Assessment Committee and other Library staff outside of the Assessment Committee as appropriate for that project.

Leaders: If feasible, a member of the Assessment Committee will lead the project team with advice and guidance from the Assessment Librarian. Team leadership will be decided on a project-by-project basis.

Project Advisory Group: A small group of stakeholders may be named for each project. Responsibilities of the Project Advisory Group include advice and support for resources, goals, and the implementation plan for the assessment project.

Project Charters: The team chairperson prepares a charter to define each project and meets with the Project Advisory Group for approval to implement.

Role of Administration

Library Administration and Department Heads play an advisory, approval, and resource allocation role to the Assessment Committee. The Assessment

Committee meets with the Library Leadership group two to three times a year to discuss the assessment plan for the upcoming period.

Role of Library Staff

This Library Assessment Plan is a big-picture plan and should not interfere with Library staff's individual and departmental assessment activities. Each department may want to explore developing an assessment plan of their own to focus on their specific assessment needs. The Assessment Librarian is available to consult on this as well as to provide individual consultations. Communication of assessment research results to the Library as a whole is valued. Staff are encouraged to share results widely and make reports to library-wide meetings. Copies of assessment research reports are welcomed by the Library Director and Assessment Librarian.

Assessment Program Priorities—FY21–23

Through meetings with Library faculty and staff, consideration of past assessment efforts and results, and guided by the Library's Strategic Plan, the Assessment Committee has identified the following areas as priorities for assessment:

Facilities

A major priority for the Library is improvement of our physical spaces. Space itself is at a premium, which means that careful consideration of how space is best used is very important. Another important issue is accessibility and ease of use. Infrastructure problems are also an issue, although in many cases this is more an issue of budget than a need for assessment. Assessment efforts focusing on facilities will largely take place after the upcoming renovations, so as not to confuse temporary issues with more permanent ones.

Planned Projects
- In-Library User Survey—Fall 2021

Collections

Collections have traditionally been at the heart of the Library's mission. Although this model is changing in important ways, the quality of our collections is still of paramount importance to our users. Access is also an important aspect of collections, as not being able to access a resource is functionally the same as not having it. Access is one area where we can improve and assessment efforts will also keep this in mind moving forward.

Planned Projects
- E-problems Audit—Spring 2022

Services

In past assessments, customer service in the Libraries has consistently been rated highly by all user groups, and service of this kind is important to and valued by users. It is important to continue to track how we are doing in this area and ensure we continue to excel.

Research services are of high importance to users. In past assessments, users have expressed concern with the ease of finding materials and the importance of an easily navigable website that allows them to access needed information without assistance, as well as a desire for easy-to-locate reference help when they do need it, both virtually and in person.

Planned Projects
- Web and Mobile Web Usability Study—Fall 2022

Culture of Assessment

An important goal of the assessment plan is to create a culture of assessment throughout the Library. Training all staff in the Library to understand what assessment is and how to do it and providing them with the tools to do it will empower staff to do their own assessment, large or small, to improve their own efforts and those of their department. In addition to regular trainings (which will themselves be assessed for effectiveness and relevance), a research/assessment skills inventory of all Library staff will help focus what training would be beneficial, as well as identify potential team members to work on assessment projects or conduct trainings themselves, and also help staff connect to work on projects together.

Planned Projects
- Staff Survey—Summer 2022
- Staff Research Skills Inventory—Spring 2023
- Ongoing trainings

Management Data and Statistics

To support fact-based decisions, it is important to have accessible and accurate management data. Additionally, the Libraries are required to report statistics to various external organizations. Data and statistics gathering and reporting is a continual process. Supplying the Library Director and others in the Library with needed data for decision-making and planning is also a part of this process and an important activity of the assessment program.

Two Year Assessment Projects Grid*

	Fall	Spring	Summer
FY2021–2022	In-Library User Survey	E-problems Audit	Staff Survey
FY2022–2023	Web/Mobile Web Usability Study	Staff Research Skills Inventory	Organizational Assessment Planning

*Ongoing assessment activities and trainings will also occur during this time.

Sample Informed Consent Form

(Note: each institution will have specific guidelines for these and other human subjects research-related forms. This example complies with our institution's guidance.)

Library User Instruction: Value to Students Informed Consent

Introduction

You are invited to participate in a study on the value of library user instruction to students being conducted by the University of X.

You must be 18 or older to participate.

The objective of this study is to assess the value of library instructional services to students in terms of development in three areas:

1. Acclimation to the Research University (UTX) and the Community of Scholarship

2. Physical (and virtual) orientation to the Library, including

3. Skills for conducting research using both proprietary information resources (e.g., subscription databases) and freely available informational material on the World Wide Web

Information about Participants' Involvement in the Study

Students who choose to participate will be asked to complete some brief assessment tools (quizzes) that will not in any way affect your course grade. You will not be asked to write your name on these tools. You are also asked to consent to allowing project staff to review assignments completed before and after you receive instruction. Again, we will not know which participant completed each assignment.

Risks

We anticipate risks involved in the project to be minimal.

Benefits

This project will contribute to our understanding of how to best help students learn about conducting research. You will hopefully benefit as well by improving your knowledge of how library resources work and where to go for help finding information. Participants will not be compensated.

Confidentiality

Any information obtained in connection with the study will remain confidential. In any written reports or publications, no participant other than the research team will be identified, and only anonymous data will be provided. Data generated in the course of the project will only be shared with the project team and will be stored in a locked file cabinet in a locked office (Bldg. Y, Room 424) for three years.

Participation

Your participation in this study is voluntary; you may decline to participate without jeopardizing your course grades. If you decide to participate, you may withdraw from the study at any time. If you withdraw from the project prior to its completion, data gathered to that point will be retained for analysis to the extent necessary for completing the research unless you request that it be destroyed.

If you have questions at any time about the study or the procedures, (or you experience adverse effects as a result of participating in this study), you may contact the primary researcher, Ms. Jane Doe [address; phone; e-mail address]. If you have questions about your rights as a participant, contact the Office of Research Compliance Officer at [phone number].

By clicking "next," I am agreeing that I am at least 18 years old and am willing to participate in the study.

Template for Recording Observation

Date: MM/DD/YEAR   Day of Week: Su M Tu W Th F Sa

Time: XX:XX AM/PM - XX:XX AM/PM

Submitted by:

Sketch room layout during observation:

⬭	Chair (soft seating)
◯	Chair (office or table)
▭	Table
△	Other (please label)
☺	Individual

Notes:

Suggested Journals and Conferences

Journals and Literature

Articles about library assessment are published in many journals, but the following are recommended.

College and Research Libraries

https://crl.acrl.org/index.php/crl

Contains articles discussing trends and developments that impact academic librarians and research libraries. Recent articles cover library instruction, World-Cat Local, and information-seeking habits of faculty. Articles are supported with tables, figures, and surveys, and each issue includes book reviews.

Evidence Based Library and Information Practice (EBLIP)

https://journals.library.ualberta.ca/eblip/index.php/EBLIP

EBLIP is an open access, peer-reviewed journal. Articles and other features provide librarians and library administrators with research that may help inform decision and policy making.

The Journal of Academic Librarianship

https://www.sciencedirect.com/journal/the-journal-of-academic-librarianship

Features articles that focus on problems and issues germane to college and university libraries.

Performance Measurement and Metrics

https://www.emeraldinsight.com/loi/pmm

Performance Measurement and Metrics (PMM) is a leading double-blind refereed, international journal, charting new qualitative and quantitative developments and techniques for measurement and metrics in information environments. The journal is concerned with planning and development in libraries and the organizations they are part of.

Portal: Libraries and the Academy
https://www.press.jhu.edu/journals/portal-libraries-and-academy
Covers current topics of interest to academic libraries such as library administration, information technology, and information policy.

LibValue Bibliographic Database
http://libvalue.cci.utk.edu/biblio
The LibValue bibliographic database includes over 1,000 individual items from library and information science literature, as well as relevant material from such diverse disciplines as higher education administration, museum assessment, and environmental economics.

Library Assessment Conferences

Past proceedings of these conferences, and in some cases posters, are available online and are a good source of practical information about a variety of assessment topics, methods, and tools.

ARL Library Assessment Conference (ARLLAC)
https://www.libraryassessment.org

Evidence Based Library and Information Practice Conference (EBLIP)
https://www.eblip10.org

International Conference on Performance Measurement in Libraries (LibPMC)
https://libraryperformance.org

Qualitative and Quantitative Methods in Libraries Conference (QQML)
http://qqml.org

Southeastern Library Assessment Conference (SELAC)
https://www.southeasternlac.info

Sample Assessment Librarian Position Description

POSTION TITLE: Assessment Librarian
DEPARTMENT: Administration

I. GENERAL FUNCTION

State briefly the general purpose of your position within the depart-ment or library.

The Assessment Librarian supports the mission of our library by fostering a culture of assessment and by leading the design and imple-mentation of a successful and sustainable assessment program. Engag-ing staff throughout the Libraries, this position analyzes systems and services for continuous improvement. Working closely with library leaders to document and disseminate assessment results, the Assess-ment Librarian helps to incorporate the knowledge gained through assessment into library strategic planning and decision-making.

II. SPECIFIC DUTIES

List the primary duties or assignments of your position and estimated percentage of work time allocated to each.

A. Assessment Activities (35 percent)

1. Plan, implement, and promote a comprehensive assessment program that informs library strategic planning and organiza-tional effectiveness.

2. Plan and implement both regular/ongoing assessment activities and unique assessment initiatives, employing a variety of evaluation techniques.

3. Prepare reports and presentations to summarize data analysis, interpret findings, and inform the planning and decision-making process in the library.

4. Work closely with outreach and public relations personnel to communicate findings and initiatives resulting from assessment activities through publications, presentations, and the library website.

5. Work closely with administration to coordinate strategic planning activities and monitor progress toward strategic goals.

6. Coordinate and direct assessment committee.

B. Data Gathering and Reporting (25 percent)

1. Coordinate library response to external requests for statistics and participate in national and regional surveys.

2. Collaborate with campus offices that collect and disseminate data.

3. Develop and coordinate a process for the collection, compilation, and analysis of statistical data for the Libraries.

4. Analyze statistical data using qualitative and quantitative methodologies.

C. Data Management (15 percent)

1. Develop, implement, and maintain a data management plan that streamlines data collection and reporting.

2. Facilitate transparency and accessibility in data processes.

D. Consulting and Training (25 percent)

1. Serve as a resource for library colleagues engaged in assessment activities.

2. Provide training, technical assistance, and consultation on specific projects.

3. Keep up-to-date on new assessment tools, issues, and best practices and share information with library colleagues.

QUALIFICATIONS

Include educational requirements, special skills, and minimum work experience.

Required:

- ALA-accredited master's degree.
- Demonstrated understanding of quantitative and qualitative assessment methodologies and their application in academic libraries.
- Experience conducting analysis and creating customized reports using statistical software applications (such as Excel, SPSS, atlas.ti).
- Demonstrated ability to work successfully in a team environment, as well as independently.
- Excellent communication and interpersonal skills.
- Strong problem-solving, organizational, and presentation skills.

Preferred:

- Demonstrated successful project management skills.
- Experience working with library-specific assessment tools in an academic or research library environment.

Glossary

This glossary includes terminology used in the text and definitions for additional terms commonly used in planning and assessment. It should not be considered exhaustive.

analysis. Process of reviewing data and drawing conclusions.

ANOVA (analysis of variance). A statistical model that measures the variation between group means. The p-value produced determines whether the results are significant or not.

assessment. Evaluation methods used to assess the needs of library users and other groups to (1) facilitate evidence-based decision-making (i.e., determine if needs are being met or what improvements should be made), and (2) demonstrate library/organizational value to key stakeholders.

baseline. The condition, status, or performance prior to program implementation or intervention.

benchmark. A standard or measure against which progress toward specific goals may be compared or assessed.

best practice. A technique or method that has consistently proven to be more effective than other techniques or methods.

bias. An attitude, opinion, perspective, or point of view that inhibits objectivity and skews the findings, results, and conclusions of an assessment.

bibliometrics. The study of citation behavior and attendant relationships between texts, authors, and ideas.

big data. A group of data sets that are difficult to analyze and process using traditional methods. These sets require advanced technology and methods to manage data.

case study. A research method in which data is collected from multiple points from a single or small number of settings to develop a representative case.

causation. The relationship between variables that establishes cause and effect: "because of X, Y happened."

census (complete enumeration). A study of everyone or everything in a population as opposed to a *sample*, which measures part of a population.

confidence interval. The likelihood that the sample you selected or the sample that responded/volunteered is representative of the population you are measuring. The standard desired confidence interval is between 90 and 99 percent, usually 95 percent. A 95 percent confidence interval suggests that, if tested again, the same results would occur every time.

confounding factor. Any element external to the phenomenon being studied that might have an influence on findings.

contingent valuation. A method of estimating the value that a person places on a good.

convenience sampling. A non-random section of the population. This occurs when not every member or unit has an equal chance of being selected for study, such as when volunteers are used.

correlation. The measurement of two variables to determine their relationship (not cause and effect). In statistics, it is abbreviated as r. The range of correlation is −1.00 (negative correlation) to 0 (no correlation) to +1.00 (positive correlation).

cost per use. Typically calculated for electronic resources. Cost of a resource divided by number of instances of some measure of use—for example, database log-ons or article downloads.

critical assessment. An approach to assessment (especially in higher education) that considers the power structures inherent in the assessment enterprise and encourages practitioners to reflect upon how assessment affects the entities being assessed, as well as the potential impact of assessment findings. Includes recognition that assessment is never value-neutral or objective.

data hacking. The practice of using open source data in innovative ways to address needs or assess a problem.

deep log analysis. A methodology that helps librarians, publishers, and other suppliers of web-based content to gain a better understanding of how consumers actually use their services by analyzing raw transactional server-side logs, for example, session length, number of content or other pages viewed, whether or not an internal search engine was used, which titles and subjects were viewed, and when an access took place. This data reflects what people actually do online and not what they think they did or what they think they ought to say to a researcher.

dependent variable. The variable that is acted upon in a research project—the variable that shows evidence of change or influence.

descriptive statistics. Quantitative statistics used to summarize the general features of the population being studied. Demographic information is one type of descriptive statistics.

direct evidence. Measurable, observable data that can be recorded without significant human intervention. *See also* indirect evidence.

generalizability/external validity. The extent to which results of a study can be ascribed to other, similar groups or real-life situations. Replication of the study using different subject populations and settings can demonstrate generalizability of results.

goal. The desired end result of an activity. Goals should be specific, measurable, achievable, relevant, and time-bound (SMART). They should be formulated before beginning assessment research or implementing a program to provide measurable variables that can be used to formulate program structure or for later assessment.

hypothesis. The supposition regarding outcome of an assessment or other research project.

independent variable. The variable that acts in an assessment or research project—the variable that exerts influence or causes change.

indicator (key performance indicator). Milestones that are created from breaking down goals into smaller steps to measure progress toward goals.

indirect evidence. Account of a phenomenon unobserved by the researcher; what respondents say they do, have done, or did. *See also* direct evidence.

inferential statistics. Probabilistic statistics used to infer or predict something about a larger population from a sample, for example, correlation.

informed consent. The process by which a research participant is informed of the potential risks and rewards of participating in a project. Also the method used to apprise participant of risks/rewards and secure evidence of participant's agreement (e.g., signature).

input. Something that goes into a system. In assessment, resources invested, such as monetary funds, staff, or operating hours.

input measure. The measure of resources such as materials, labor, etc., that are used to generate an output.

institutional review board (IRB). An ethics committee that reviews research proposals to assess the risk to subjects and enforce ethical standards. IRBs have the authority to reject or suggest revisions for research proposals at their institutions.

instrument. A tool for collecting data, often a survey.

internal consistency. The extent to which an instrument collects the evidence it is meant to collect.

internal validity. The extent to which a researcher's hypothesis is proven by the research they conduct.

inter-rater reliability. The extent to which different raters agree on a score or measurement assigned. If scores are similar, then a problem exists with the measurement or standards have not been well defined to judges.

learning outcome. A broad educational goal that the student is expected to achieve by the end of the course, relative to some knowledge or skill. Outcomes may be broken down into smaller and more specific learning objectives.

linear regression. A statistical method that models the relationship between the dependent variable (y) and one or more independent variables (x). It can be used to predict results based on the model's linear representation of data, or to determine the relationship between the dependent and independent variables.

longitudinal analysis. A study that takes place over a long period of time.

margin of error. The percentage of possible errors in a sample size, between 1 and 10 percent—usually 5 percent. If 40 percent of your population answers "yes" on a survey and your margin of error is 5 percent, then 35 to 45 percent of the population would respond "yes" for that item.

measures. Individual proxies for activity, quality, value, or usage.

method. A specific approach to collecting data.

methodology. A theory or approach to research design, execution, and analysis.

metric. A meaningful, verifiable measure, which may be qualitative or quantitative.

metric. A unit of measurement.

mission statement. An organization's statement of its purpose for existing.

mixed methods. A project that employs multiple methods of data collection.

moderator. The individual who directs a focus group.

open data. Data that is freely available to the public and can be used and republished by anyone without legal barriers of copyright, patent, or other restraints, although attribution is still required.

operationalizing. Identifying the event or entity that can stand in for a variable in a research project.

outcome. The observable impact of an intervention.

output. Things that are generated by a system. In libraries, book circulation and electronic resources usage statistics are examples of outputs.

output measure. The results of an activity measured in quantitative form.

paired T-test. Like the margin of error, usually set at 0.05 and the degrees of freedom (i.e., the sum of persons/units in both groups minus 2).

participant. An individual taking part in an assessment or study.

performance measurement. Used to measure quality or suitability of purpose, of a library product or service. High-quality performance is measured based on the users' needs and expectations, which may be relative to an institution.

pilot study. A test run of a study with a small group of participants.

pre- and post-test. Instruments administered before and after an intervention (e.g., a library instruction session) to determine its success.

primitive concept. A concept so fundamental that it is impossible to further define it.

Project COUNTER. A code of practice used by vendors and publishers to generate consistent electronic resource usage reports. *See also* SUSHI.

protocol (interview or focus group). The script of questions an interviewer or focus group moderator uses.

p-value. A number from 0 to 1 used to calculate the probability that the results of a study are significant. This means the results obtained are more likely due to correlation or causation (alternative hypothesis) than chance (null hypothesis). A significant p-value is usually considered to be less than 0.05 or 0.01, depending on the stringency of the criteria.

qualitative. Non-numeric data, typically text-based. Qualitative, or interpretive, analysis considers participants' accounts of lived experience.

quantitative. Numeric data. Quantitative analysis is statistical in nature.

random sample. Every member or unit has an equal chance of being selected for the study.

regression analysis. A powerful statistical method that allows you to examine the relationship between two or more variables of interest. Although there are many types of regression analysis, at their core, they all examine the influence of one or more independent variables on a dependent variable.

reliability. The extent to which a method consistently measures the same variable; the extent to which a research design generates consistent results.

representativeness. An estimate of the probability of the recurrence of a study's results based on the degree to which the sample is an accurate representation of the population measured in the study.

research question. The area of interest at the foundation of a research project.

respondent. A research study participant. A term often used in the context of a survey.

response rate. The percentage of possible participants who completed the research-related task. If a survey was distributed to 100 people and returned by thirty, the response rate would be 30 percent.

return on investment (ROI). An assessment of the extent to which resources allocated to library resources and services generate a positive dividend. Typically a financial metric.

rigor. A quality of well-designed and executed research.

rubric. A tool to record and score individual performance.

sample. The group identified to participate in a study.

sample size (survey sampling). The percentage of the population that responds to your survey. For your sample size to be representative of your desired population, you must calculate your desired margin of error and confidence interval.

sampling method. A scientific method for selecting units to test that will be used to make inferences about a population.

selection bias. An error in the choice of individuals or populations included in a study, which distorts results.

self-selected sample. A sample that is determined by whether the members of a population can agree or decline to participate in the sample, implicitly or explicitly.

snowball. A method of identifying participants in which current participants identify other potential participants.

stakeholders. Any and all populations that may be involved with the library directly or indirectly, including but not limited to users, schools, partner organizations, government agencies, etc.

standard T-test. A method that determines whether the means of the results of two independent groups or variables are statistically different from one another.

statistical significance. The probability that the results of a study are due to cause and effect or correlation rather than to chance. This measure generally rejects the null hypothesis (that results are due to chance) if a p-value less than 0.05 or 0.01 is obtained.

SUSHI (Standardized Usage Statistics Harvesting Initiative). A protocol for collecting standardized electronic resources usage statistic data. *See also* Project COUNTER.

table study. The study of in-house use of library materials in which patrons are asked to leave materials pulled from shelves on library tables rather than reshelving them. Items are recorded by library staff.

theoretical framework. Assumptions for research based on ontological and epistemological understanding.

theory. Formally, a construct that shapes a researcher's worldview or view of a research project.

transaction logs/transaction log analysis. Records of individual searches conducted on webpages or in electronic resources (e.g., databases).

triangulation. Approaching a research question by using more than one method to collecting data.

usage. Metrics for measuring engagement with electronic resources. Typically includes database log-ons and downloads, sometimes more finely grained data.

validity. The extent to which a method accurately reflects or measures the specific concept that the researcher is assessing.

values statement. An organization's statement of priorities, ethics, and beliefs.

vision statement. An aspirational description of an organization's ideal state.

Index

f denotes figures

#
80/20 rule, 88

A
academic libraries
history of assessment in, 24, 25–27,
33–36
return on investment of, 86
surveys for, 182–183
actionability, as guiding principle, 52, 53,
221
administrative science, 21–22
aesthetics, in reporting, 190–191
agility, need for, 37–38
ALA Bulletin, 23
American Library Association (ALA)
Committee on Post-War Planning, 23
Core Competencies of Librarianship,
19–20
history of assessment and, 23, 25, 28,
29
Library Bill of Rights, 176–177
analysis
data, 70–71, 157–172
SWOT, 54–56
Anthony, Robert N., 23
ARL Library Assessment Conference
(ARLLAC), 234

Asantewa, Doris, 24
assessment
approaches to, 81–96
collaboration in, 186, 216–219
collecting data for (*see* data collection)
concept of, 1–5, 239
critical framework for, 9, 35–36, 73–74,
85, 240
culture of, 202–209, 225–226
vs. evaluation, 2
guiding principles for, 10–17, 52–54,
63–78, 221–222
history of, 19–20, 24–38
organizational structure of, 210–216
plans for, 57–61, 208, 221–226
purposes of, 7–10
vs. research, 65, 79
rigor in, 10, 15–16, 65
timeline of, 59
See also planning; surveys
assessment librarians
as matrix leaders, 215–216
position and title of, ix, 206, 210, 222,
235–237
sample job description for, 235–237
soft skills needed by, 201–202*f*
surveys of, ix, 20, 67, 71, 81, 173,
202*f*
assessment-generated data, life cycle of,
177–178

Association of College and Research
    Libraries (ACRL), 19–20, 27, 28,
    34–35, 84, 182
Association of Research Libraries (ARL),
    24, 25–27, 33–34, 84–85, 141,
    182–183
audience, knowing your, 188–190

B

Baltimore County Public Library (BCPL),
    107
Bekkerman, Anton, 100
Belanger, Jackie, 35
Belmont Report, 72–73
benchmarks, 84–85, 239
beneficence, 72
bias, 74, 84, 115, 239
bibliometrics, 239
big data, 240
Birks, Melanie, 172
Bookstein, Abraham, 101
Bryson, John, 50

C

case studies, 153–154, 240
causation, 64, 240
celebration of successes, 204, 209
challenges, failure to face, 47–48
Chao, Zoe, 100–101
Choi, Namjoo, 100–101, 102
choice, in good strategies, 49
The Chronicle of Higher Education, viii,
    36
Chun Tie, Ylona, 172
circulation data, 4, 25, 70, 88, 106–109,
    112
citation, 88, 112–113, 115, 116f–117f
cognitive turn, 29
coherent action, 49
Coleman, Anita, 112
collaboration, 186, 216–219
College and Research Libraries journal, 233
committees, 211–215, 222–223
Common Rule, 73
communication of results, 188–192, 195
community priorities, 10–15
complexity, planning as response to, 5–6

concept codes, 164–167
conferences, 234
confidence intervals, 240
confounding factors, 94, 240
consent, informed, 73, 227–229, 242
constraints, faced by libraries, 4
constructivism, viii
context, assessment in, 10–15
contingent valuation, 87–88, 240
convenience sampling, 240
Corbin, Juliet, 172
Core Competencies of Librarianship
    (ALA), 19–20
correlation, 240
correlation coefficient, 162
cost per use (CPU), 89, 240
cost-benefit analysis, 86
COUNTER project, 32–33, 110, 244
creativity, supporting, 12–13
critical assessment, 9, 35–36, 73–74, 85,
    240
critical librarianship, 73–74
Crunden, Frederick, 21
culture of assessment, 202–209, 225–226

D

Dana, John Cotton, 21–22
data
    integrity of, 74–78, 187
    preservation and storage of, 177–180
    privacy and, 176–177
    qualitative, 69, 106, 111–120, 158,
        163, 172, 244
    quantitative, 69, 106–111, 158, 172,
        244
    reporting and presenting of, 182–192
data analysis, 70–71, 157–172
data collection
    data management and, 178
    for direct evidence, 105–120
    for indirect evidence (*see* indirect
        evidence)
    principles underlying, 99–103
data definitions, 183–184
data inventory, 180–181
data life cycle management (DLM),
    177–178

data management, 173–176, 178, 236
data points, 25–27, 69*f*, 181, 183–185, 196–197
data sets, preexisting, 154
data visualization, 192–198
Davis, Chrispin, 110
deadlines, for reporting, 184–185, 186
decision-making, support for, 7–8*f*
deep log analysis, 241
Demarais, Ann, 218
demographic questions, 132
dependent variables, 67, 68, 70, 118, 241
Dervin, Brenda, 30, 36, 102–103
descriptive statistics, 158–159, 241
direct evidence, 68, 105–120, 241
dishonesty, in data presentation, 75–78
door counts, 82, 108, 111
Douglas, Veronica Arellano, 35
Dworak, Ellie, 91–92

E
economic models, 85–90, 96, 100
Edgar, Bill, 142
Efficiency Movement, 21
electronic journals, 33
electronic resources assessment, 32–33, 34, 110, 159–160
Emery, Ann K., 194–196, 198
E-Metrics Project, 34
Encyclopedia of Case Study Research (SAGE), 66
ethical assessment, 16, 84
evaluation vs. assessment, 2. *See also* assessment
Evidence Based Library and Information Practice (EBLIP), 233, 234
evidence gathering, 68–69
evidence-based assessment, 52, 222
Excel, 171, 185, 194, 197
existing data sets, 154
experimentation, 118–119
external validity, 70, 241
external *vs.* internal factors, 7–8*f*
eye-movement tracking, 169f, 170*f*

F
Faber, Maggie, 35
Facebook, motto of, 5
facilities usage, 133*f*, 168–171
factors, confounding, 94, 240
failure, 17, 218–219
Farkas, Meredith, 35, 204
"feedback, not failure" motto, 218–219
file names and formats, 179
financial value, 85–88, 90
First Impressions (Demarais and White), 218
Fleming-May, Rachel, vii–viii, 15–16, 107–109, 120, 150, 160
fluff, 47
focus groups and interviews, 143–153, 163–165
Francis, Karen, 172

G
Gaebler, Ted, 51
Garfield, Eugene, 112
generalizability, 66, 70, 241
George, Claude S., 20–21
Georgia, data manipulation by, 77–78
Gerould, James T., 25–27, 34
The Gerould Statistics (Molyneux), 27
Gilpin, Gregory, 100
goals
    mistaking for strategy, 48
    SMART, 48, 241
    in strategic planning, 57
Gonick, Larry, 172
Good Strategy, Bad Strategy (Rumelt), 46–47
Graduate Library School (GLS), 22, 101
grant applications, 86
graphic design, 190, 193, 195
graphs
    best practices for, 196–197
    data manipulation in, 75–78
Griffiths, José Marie, 8–10, 31
grounded theory, 71
guiding principles, 52–54, 221–222

H
heat maps, 133, 170*f*–171

The History of Management Thought, 21
honesty, in data presentation, 75–78
Hoover, Herbert, 23
human subjects, protection of, 72–73
hypotheses, 66, 70, 162–163, 241

I

implementation, in planning cycle, 2,
    3*f*, 5
incentives, 140, 146
inclusivity, viii, 14, 53, 213, 222
independent variables, 67, 70, 118,
    241
indicators, key performance, 241
indirect evidence
    case studies for, 153–154
    defined, 68, 123, 242
    interviews and focus groups for,
        143–153
    surveys for, 123–143
inferential statistics, 158–159, 160, 242
informed consent, 73, 227–229, 242
in-house use, 68–69, 109, 246
inputs, 82–85, 96, 168, 242
Institute of Museum and Library
    Services (IMLS), 34, 92
institutional review boards (IRBs), 16,
    65, 73, 74, 79, 152, 242
instruments, defined, 69, 242. *See also*
    surveys
Integrated Postsecondary Education Data
    System (IPEDS), 28, 182, 184
integrity
    of data, 74–78, 187
    as guiding principle, 53, 217, 222
internal consistency, 129, 242
internal validity, 70, 242
internal *vs.* external factors, 7–8f
International Conference on Performance
    Measurement in Libraries
    (LibPMC), 36, 234
inter-rater reliability, 71, 165, 242
interviews and focus groups, 143–153,
    163–165
inventory of data, 180–181
Ithaka S+R Surveys, 36, 136

J

jargon, avoiding, 47, 134, 189–190
Jewett, Charles Coffin, 28
job description, sample, 235–237
Joeckel, Carleton B., 22
Joo, Soohyung, 100–101, 102
Journal Citation Reports (JCR), 112
The Journal of Academic Librarianship,
    233
journals, recommended, 233–234
just and ethical assessment, 16, 84
justice, 72–73

K

Kaufman, Paula, 86
Kemp, Brian, 77
Keyes, Kelsey, 91–92
Kidston, James, 101
King, Donald W., 8–10, 31, 33
Kotter, John, 191–192, 205
Kupersmith, John, 134
Kurtz, Michael, 112

L

land grant universities (LGUs), 11–12
leadership, matrix, 215–216
"Leading Change" (Kotter), 205
learning outcomes, 242
LibInsight, 176
LibQUAL+, 34, 141–142
librarians
    assessment positions and titles for, ix,
        206, 210, 222, 235–237
    data points on, 26
    soft skills needed by, 201–202*f*
    surveys of, ix, 20, 67, 71, 81, 173,
        202f, 204
libraries
    academic (*see* academic libraries)
    public (*see* public libraries)
    reasons for lack of planning by, 3–5
    surveys for, 182–183
library administration, role of, 223–224
Library and Information Science Source
    (LISS), 24, 100
library assessment conferences, 234
Library Bill of Rights (ALA), 176–177

Library Evaluation (Wallace and Van Fleet), 7–8
Library Investment Index (LII), 84–85
Library Journal, 25
"Library Privacy Policies" (Vaughan), 177
Library Services Act, 28
Library Services and Construction Act, 24
"Library Terms That Users Understand" project, 134
library-generated data, life cycle of, 177–178
LibValue, vii, 34, 234
life cycles, of data, 177–178
likert scale questions, 126–129, 161*f*
Lilburn, Jeff, 35–36
linear regression, 242
longitudinal analysis, 140, 175, 243
long-range planning, 23–24
Luther, Judy, 86

M

MacAyeal, Greg, 203
Magnus, Ebony, 35
Mahoney, Michael, 192–193
Malone, Cheryl, 112
management science, 21–22, 29
margin of error, 138, 243
marginalized groups, 13–15
matrix leadership, 215–216
Matthew Effect, 88–89
Matthews, Joe, 46–47
Mays, Regina, vii, ix, 191, 192, 216, 217, 219
meaningfulness, as guiding principle, 52, 53, 221
Mellon, Constance, 71
Membership Criteria Index (MCI), 85
Merriam, Charles, 21
Merriam-Webster, 15
Merton, Robert K., 88
metadata, 179
metrics-based approaches, 82–85
Microsoft Excel, 171, 185, 194, 197
Microsoft PowerPoint, 194–195
Microsoft Word, 171, 195, 197
MINES surveys, 34, 141, 143
Mintzberg, Henry, 50

MISO surveys, 141, 142
mission statements, 10–14, 50–51, 165–167, 243
mixed methods projects, 154, 243
moderators, 152–153, 243
Molyneux, Robert E., 27
Molz, R. Kathleen, 22
"move fast" motto, 5
Multicultural Student Life (MSL), 14
multiple choice questions, 125–126, 131, 161*f*

N

National Center for Education Statistics (NCES), 28, 182, 183
National Research Act, 72
national statistical programs, 27–28
National Teacher and Principal Survey (NTPS), 183
necessity, as guiding principle, 52, 53, 221
New Measures Initiative (NMI), 33–34
Nielsen, Jakob, 114
"no failure, only feedback" motto, 218–219
null hypotheses, 162, 244, 245
NVIVO, 167–168*f*

O

Oakleaf, Megan, 34–35
observation, 113–114, 168–169, 231
Office of Multicultural Student Life (MSL), 14
open data, 243
open text questions, 130–131, 161*f*
operational planning, 42–43, 45
operationalization, 68, 243
opportunities, in SWOT, 54f, 55
organizational structure, 210–216
Osborne, David, 51
Osburn, Charles, 107
outcomes, 61, 92–96, 208, 243
outputs, 82–85, 96, 111, 168, 243
outreach, as mission statement, 11–13

P

paired T-tests, 243

Palmour, Vernon E., 24
paper surveys, 136–137
participants
    in focus groups, 145–147, 149–153
    informed consent for, 73, 227–229,
      242
    protection of, 72–73
    soliciting of, 147
patrons
    from marginalized groups, 13–15
    observation of, 113–114, 168–169, 231
    privacy of, 95, 142
    surveys as public relations tool for, 10
Pearl, Nancy, 107
performance measurement, defined, 243.
    See also assessment
Performance Measurement and Metrics
    journal, 233–234
Pew Research Center, 154
pilot testing, 149, 243
planning
    for assessments, 57–61, 208, 221–226
    concept of, 1–5
    history of, 19–24
    importance of, 5–6
    strategic, 23–24, 41–46, 50–58
    types of, 41–45
    See also assessment
Planning and Control Systems (Anthony),
    23
A Planning Process for Public Libraries
    (Palmour), 24
political positions, strengthening, 7–8*f*
Portal: Libraries and the Academy, 234
post-testing, 114–115, 119*f*, 244
PowerPoint, 194–195
preexisting data sets, 154
preservation of data, 177–180
pre-testing, 114–115, 119*f*, 244
primitive concepts, 68, 244
principles and values, 52–54
print materials, canceling, 160
privacy, 95, 142, 176–177
professional development, 204, 208
program attendance, 111
Project COUNTER, 32–33, 110, 244
project teams, roles in, 223

protocols, in focus groups, 148–149, 244
public administration, 21–22
public libraries
    history of assessment in, 24, 25, 28, 30
    return on investment of, 86
    surveys for, 182
Public Libraries Survey (PLS), 182
public relations, 10, 79, 236
p-value, 162, 244

Q
Qualitative and Quantitative Methods in
    Libraries Conference (QQML), 234
qualitative data, 69, 106, 111–120, 158,
    163, 172, 244
quantitative data, 69, 106–111, 158, 172,
    244
quasi-experimentation, 118–119
questions
    in interviews and focus groups,
      143–144, 148–149, 152
    in research projects, 66–68, 69*f*, 244
    for surveys, 124–135, 161*f*

R
random samples, 244
ranking questions, 130, 161*f*
real-time dialogue, 143–149
Recent Social Trends in the United States
    report, 23
reference statistics, 83, 111
regression analysis, 161*f*, 244
regrouping, in planning cycle, 2, 3*f*
relationships, managing, 186, 216–219
reliability, 70–71, 129, 244
reminders, 140, 147
repetition, in communication, 191–192
reporting of data, 182–192
representativeness, 138–139, 244
research
    grounded theory and, 71
    as mission statement, 11–13
    protection of human subjects in,
      72–73
    questions in, 66–68, 69*f*, 244
    relationship to assessment, 63–65,
      79

respondents, questions for, 124–135,
    148–149, 161*f*
response rates, 136–140, 245
return on investment (ROI), 30–32,
    86–87, 95–96, 245
revising, in planning cycle, 2, 3*f*
Riggs, Donald E., 24
rigorous assessment, 10, 15–16, 65
Robinson, Charles, 107
rubrics, 114–118, 245
Rumelt, Richard, 46–47
RUSA Guidelines, 91–92, 120

S
SAGE, 66, 172
sample size, 137–138, 245
scholarly communication, 33, 88
scholarly sources, 116–118
school libraries, surveys for, 183
scientific method, 66–69
selection bias, 245
services and facilities usage, 133*f*,
    168–171
Shera, Jesse Hauk, 23
Shneiderman, Ben, 193
simplicity, as guiding principle, 52, 221
SMART goals, 48, 241
Smith, Woollcott, 172
social return on investment (SROI), 95–96
soft skills, 201–202f
Southeastern Library Assessment
    Conference (SELAC), 234
Spaulding, Frank L., 30–31
SPEC Kits, 24
special libraries
    economic models of, 85, 90
    return on investment in, 30–31
    surveys for, 183
Special Libraries (Griffiths and King),
    8–10, 31
Special Libraries Association (SLA), 21,
    28, 30–31
SpringShare, 176
staffing
    for committees, 211–215
    for interviews, 152–153
stakeholders, 7, 9, 150, 188–190, 245

standard T-tests, 245
standardized surveys, 34, 140–143
standards-based assessment, 91–92, 96,
    119–120
statistical analysis, 158–159, 160, 194
statistical programs, 25–29
statistical significance, 245
storage of data, 177–180
strategic analysis (SWOT), 54–56
strategic planning, 23–24, 41–46,
    50–58
*Strategic Planning Basics for Special
    Libraries* (Asantewa), 24
Strategic Planning for Library Managers
    (Riggs), 24
strategy, defined, 46–49
Strauss, Anselm, 172
strengths, in SWOT, 54f, 56
structured interviews, 148
"The Study of Administration" (Wilson),
    21
Sullivan, Gordon R., 47
survey movement, 28–29
surveys
    overview of, 123–124
    analysis of, 160–163
    best practices for, 132–135
    creation of, 124–132
    distribution of, 137–140
    history of, 28–29
    of librarians, ix, 20, 67, 71, 81, 173,
        202*f*, 204
    for libraries, 182–183
    on paper, 136–137
    public relations benefit of, 10
    standardized, 34, 140–143
    on use, 100–102
    web-based, 135–136
SUSHI initiative, 32–33, 110, 246
SWOT analysis, 54–56

T
table studies, 68–69, 109, 246
tactical planning, 43, 44, 45
Taylorism, 21
team members, choosing, 212–213
Tenopir, Carol, vii, 33, 86

testing
    pilot studies, 149, 243
    pre- and post-tests, 114–115, 119*f*, 244
    usability studies, 53, 114, 169–171
textual analysis, 163–168*f*
theoretical framework, 66, 246
theory, grounded, 71
threats, in SWOT, 54*f*, 55
timelines, 59
Towards Electronic Journals (Tenopir
    and King), 33
transcription, 151
triangulation, 69, 94, 246
Trueswell, Richard, 88
Tufte, Edward, 193

U
University of Chicago, 22, 101
University of Tennessee (UTK), 11–14,
    34, 87, 165–167, 169*f*–170*f*
unstructured interviews, 149
usability testing, 53, 114, 169–171
usage measurement, 107–110, 159–160,
    168–171, 246
use, as primitive term, 100–102
user experience (UX) testing, 114
user-centered assessment, 53, 222
users, focusing on, 102–103

V
validity, 70, 241, 242, 246
value, economic, 85–88, 90

Value, Outcomes and Return on
    Investment of Academic Libraries
    (LibValue), vii, 34, 234
The Value of Academic Libraries
    (Oakleaf), 34–35
Value Report, 35
values and principles, 52–54
Van Fleet, Connie, 7–8
variables, 67, 70, 118, 241
Vaughan, Jason, 177
video recordings, of interviews,
    151–152
vision statements, 47, 50, 51–52, 246
visualization, data, 192–198

W
Wallace, Danny, 7–8
weaknesses, in SWOT, 54*f*, 56
Web of Science, 112
web-based surveys, 135–136
Weiner, Wendy, 203–204
Weiss, Carol H., 2
White, Valerie, 218
Williams, Robert, 27–28
willingness to pay, 87–88
Wilson, Woodrow, 21
Word (Microsoft), 171, 195, 197
word association questions, 133–134*f*

Z
Zuckerman, Harriet, 88
Zweizig, Douglas, 30, 36, 92, 102–103